The Journey

John Dearman

with
David McClure and others

SCARABSKIN

For more information, write to this address: scarabskinbooks@gmail.com.
First paperback edition February 2024
First digital edition February 2024
Cover design by Scarabskin Books
ISBN (paperback) 979-8-9891199-3-6
ISBN (ebook) 979-8-9891199-2-9
Published by ScarabSkin Books

www.scarabskinbooks.com

For my mom, Jessie Mae Evans, for always believing her sons would have fantastic lives. We did it.

Contents

Foreword

Do you know the difference between lucky and being blessed?

Lucky refers to **Luck** which is defined as the phenomenon and belief that defines the experience of improbable events, especially improbably positive or negative ones.

Blessed is defined: In religion, a blessing (also used to refer to bestowing of such) is the impartation of something with grace, holiness, spiritual redemption, or divine will.

I never really thought about the difference or similarity until forty years ago, my friend Bill Badger, posed the issue to me. I have known Bill for sixty-three years of our lives in Saginaw, Michigan. Bill thought that I had been blessed.

Bill and I were born in 1950 in Saginaw, to separate families. Bill's parents emigrated to Saginaw from Mississippi. Saginaw was a town that offered "better" living for the young, adult population of the South migrating to the North. My parents and brother were a part of it like the thousands of Black people who sought to escape the South. Were we blessed or lucky that our parents sought a better life up north?

Foreword

Both my mother and brother, John, whose nickname, among others, was Little Brother, were born in Falls County, Texas.

This is where this story begins. Rose Ward Banks, our maternal grandmother was born in Falls County, Texas in 1874. Her second and third children were twins, Johnnie and Jessie, girls born in 1914. Their father, John Banks, was killed in 1920. That left Rose with five children to raise at a time when the KKK and cotton were kings in Texas. It was in 1931 that Jessie found herself as a seventeen-year-old cotton picking sharecropper with an infant who spent his formative months riding on a cotton sack. After a while, Jessie left John with Rose and went to Waco to work as a domestic. It was only when John was big enough to help on the farm (according to my aunt Ceola) that Jessie came to get him to take John to Waco to live with her in the white people's house. Was that luck or a blessing? Jessie had dreams that did not include cotton picking for her son, but rather an education.

Was John blessed or lucky to have been born to Jessie?

I am the other little brother, but known as Junior. I was born in Saginaw, Michigan in 1950, unexpected but wanted. I am the second child born to Jessie. I was born on a weeknight, and first announced by Jack Banks, my mother's brother, to my father, Robert Sr. and my brother John Dearman as they left the Chevrolet Grey Iron Foundry after their shift. My dad worked there, my uncles, my brother, and I along with many of my contemporaries. It was hard work, dangerous, dirty, hot and loud.

Saginaw, in 1950, was a small midwestern town dominated by the auto manufacturing business but especially General Motors. It served as a refuge for black men and women who wanted to escape the indignities of the sharecropping south. It was a place where you could work, earn a reasonable wage, and raise a family.

Obviously, Robert & Jessie were the greatest influences on my life as I knew it from that time but I only have two recurring memories from before I started school.

When I was born, my parents lived in a two room apartment along with Robert, Sr., Jessie, and Jack. John was off to college soon thereafter. My first distinct memory was moving from those two rooms to the house where I would live exclusively until I moved to California.

I remember that house fondly. It was a big house with a second floor and a basement, as did most houses in the Midwest. It even had a garage. When we moved there in the early 1950s, all the neighbors were Caucasian, although that didn't last long.

The ability to purchase a home in the south was almost universally unavailable to sharecroppers in Texas. My dad was a World War II veteran but couldn't buy a house in Texas. But my parents had great pride in what they were accomplishing once freed from the indignities of the South. They were homeowners, supporting a child in college, working for reasonable hours , and being paid a reasonable wage.

Saginaw is about ninety-five miles due north from Detroit. Whenever anything big happened in the state, it happened in Detroit.

My second distinct memory involves traveling from Saginaw to Detroit in my parents' 1956 dark blue Chevrolet. I remember the ride, so far to travel. I remember going to a large room, which turned out to be an auditorium, to see my brother graduate from law school. He was twenty-six, and I was seven. Little did I know at that time how much influence that ceremony would have on my life. John had graduated from Wayne

State University Law School, and soon passed the Michigan bar exam. He was the first in our family to obtain a graduate degree.

Coincidentally, a few years earlier, Henry Marsh, who would become the first black mayor of Saginaw in 1967, graduated from Wayne State University Law school. His oldest child, Thomas Michael Marsh (aka Happy), also born in 1950, became my good friend and college apartment roommate at the University of Michigan. I have known Happy since 1963. Happy became a lawyer in Michigan. Happy's parents, Henry and Ruth, emigrated to Michigan from Mississippi and Tennessee, respectively.

Of course, there was brotherly competition between John, who I referred to as "Ba" because of my inability to say brother. He was the first person to refer to me as Robert which has been the case since.

I always considered myself the better athlete but John has always been faster with more running endurance than I ever had. That has always been a point of laughter for both of us. John has always been able to outrun me. The first race I remember was outside our house in Saginaw. I probably challenged him. I was a baseball player all of seven or eight. Full of myself. John dusted me in about a half of a block. That was our last "race" until 1972, shortly after I moved to San Francisco.

Another aspect of John's personality is his commitment to fitness. He jogged every day. This was before jogging became "a thing." He ran the track at the Polo Fields. The track was about a mile in circumference. He would go in the morning in his black Porsche, run, and then go to his law office. One morning he invited me to go to the Polo Fields. I was twenty-two, John was forty-one. I went along. John challenged me to a race. Knowing I had no chance (he knew it and so did I), John ran the circumference of the track first, got back to my position, and the race started. It lasted only 100 yards or so! He dusted me again. I'm still puffing today.

I don't know how Jessie came to know lawyers in Saginaw however she did. She knew Carl Posten, who was Henry's law partner, and Peter Cincinelli, another local lawyer. But she did. Even though she worked hard as a domestic, she worked harder with the pride of the mother of a professional man. It's the truth that it was a unique experience for a former cotton picker to have a child who was a professional man protected from the indignities of the South.

It is from that time that I knew that I had a brother who was also a lawyer, and what that meant in the black community! From that time until the present day, the original Lil Brother, my Ba, has been one of three people upon whom I've ever relied. That was the other end of promises made, promises kept. My success, and by extension, my nieces, nephews, sons' and daughter's success is connected to the promises made and the promises kept by Jessie. I will support you as long as you get your education was her refrain.

The kids in my neighborhood had siblings, too. But their sisters or brothers lived with them, and went to the same school.

For me, John was an idea. I was always raised to be like John. But John was taller, slimmer, combed his hair backwards. I didn't understand then. Was I lucky or blessed to have a brother as an example that I could aspire to? The idea to follow John's example was drilled into me beginning at an early age. I came to San Francisco and became a lawyer. Jessie would be so proud. Her first child became the longest serving judge in the history of the Superior Court of San Francisco County, and her baby became an attorney as well.

I had an example of what was possible if you worked hard.

That was the attitude that Jessie embodied. That woman worked hard every day, and she was successful.

So, have John and I been lucky or blessed?

-Robert Coy Evans, Jr.
　　the other little brother.

Chapter 1
The Beginning

Some people live where they work. But I've always thought that was a good idea turned on its head.

Me? I've chosen to work where I live.

And I chose San Francisco. After just three days here, it already felt like paradise. I have never regretted my choice. I now live with my family on Mount Olympus and have a panoramic view of the city.

But I am getting ahead of myself. Let's start at the beginning.

I was born a Negro on March 28, 1931, to a seventeen-year-old unwed mother who was two generations away from slavery and had a fourth-grade education. A midwife delivered me, helped by my grandmother and aunts, and I took my first breaths in a three-room sharecropper's shack on a hardscrabble farm located miles down a dusty dirt road in Falls County, Texas, twenty-five miles south of Waco. As was the custom for blacks then, my birth was recorded in the family Bible, not in county birth records. It was finally recorded in Austin decades later by the state of Texas in response to a court order based on my school records and an affidavit signed by my grandmother, my mother, and two aunts.

I began to work in the cotton fields almost as soon as I could walk. Before I could walk, my mother would put me on top of the coarse cotton bag and I would sleep as best I could while she picked cotton, pulling the bag along. I watched her and would mimic picking myself, except I was too young and weak to succeed. All I managed to do was cause grief for my mother as I hung onto a boll or two from time to time, preventing her from moving the sack.

When I was about five, I started picking cotton myself. We started when the sun came up and worked until dark most days, with only a break for lunch, avoiding the hottest part of the blistering Texas summer days. There were times in the broiling Texas sun when I thought I wouldn't be able to reach the end of a half-mile-long cotton row before I gave out. I pulled a coarse three-foot-long bag between rows while I filled it with the cotton I picked from plants taller than I was. It took a month every year for my child-soft hands to toughen up enough to withstand the cuts, pricks, and scrapes the stiff parts of the cotton bolls would make as they attacked my moving limbs.

It was the depths of the Depression when I came into the world, and my family felt lucky to make $200 a year. When I was five, my mother moved to Waco to work as a domestic. She couldn't afford to take me with her, so the first lifesaving event of my young life came when I stayed on the farm and moved in with my grandmother, Rose Banks (also known as Rosie). She took in at least five close relatives during the seven years I lived with her—maybe as many as nine. There were times when I went to bed hungry and times when my family and I spent huddled around our small single-burner pot bellied stove through the sometimes-freezing Texas winter nights with the rest of the family in the one room we could heat. However, those seven years introduced me to the first of my lucky stars, my grandmother. During this time, I learned the value of hard work while she taught me the difference between right and wrong. Her early lessons set the moral boundaries that have guided me through life.

I was the first in my family to graduate from high school, the first to graduate from college, and, amazingly, the first to graduate from law school. And all this after I had quit grammar school at age eleven like many around me, sure that we knew enough to be successful Texas farmers—the highest ambition we had.

The second lifesaving event occurred when I was twelve. One dark October night, my mother woke me from sleep at my grandmother's house, where I was still living. "Get dressed, John," she said. "You are coming to live with me in Waco, where you can go back to school and finish your education. I don't want you to have to make a living cleaning other people's houses like I do." And so I went to live in Waco with my mother, who worked for the Schmidt family.

The author as a small boy in Texas

I experienced this type of lifesaving event several times throughout my life, mostly via people who pushed me in different, better directions. They were guides, lucky stars. They must have known what they were doing since I would go on to know and call among my friends the Speaker of the California Assembly, the Speaker of the US House of Representatives, several San Francisco mayors and California governors, and

many national and state politicians. I would rub shoulders with famous actors, successful barristers and politicians, well-known businessmen, and a few presidents.

As an attorney, I was able to give legal representation and seek justice for people who otherwise could not afford an attorney, or who could pay very little. As a judge with the San Francisco Superior Court, I ruled on issues that affected, and hopefully helped, thousands of people suffering from asbestosis. I also made rulings related to the unequal application of corporate power and cases that pitted the well-funded against others less fortunate. In all my time as a judge, no one—right or left, individual or corporation, black or white—avoided my court. After I had been making rulings for a few years, everyone knew they would get a fair shake in my court, which was impartial and by the letter and spirit of the law.

Jessie Mae Evans, the author's mother.

It has been an amazing journey, especially for me, the one taking it. To deny my part in my version of success would be disingenuous. But to claim sole responsibility for my success would be worse. For that would foreswear the immense debt of gratitude I owe to many people who guided, pushed, pulled, suggested, demanded, and otherwise showed me the way as I sometimes ran but often stumbled along.

So, this is really our story: it's mine, but it's also the story of those who helped me, from my birth family to the one I created

4

with the woman I married, Ina Flemming. From my determined mother to my beautiful wife to my accomplished children to all those whom I am privileged to call friends, this is our story. It is but one example of what can be achieved by those who are willing to apply themselves, work hard, work smart, take advice, and accept help in situations like mine—the often contentious but just as often serendipitous conditions I found myself in as life moved along.

The author as a young man

Chapter 2
Falls County, Texas

Falls County, where I was born, is about twenty-five miles south of Waco, Texas, the nearest town. Waco had a population of about 60,000 then, and it's located 125 miles south of Dallas, the nearest major city. During my early years, I was raised in Bell County, the adjacent county to the southwest. I lived in the country, and the nearest town, just a few miles from my home, was Troy, with a population of about 900.

When I was growing up in the '30s and '40s, the nearest city was Temple, with a population of about 40,000, located eight miles from Troy. In 1942, Camp Hood (later changed to Fort Hood and now named Fort Cavazos) was established just outside of Killeen, Texas, sixty miles south-southwest of Waco. Fort Hood was named after a Confederate general, John Bell Hood, and when it was finished in August 1942, there were about 90,000 troops billeted there.

When I was born, people were still alive who had fought in

the Civil War. And there were many who had yet to admit that the South had been beaten. Every town in the South big enough to have a town square—and some even smaller—had a statue dedicated to the Civil War soldier and a monument to "our honored dead." This quote from one such statute expresses the sentiment that much of the Southern white population still felt:

> *The world shall yet decide,*
> *in truth's clear, far-off light,*
> *that the soldiers who wore the*
> *gray, and died*
> *with Lee, were in the right.*

Texas was also the place where many of the soldiers most unwilling to admit defeat retreated and settled after the war. When I was young, there was still a contingent of Confederate veterans who proudly marched beneath a Confederate battle flag in the Veterans Day parade along with the younger Sons of Confederate Veterans, who just as proudly marched under the same flag. To them, the Confederate flag was sacrosanct. It was everywhere.

But to us blacks growing up there, that flag evoked different emotions. Like other states' Confederate documents, the February 2, 1861, Texas Declaration of Causes for Secession focused mostly on the threat to whites' right to own slaves as property and dominate "the African race . . . as an inferior and dependent race."

That feeling still permeated many whites during my early years in Texas. They used it to justify inferior public facilities and services, shameful acceptance of squalid living conditions, poverty wages, few jobs, and a racist culture that rivaled that of any other Southern state. The Ku Klux Klan (KKK) was alive and active, and many whites were proud members. It seemed they were determined to prove us inferior and keep us dependent.

Waco was the site of one of the most horrific lynchings in US history. In 1916, a white mob of 10,000—including the mayor and police chief—cheered as Jesse Washington, a seventeen-year-old illiterate and mentally disabled black farmhand, was dragged from his cell, hanged, dismembered, and burned while the mob celebrated. Whether guilty or not, he had confessed to the rape and murder of a white woman and signed his "X" on the bottom of a confession he did not write and could not read. He was convicted by an all-white jury that deliberated for four minutes.

1922, just nine years before I was born, was the first year since 1885 without a recorded lynching in Texas. And other lynchings came later. Texas has the third-highest number of lynching victims in the US, after Mississippi and Georgia. The eleven counties on the Brazos River between Waco and the Mexican border account for 20 percent of all lynchings in Texas. Falls County lies solidly along this line. For us, the Confederate flag evoked thoughts of a hanging tree more than anything else.

I don't recount these despicable incidents to condemn the state or its citizens, for that behavior was commonplace throughout the South. I bring them up to make more vivid the culture I was brought up in. There, racism, an evil birthed by local slavery, was as pervasive as air.

But just as a fish doesn't wonder why the water is so dark or so polluted, a youngster has nothing for comparison when he considers the time and place he grows up in. They both just keep swimming. And that is what we did there in Bell County. We had meager circumstances, but we also had each other, so we just kept swimming. Like people in many other situations, we didn't think about it too much. That was just the way it was. We simply tried to make the best of it and enjoy our lives. For the most part, that is what we did.

Chapter 3
The Family

I was named after my maternal grandfather, whom I never met. He died of a gunshot wound in 1929 or 1930. His son-in-law, my uncle George and the father of my best friend, DV, killed him.

DV was my best friend growing up. He was my cousin, and he was three years older than me. We went everywhere together and did everything together. When my grandfather was killed, George, DV's father, was having trouble accepting the breakup of his marriage to Ceola, DV's mother and my aunt. For some reason unknown to me, he blamed my grandfather for the breakup.

From what I have assumed based on listening to stories from my aunts and uncles when I was growing up, it must have happened this way:

It was a balmy summer evening when George crept onto the porch of my grandfather's house at suppertime. My grandfather and the rest of the family were having supper inside. Thousands of crickets surrounding the house filled the warm Southern night with a cacophony of chirping. The full moon was rising over the farm—an area entirely devoid of streetlights. The moon made the night as bright as day, and an occasional night owl hooted expectantly in the distance. George carefully opened the unlocked screen door a crack and reached inside, wrapping his hand around the shotgun my grandfather kept standing by the door. Carefully, ever so slowly, he lifted the gun off the floor and took it out of the house. He set the weapon down beside him and knocked.

"Mr. John," he said. "John, this is George. I am sorry to bother you during suppertime, but I would like to speak to you."

"OK," my grandfather said. "Comin'."

Ceola listened with trepidation to her stepfather's footsteps as he walked into the other room and towards the door.

"What is it, George?" he said through the screen door.

George said nothing. He simply raised the shotgun and fired. The sound of a single-barrel twelve-gauge shotgun boomed through the house.

The noise startled and silenced the cicadas, and all anyone heard was the sound of my grandfather's lifeless body hitting the floor and George's feet hitting the dirt road as he ran away. Ceola ran into the front room and stood there frozen before her stepfather's body, afraid to move. The family believed in ghosts. They believed the spirits of the dead would return, and some even believed they could see them. They assiduously avoided graveyards, especially in the dark, as was common for black country folk back then.

Grandfather John's death changed the family forever. Suddenly, our family lost one of its great providers and the proven head of the family, whom the whole family loved and respected. My grandmother took his place, moved into her new role as head of the family, and immediately began proving she was meant for the job. Though she wasn't very old when her husband was killed, she lost all interest in men and never married again.

George ran. He wasn't chased and wasn't arrested for the murder even though there were witnesses. My grandmother and Aunt Ceola spent hours at the police station, uncharacteristically begging them to find him. Back then, the all-white police force didn't spend much time bringing justice to Negroes.

Ceola Banks, the author's aunt, and mother of her only child, DV.

My mother saw George some years later in a south Texas town not too far away where he had, undoubtedly, run to. He seemed to be leading a life quite unencumbered by keeping out of sight.

Where I lived in Texas, the culture was fairly violent. In Troy, for example, without the benefit of any official person whose job was to maintain law and order, the black community enforced its own ideas of right and wrong. The often violent results were frequently sparked when people insulted or wronged one another, real or perceived. And without active policing, routine crime can easily grow violent. I saw several examples of this during my early childhood. They were among my earliest lessons in the use of violence to settle disputes, and they would stay with me throughout my life, influencing my regard for the unqualified necessity of fairly applying the law.

Every month or so during the summer, someone would rent a vacant house from one of the white landowners and throw a party on a Saturday night. There was usually home brew, regular beer, and wine—and always moonshine. People from miles around would come, and there was singing, dancing, drinking, and gambling (usually a dice game) well into the night. Not always, but often, a fight would break out and someone would be stabbed. Not too many people carried guns then or there would have been much more killing. In my day, the sight of blood spurting from a generous wound would normally end a fight.

In Troy, Mr. Thompson, a much-admired black man and a friend of the family, chased a young man down for some reason I never knew. He caught him, shot him in the back in the middle of the street, and killed him. Mr. Thompson was never arrested, and although there was a lot of talk about it, no one seemed upset or thought it unusual that he had "gotten away with it."

Uncle Jace, whose given name was Dave, once got into a fight with Plunk, a local tough who bit off part of Jace's lip while escaping his grasp. Plunk went on to kill someone a few months later and was arrested for the murder, but he only served a few months in jail before being released.

My family in general, and my uncles in particular, were never ones to back down from a fight. It just wasn't considered the honorable thing to do. How many of those fights they themselves started, I never knew.

David Banks, known as Jace

I didn't see a black police officer until I was eight or nine years old because there weren't any. The county chief of police in Temple finally hired a black officer to patrol the black community, but we were quickly disabused of the idea that it was a good thing for us when the officer began beating up other blacks for no reason except that he could. He may have been establishing his reputation as no one to mess with, but in the vernacular of my uncles, he was really just a "mean bastard." In fact, I recall Uncle Jack, at six foot four and 220 pounds, saying, "Someone is going to kill that son of a bitch." I took it to mean he just might be the one to do it.

Uncle Jack's given name was Beverley, but he so disliked that feminine name that he was known to fight anyone who called him that. He changed it by only using Jack, especially on official paperwork. Even his army paperwork recorded him that way, with no mention of Beverley.

Both of my uncles, Uncle Jack and Uncle Jace, would fight at the drop of a hat. Jace was almost as big as Jack, and he was just as strong.

My grandmother was deathly afraid one of my uncles would have an encounter with the black cop that would not end well for our family. Somehow, we avoided it, and that new danger in the neighborhood missed us altogether. But Rosie's fears were not unfounded. Both of my uncles gambled and drank, though neither carried a weapon. However, if there was trouble that required a gun, they might go get one. Jace loved to gamble and he was pretty good at it, seeming to win much more than he lost. He always said he needed to do

Anna Banks

something in addition to his work to feed his family, and that was it. He was killed one night at a dice game after he lost all of his money, accused someone of cheating, and got into a fight over it. He was shot during the fight. Then he walked half a mile to his home, where he collapsed and died, leaving Anna, his wife, with thirteen children.

She remarried a few years later and had two more, for a total of fifteen children that were birthed at home with the help of a midwife. There was no birth control back then so families were large, but Anna's was exceptional. My cousin Doris, was born February 16, 1933 and had eleven children. I always thought that if Uncle Jace had gone north and worked in the auto plants where he could make a living with one job, he might have lived longer. Maybe he would have stopped gambling and not been killed.

My grandmother is as far back as my known family tree goes. I believe my great-great-grandfather and great-great-grandmother were both brought to one of the South Carolina, Georgia, or Florida slave markets on a slave ship from West Africa in the early 1800s, but I don't know that for sure. I once took a genetic test that shows my genetic makeup going back "beyond five generations and well beyond 500 years." It doesn't shed any light on my specific ancestors. The following are the results from a cheek swab analyzed by CRI Genetics:

African (Tribe/Country) 95.9%

Esan in Nigeria	39.4%
Yoruba in Nigeria	16.2%
Luhya in Kenya	12.4%
African Caribbean	10.0%
Mende in Sierra Leone	9.7%
Gambian	6.1%
African American	2.1%

The Journey

European 1.5%

British Isles	0.5%
Iberian	0.5%
Northwestern European	0.2%
Toscani Italian	0.2%
Northern European	0.1%

Mixed American 2.0%

Peruvian	1.9%
Colombian	0.1%

East Asian 0.5%

Japanese	0.2%
Southern Han Chinese	0.2%
Northern Han Chinese	0.1%

South Asian 0.1%

Punjabi	0.1%

I learned a bit about my family history when Grandmother Rose told stories from her childhood. Apparently, her mother, my great-grandmother, was a field hand under slavery in the Falls County area. One day in 1865, the plantation overseer rode his horse into the fields and told them they were free. As Rose told it, the field hands took in the news and then went back to work since they didn't have anywhere else to go. They probably stayed there for years working under a labor contract with the plantation owner without much change to conditions.

There were seven children in Rose's family, three sisters and four brothers. One brother was hit by lightning when he was a teenager. His body was brought into the house and laid out on a table in the back room with a sheet over it since there was no embalming back then, and no undertakers, either. Later that day, when someone went into the back room, he rose into a sitting position with the sheet still over him. Apparently, the lightning had slowed his heart to the point where they couldn't hear the heartbeat. After they had all run screaming from the house, he walked out and asked what was wrong, having no recollection of anything after he left home for the fields that morning.

My grandmother's mother died when Rose was in her early teens. Her father remarried, moved in with his new wife, and had several children with her. Rose was never close to her stepmother or any of her step siblings, but she remained close to her full brothers and sisters until they died.

Grandmother Rose had two girls with her first husband. Ceola, the oldest, became my best friend DV's mother. The second girl, whose name I don't know, died in childhood from causes I am not aware of. While I don't remember her given name, I do remember we always referred to her as Daughter. Rose had four more children with her second husband, John, my grandfather, who had one son from his first marriage. That was Dave, whom we called Jace. Everyone I knew had a nickname; in most cases, that was only the name we knew them by.

Beverly, known as Jack, the author's uncle. He was married to Anna's sister, Ocie. Ocie brought one child to the marriage, Otis Griffin, nicknamed Duke.

My mother, Jessie Mae, was a twin, and her twin sister was named Johnnie Mae. They were born January 18, 1914. Annie Mae was born next, on March

28, 1916. We most often called her by her nickname, Punk. In April 1918, a son was born. This was Beverley, who went by Jack. So, I had three aunts and two uncles growing up.

I asked other members of my family to send me information about our relations, I received the following from a cousin:

My name is Laura Ann Ward Holiday. I am the only child of Gladys Marie Cross Ward and Willie Lee Ward. My father was the grandson of Nathaniel Ward and Amanda Shields Ward. He was the son of Nathaniel and Amanda's first born, a son, John Henry Ward.

I would like to tell you a story. A story that affects every member of this family and but for this story you would not exist. It begins with a boy referred to on the 1880 United States federal census as Nathanial Ward. The spelling of Nathanial was later changed to Nathaniel. On the 1880 census he stated he was born in Louisiana to unnamed parents about 1842. On later census records, according to his recorded age, he was born about 1844. To put Nathaniel's story in perspective, let us explore what was happening around the time of his birth.

The Republic of Texas was established in 1836 and Falls County, Texas was established on January 28, 1850 when he was approximately eight years of age. Falls County is located in Central Texas and is surrounded by Limestone, Robertson, Milam, Bell, and McLennan counties. Marlin, the largest town and county seat, is 24 miles south of Waco and 121 miles south of Dallas. The county was named after an area where waters of the Brazos River cascade over rocks creating a waterfall which was a fording and camping area for both Indians and white settlers. In the early 1880s the area was still a part of Mexico. Indian tribes such as the Wacos, Tawakonis, Andarkos, and Commanches were also in the area. Although illegal, nine white families settled in the area by 1830. By 1834–35 there was a permanent settlement of the Cherokees and white settlers in the area. On January 28, 1850, the Texas state legislature formed Falls County from Limestone and Milam counties. Marlin, located on the east bank of the Brazos River, became the permanent county seat.

Nathaniel and other people of African descent lived and worked on the west bank of the Brazos River commonly known as the Brazos River bottom. Nathaniel would grow up, raise his family and die there. The white settlers of Falls County came from the slaveholding South, primarily Mississippi, Tennessee and Alabama. Four years after the creation of the county in 1854, records show there were 647 slaves which were valued at $335,300. By the census of 1860 the county had 1,716 slaves (forty-seven percent of the total population) and 504 farms and plantations. Four years before the signing of the Emancipation Proclamation, there were 1,654 slaves valued at $987,980. By the time news of the signing of the proclamation reached Texas on June 19, 1865, Nathaniel was twenty-three years old.

Nathaniel Ward showed up on the June 2, 1880, United Federal census. He was 38 years old. How he arrived in Texas is unknown, however, there is a family story which states he was brought to Texas at an early age by a slaveholder and given as a gift to his wife to work as a house boy. He grew up near the Brazos River, only miles from the present town of Lott, Texas. As the story goes, he was forced to go to the Civil War by this slaveholder; however, he ran away and returned to the plantation. Not knowing of his return, the slaveholder wrote a letter to his wife stating that Nathaniel had been killed on the first day of their arrival. As legend has it, the wife hid him until the war was over. Slavery ended when Nathaniel was twenty-three years old. He could not read or write. At age twenty-five, two years after the signing of the Emancipation Proclamation, he married Amanda Shields in Falls County, Texas, August 3, 1867. On the 1880 census, he listed his occupation as farmer.

Amanda Shields, also known as Manda, was thirty-five years of age on June 1, 1880. According to this census, she was born in 1845 in Texas and listed her father's birthplace as Texas and her mother's birthplace as Louisiana. It appears Amanda may have grown up in the same area as Nathaniel. At age six, one of the largest plantations in the area was established by B.G. Shields of Alabama, and she may have lived on that plantation and took the last name of Shields, a common custom at that time. B.G. Shields, known as General Shields, was a slaveholder from Alabama. He was elected to the United States Congress and served as a representative from Alabama from 1840 to 1841. An associate of President Andrew Jackson, he was appointed as a diplomatic official at Caracas, Venezuela by President James K. Polk and appointed collector of customs at Galveston, Texas, in 1874 by President Ulysses S. Grant. When slavery ended, Amanda was twenty years old and could not read or write.

At age twenty-two, she married Nathaniel Ward and on the 1880 census, she listed her occupation as housekeeper. It is possible that both Nathaniel and Amanda were slaves on the Shields plantation. After slavery ended, Nathaniel and his brother George entered into labor contracts as freedmen and worked for ex-slave holding families. He also purchased approximately 33 acres of plantation land from the ex-slave-holder B.G. Shields.

By June 1, 1880, after thirteen years of marriage and at ages 38 and 35, Nathaniel and Amanda were the parents of seven children; four girls, and three boys: Henrietta, age 11; John Henry aka J.H., age 10 who later became my grandfather; George, age 8; Nathaniel, age 6; Roberta, often referred to as

Rose/Mama/Mama Rose, [my grandmother] age 4; Lou J., age 2; and Ettie N., age four months.

After 1880, a son, Nathan was born March 14, 1881, Indiana born May 1883, Chilton born April 1885, Sallie born March 1887, and Violet born January 1890. It appears Amanda died sometime after the birth of her last daughter and twelfth child because by 1900, Nathaniel was married to Amelia Hardy and four children remained in the household. According to records, he married Amelia Hardy in 1896 in Lott, Texas. Nathaniel Ward did not appear on the 1910 federal census. He apparently died between June 8, 1900, and 1910.

My grandmother, Rose Banks, was a feisty, God-fearing woman born April 25, 1874, in the area of Falls County. She was practical and stubborn, and she worked hard to keep us together. From time to time, she would take grandchildren in when their parents found it too hard to both work and take care of them. During particularly hard times, her children—and sometimes their families—came back to live with her, too. During my childhood,

The author's grandmother, Rose Banks, at about eighty years old. She lived from 1874 to 1974.

Rosie always seemed to have someone else's baby on her hip, and she usually had anywhere from three to seven additional people living in her three-room house. She dipped snuff, quoted the Bible (though her ability to read it was limited), and was a master with a switch if she thought we had done wrong and needed a lesson. She was lively and nurturing, and she could run as fast as the wind. Trying to outrun her to escape her correcting punishment was always futile. She lived to reach 100 and died in her kitchen making her daughter Ceola breakfast in November 1974.

As I mentioned earlier, I lived with her from the age of five, when my mother moved to Waco for work, until twelve, when my mother took me back to Waco to live with her. My grandmother was the source of my early childhood lessons in civility, independence, hard work, self-preservation, and the clear difference between right and wrong. The boundaries she established between right and wrong, and our place amidst them, were very clear. Her enforcement was also consistent and, for the most part, well-deserved. She was the one constant in her children's and grandchildren's lives, and she successfully held the family together despite all the hardships.

My biological father was a Baptist preacher who impregnated my sixteen-year-old mother in 1930 but took no responsibility for either her or his child. Mother always said that had her father been alive during that time, "he would have taken his shotgun and had a talk with that preacher so [she] never would have been an unwed mother." While there was little talk of him as I grew up, there was enough for me to understand he was the cause of some pain for me during my early years in Bell County, when I was regularly called a "little bastard," sometimes even by my cousins, aunts, and uncles. It was their way of putting me in my place when there were disagreements around the house. To this day, I don't believe they meant to hurt me as deeply as that epithet did—I think they merely used it to end our disagreements.

My earliest recollection of hearing that hateful name is from shortly after I moved to Grandmother Rosie's. DV and his family were living there, too, and one day, several of our cousins and some other kids were there as well. They were picking sides for a game, and since I was the smallest, no one wanted me on their side.

"You take that one," someone said.

"No. I don't want that little bastard," another said.

I didn't know what the name meant, but soon enough, they were hurling "little bastard, little bastard, little bastard" at me. From the way they said it, I could tell it was a bad name. Finally, someone spat out, "Why, you ain't got no daddy. You are nothing more than a lil' bastard. Who would want you on their team?"

Feeling the sting of those words, I ran across the road and sat, crouched on my haunches, between two rows of cotton with my fists tightly balled up, muttering "I ain't no little bastard" over and over. Soon I heard DV's voice from across the road, rising above the others.

"You stop calling lil' brother that name," he said. I had a protector. Everyone called me Lil' Brother. The last time I went back to Texas, I was over seventy years old and people still called me Lil' Brother. "He didn't have nothin' to do with it. It ain't his fault and he can't do nothin' about it. What makes you all so sure your daddy is your real daddy, anyway?" He said this with some force.

"We'll take him on our team," DV said before walking across the road to where I sat, still muttering in anger.

"Come on, lil' brother," he said. "You're on our team."

I don't know why DV stood up for me that day. But he did, and I remain grateful to this day. I have always believed it came out of the goodness of his nature, which he demonstrated many times as we grew up together there in Troy. Kids can be harsh to each other, and as the son of an unmarried single parent, I did stand out. DV's simple act of kindness helped me fit in, and that was what I wanted more than anything at the time.

As I grew older, my biological father's actions significantly colored my view of the church. This happened in spite of my grandmother's vocal reliance on Bible verses she could hardly read to bolster her notions of right and wrong and despite my mother's weekly attendance at the church services to which she regularly took me.

David V. James, Sr.

DV in his Army uniform.

Consequently, I have never acknowledged that morally challenged gentleman as my father. My relation to him is one of accident only, and I can honestly say he never had any intentional part in raising me. However, his actions did provide significant and lasting instruction in how a man should not act and how a person in authority should not treat women or those who look up to him morally, or in any other way. Ironically, that bitter lesson informed me greatly as I moved through life. I recognized boundaries and restrictions, and I endeavored to always do the right thing by others. All in all, I believe both his malfeasance and DV's kindness made me a better man.

Melvin Dearman, my first stepfather, was, conversely, a monument to right actions. From the time he gave me his name through common law adoption to the time when he and my mother separated a few years later, he gave me the full support of a loving father, always modeling the actions of a faithful, hard-working family man. He was never as happy as when he was providing for his family and when he could see us happy and content. I consider him one of my lucky stars, too, without whom I would never have succeeded.

Melvin worked hard and never complained. He worked in the fields driving the mules or driving a tractor during the growing seasons. He picked cotton and did the other activities necessary to keep a farm working. Like every Negro I knew, he did not own the land he worked but farmed it for the landowning whites. When he wasn't farming, and in the offseason, he worked as a mechanic maintaining and repairing farm equipment and cars belonging to Negroes in the area. My strongest memory of Melvin is of him sliding out from under an automobile with a smile on his face as he wiped the grease from his hands on the rag he kept in the back pocket of his overalls. I took to mimicking him by keeping a greasy rag in the back pocket of my overalls, too, and pretending to repair cars like he did. I learned to slide under cars next to Melvin, and though I am sure I must have been a nuisance and in the way most of the time, he never scolded me or told me to leave him to his work. On the contrary, he always encouraged me, explaining exactly what he was doing. He seemed to enjoy my being there as much as I did.

Mother wasn't happy that her young son insisted on rubbing grease on his face and clothes as he pretended to be a grease monkey like Melvin, whom I called Daddy. But she didn't protest too much. I believe she thought it a small price to pay for having her son so happily attached to as good a man as Melvin was.

By the time I was about four, the Depression had driven cotton prices down to less than half of what they had been before it started. Unemployment was rampant, so Melvin, my mother, and I moved south to Edinburg, Texas, near Brownsville on the Mexico border in the Rio Grande Valley to find work. Even DV lived with us for part of the time when we were there.

In Edinburg, I got to know some Mexican farmworkers for the first time as there was a sizable Mexican population. (There had been none living in Bell County that I was aware of.) They all seemed like industrious, family-oriented people with whom we got along quite well. We stayed in the Rio Grande Valley for a while. Then, when prospects in Bell County got better, we moved back.

One day, after we returned to Bell County, Melvin spent the day plowing the fields around the house with a two-mule team, a tiring task in the searing summer sun. He was making his way back to the house behind the mules when I saw him coming and ran up the hill to meet him. Instead of sending me away, he put me on his lap behind the mules, letting me hold the reins to "drive" them the rest of the way to the house and on to the barn, where we put them up for the night. That is only one of my many fond memories of Melvin, a man I have always considered to be my real daddy. It was characteristic of the gentle, caring way he always treated me.

Our bond was strong and nobody questioned my integration into Melvin's side of the family even after he and my mother broke up. Some ten years after I finished law school and moved to San Francisco, my mother located and introduced me to Joe Dearman, Melvin's brother and my adopted uncle. She was always proud of my accomplishments and never shied away from introducing her "lawyer son." Like Melvin, Uncle Joe was a very good man who worked hard and took care of his family. I was honored when I was asked to speak at Uncle Joe's funeral when he died.

Joe's family lives in the San Francisco Bay Area to this day, and I have kept up the practice of attending some of their family events like weddings, reunions, and other notable occasions. They have always treated me as a part of their family because . . . well, I am. My love of them springs directly from how Melvin, my stepfather (but really my daddy) and a very good man, treated me and my mother for those few short years so long ago.

My personal experience of being a family member by choice has also informed my treatment of others, especially those who came before me when I was a judge in court. There, I used that understanding to help me make the right decision, particularly in probate court, where I served for nine years. There were many occasions in probate when there was a family dispute and I spent considerable time trying to preserve family ties. For my money, there is nothing more precious than family, and I have never hesitated to fight for mine.

When I was about thirteen, I met my biological father for the first time. One of my close friends had drowned, and Mother and I went to the funeral. My biological father gave the eulogy; Mother knew he was going to be involved in the service, so she prepared me the night before.

"Your father will be at tha' service, John," she said. "He's your father, son, so Ah' want you ta' be nice ta' him."

"OK."

"He's tha' man who got me pregnant and then wouldn't marry me," she said. "I know you've heard me and your aunts talk about him and how much we don't like him, but regardless, Ah' want you to talk to him just like you would any preacher in tha' church. You know, John, if somebody's done you wrong, unless there is something you can do about it, you should never let on that you are hurt or mad at them. That just reminds everyone else that they have put one over on you and lets them know that they still get to you. Don't let them win again by showing you are hurt."

"Yes, ma'am," I said.

That night, I thought about how this man I had never met was the source of many personal and hurtful insults that I had endured for years. It made my blood boil, just as it did every time someone called me a bastard. And I thought about how much harder my mother's life must have been because he wouldn't marry her.

But then I thought about what my mother had said about treating him like I would anyone else, and I vowed to do what she asked, no matter how hard it might be. So, I began practicing.

"Nice to meet you, Reverend," I said.

"Nice to meet you."

"Nice to meet you, sir."

"Hello."

"Yes sir."

"Thank you, sir."

I practiced these phrases many times together with the accompanying handshake until I felt comfortable with the one I liked best. I was going to do what Mother had said. I wasn't going to let her down by letting this man know how much he had hurt her . . . and me.

So, the next day, the reverend gave the benediction at the end of the service. After it was over, we all walked outside. Mother took my hand and led me over to where he was talking to some men.

"That was a nice benediction, Reverend. I'd like you to meet my son, John," Mother said.

I stuck my hand out. "Nice to meet you, sir," I said using my best grown-up voice while looking directly into his eyes trying not to let my anger show in mine.

As we turned and walked away, we held our backs straight and our heads high. Mother looked down at me, caressed my head for a second, and smiled. It felt good to know that I had not embarrassed her or myself that afternoon. As far as I remember, she never mentioned him to me again.

I met him again when I was older, and I remembered her advice. When I was seventeen, I was living in Saginaw, Michigan, but returned to Waco for the summer. One day, we ran into each other in a downtown clothing store when we unexpectedly found ourselves face-to-face between coat racks.

"You back?" he said.

"Yes sir. Just for the summer."

"Well, you should come to church sometime."

"I might do that," I said, knowing that if I did, it certainly wouldn't be at his church. "I'll see you around," I said and headed out of the store into the fresh air. To my recollection, that was the last time we spoke. It was more contact than I'd wanted at the time.

Chapter 4
Early Life

My early life was hard in both Falls and Bell County since our family, for the most part, had no reliable income save that from picking cotton. In the 1930s, according to government anthologies, white workers in the US who were lucky enough to have a job averaged $2,000 a year whereas black sharecroppers in Texas averaged about $200 a year. Even then, that qualified as "slim pickings."

Our financial arrangements with the landowners were nearly identical to those of sharecroppers in that the landowner supplied the land, seeds, tools, farm animals, housing, and all necessary capital. However, we weren't technically sharecroppers because we didn't share in the cotton crop. I suppose we were a cross between sharecroppers and tenant farmers because the entire crop went to the white landowner, and we were paid by the yield at so many cents per 100 pounds we picked. The white landowners would advance us money to get us through the winter, and we worked the fields in summer to pay it back. We lived in a ramshackle two- or three-room house on the landowner's properties, and we moved often—whenever we found better work on another farm, mostly in Bell County.

Although we lived in four different houses while I was there, none were more than four miles away from the small town of Troy, all down a hard-packed dirt road. Highway 81, a two-lane blacktop, ran through the middle of Troy between the two gas stations, one of which had a small restaurant attached. DV's mom worked there as a short-order cook during the farming offseason. The small lumberyard and the cotton gin/warehouse were the two industries in Troy. Cotton was brought to the gin, which sat right beside the railroad tracks. The cottonseed was ginned there, separating the seeds from the cotton fibers. After that, it was baled, stored, and finally loaded onto rail cars that pulled up alongside the building for shipment to textile mills in other towns.

Our family was on the same continuously repeating cycle of poverty as the other land-poor and sharecropper Negroes in the South. We were not paid directly for our labor but were paid for what we produced. In our case, it was by the pound for the cotton we picked. This system replaced slavery after the Civil War as a way of controlling Negro families, keeping us all working and beholden to our employers—our former owners.

The pay was so low that we were always in debt. We lived in the owner's house, such as it was, and the rent was free. (That is, it was considered in establishing our income.) He extended credit to us in the offseason, which we paid back as soon as we could after the growing season started. Everything revolved around having a little money in the growing season and living on credit in the offseason. My recollection is that, except for a few months in the growing season, we were always in debt, dependent on the largesse of store owners to extend us credit in the offseason.

Adults were paid less than one dollar per day for chores and attending to animals in the offseason if they performed those jobs.

We were allowed to work for other landowners if all our primary landowner's work was done, which it often wasn't. This usually applied to picking cotton.

Thackston's General Store was one of the two stores in Troy, and Mr. Thackston gave us credit outside of the cotton season when we sorely needed it. In the winter, we put groceries and other staples on credit at Thackston's and other local stores, and we always paid it off as soon as we could after the growing season started in the spring and we were making money again. Aside from the right and the wrong of it, there was never any thought of not paying back the advance or credit. Word carried fast and far in those communities, and reneging on a debt owed to a white man meant being blackballed from future work, housing, and credit—or worse.

There were two schools in Troy, an elementary school for blacks and another for whites. There was a white church but no black church; consequently, we traveled about eight miles to the nearest black church to attend services. My grandmother usually attended every Sunday, and sometimes other family members would go with her, usually piling into an old car that someone had. This included my mother and me. We would go with her every couple of weeks while we lived there.

I started picking cotton when I was about five. At that time, my mother, Melvin, and I lived on a farm near my grandmother's house. Then, for some reason unknown to me, Melvin and my mother split up, so Mother and I went to live with Grandmother Rosie again. It was cotton-picking season when I moved there, and the rest of my family members were in the fields from sunup to sundown picking cotton. They took me with them and I tried to do my part. That may seem harsh, but Mother was just twenty-two and trying her best to make a living as an uneducated, unwed black mother with a young child. And living with my grandmother never seemed unusual to any of us who were raised by her.

My earliest recollection of the pay for picking cotton was that it was about fifty cents per 100 pounds in 1942. I remember that because when I was eleven, I earned the princely sum of one dollar for picking two hundred pounds between sunup and sundown—about twelve hours' work. Like the other family members, I proudly turned it over to my grand-mother, who managed our accounts. The most I ever picked in one day was 300 pounds, shortly before I reunited with Mother in Waco. I felt quite manly the day I picked the 300 pounds. I was never afraid of work, nor was I shy about putting my back into it. In fact, when I was a youngster, it seemed like I was always trying to prove myself by turning in a good day's work. That was the best way to earn respect in a farming community.

Like the other family members, I started picking cotton seri-ously when I was big enough to drag a cotton sack between the rows by myself. Uncle Jack would drive a two-mule wagon or a tractor-drawn wagon along one end of the cotton field. When we reached the end of a row, we'd carry our cotton sacks to the wagon, weigh them on the wagon's scales, then hump the sacks over the wooden slats and into the wagon bed. Those were long days, and we often worked in ninety-five-degree heat with very high humidity between June and September. To say it was back-breaking work is an understatement, but it was what we knew and all we had. Though we would complain (especially the chil-dren), we were grateful to have it. And we slept very well at night.

We children started picking cotton using a two- or three-foot sack since that was as much as we could drag along between the cotton rows. As we got older, bigger, and stronger, we gradually graduated to six-foot sacks, or even seven-foot sacks for the strongest. (We considered them "real studs.") We would drag the sacks behind us, filling them as we moved along between the rows. In a large field, that could be half a mile. Naturally, I was always trying to be thought of as one of the studs. We had about four weigh-ins each day, and good cotton pickers averaged forty to fifty pounds per weigh-in. The "real cotton pickers" averaged more,

There are no pictures from that time in my life, but I was about this boy's age when I started hearing "ticket, ticket, ticket."

but few averaged as much as Thousand Pound Red, the mythical monster picker who was as famous and respected in our neck of the woods as Paul Bunyan was in his.

Still, even then I was thinking about leaving.

"Hear that train whistle," I would say to DV as we worked. "You hear *chugga, chugga, whistle,* but I hear *ticket, ticket, ticket.* One of these days, I'll pick enough cotton for a real ticket and I'll get on that train and leave outta here. Then, after a while, I'll come back with a pocket full of money, drivin' a big car! Hear that? *Ticket, ticket, ticket!*"

Outside of the cotton season, we did the tilling and planting, along with general farm and equipment upkeep. We were paid by the day, which ran from sunup to sundown. My recollection, again probably from the late '30s and early '40s, was that adults earned less than a dollar a day and children less than fifty cents a day. Outside of picking cotton, the children worked without pay and helped their parents until they were about ten years old, at which point they started getting paid.

Johnnie Mae, my mother's twin, got DV and me our first official payday by negotiating with the landowner when we reached ten years old. We got a dollar a day for the two of us. DV and I had always been paid for the cotton we picked as cotton was paid by the pound, but the other work we'd done was gratis until then. The cotton growing and picking season usually ran from June to September and was intermittent depending on the weather. As much as we complained, and as unfair as much of it was, it did teach us the value of hard work. We developed the ability to push through and finish, no matter how difficult it might be—a trait I would find very useful many times later in life.

Johnnie Mae Banks, twin sister of the author's mother. She was the mother of three girls, Earlene, Mary Lou, Eula Ruth, and one son, Jake. (I was their babysitter. Eula is alive and well and her two sisters and brother are deceased.)

Although rent was free, our housing was, at best, basic. There was no running water in the houses. We drank from containers that we filled from nearby springs, creeks, or a spigot in the yard (if there was one) that was used to fill the animal troughs. There was no indoor plumbing, and if we had an outhouse, it would be a single building in the back. However, there were times when we had to go to the woods or use the fields because there was no outhouse.

We never owned a radio, and by the time the first television station in Texas started operating in September 1948, we had moved to Saginaw, Michigan. Nor did we ever subscribe to a newspaper or a magazine. We got our news through word-of-mouth and from the out-of-date newspapers and magazines that white families gave us from time to time. On the farm, we put the newspapers in the outhouse and used them for toilet paper. Most of my family members didn't read well anyway, so they never missed having access to printed news.

There are no photos of any of our houses, but this is a close approximation.

I lived in many houses during the time when I lived with my grandmother. These were all small country houses—more accurately, ramshackle shacks representative of the housing other country Negroes lived in at that time. Every one of them was a poorly built clapboard affair with weathered or no exterior paint. The doors and windows were poorly fit and thus drafty. The tin roofs leaked, and there was no insulation in the walls— poor shelter for winters that could dip to below freezing between November and March. Inside, the studs had thin pine boards nailed on them, and there were gaps between them. There were also gaps in the exterior clapboard siding. It made for a very drafty house that was difficult to heat. Grandmother Rosie tried to prevent these drafts by making a water-and-flour paste that she used to hang newspaper and magazine pages that served as wallpaper. This "wallpaper" covered the cracks and kept the house a little warmer. She was very neat about it, and all of the pages were hung with the print right-side up. It did help cut the drafts, but the flour paste attracted bedbugs, and sometimes the children (including me) would pick at the newspaper, opening more cracks. As I was learning to read, I perused the newspaper and magazine articles on the walls before I went to sleep at night. That probably helped me learn to read earlier than most.

Grandmother Rose always had a big bed that the small children shared with her on cold nights. There was almost always another bed that DV and I slept in, and other kids would also pile in when they were there. The highest number of kids I remember sleeping in the same bed is five: three at the top and two at the bottom, with our feet facing each other. That would just be for a night or two, though.

At that time, in that part of the world, it was customary for whites to call blacks by their first or last names, but whites never addressed blacks as "Mr." or "Mrs." Even small white children would address much older black people by their first names only while any white boy who could even think of growing a mustache expected us to call him "Mr." But if a black boy called a white girl or woman by her first name, it could be seen as an aggressive invitation for a beating or worse.

By some accounts, that is how the 1955 Emmett Till incident started in Mississippi. It ended with him being kidnapped, beaten to death, then shot in the head. A large fan was tied around his neck with barbed wire before his mutilated body was thrown into the Tallahatchie River. When I got older, it used to gall me no end to see a six- or eight-year-old white kid call my seventy-year-old grandmother by her first name, showing her no respect, while his whole family expected her to address him as "Mr." That is just one simple example of how even the smallest of everyday customs clearly reinforced the subservience of our race.

By the time Aunt Ceola died at eighty-three, she and her husband, L.E., were divorced, but they remained friends. I took my whole family back to Texas for her funeral and had some experiences that were good examples of old-timey, small-town Texas country meeting modern, big-city San Francisco. When I saw L.E., I introduced him to my wife and twelve-year-old daughter. "Unc, I would like to introduce my daughter, Kelly, and my wife, Ina," I said. "Ina, this is Uncle L.E.."

"Just call me Nig!" he said to the two shocked women.

Years earlier, someone had nicknamed L.E. "Nigger," and he always preferred "Nig" because it was shorter and more familiar. He was never bothered by the name, but my modern San Francisco black women were mightily offended by it.

"Dad, I just can't call him that," Kelly said.

"Why not? He doesn't mind," I said. "In fact, he likes it."

"Well, I do mind!" Kelly said.

"So do I," Ina said. "I won't call him that no matter how much he likes it. I just can't say that word. It isn't right!"

Neither I nor they brought it up to LE, but we all called him LE until we left. He must have thought we were just more formal out in San Francisco.

Just before I moved to Waco with my mother, my grand-mother lived in a house that had five rooms, and we used three of them for bedrooms. My cousins DV, Duke (Otis Griffin), and I shared a bed in one of the bedrooms.

DV, his mother, and his stepfather were also living with Mama when I moved in. DV was eight years old then, three years older than I was. He was also much bigger and already going to school. School started a few months after I moved in with Mama, and, at five, I began going to school with DV. I kept him company, and it also kept me out of Mama's hair during the day and freed her up to work the fields with everyone else. In truth, I started as soon as I was able to walk the three miles to school as it meant free babysitting in a crowded household that sorely needed it. For me, it meant I unofficially started school a year early and I spent my days in that one-room schoolhouse listening to the same lessons as the older kids. I wasn't enrolled, but the next year, when I formally started school, I had already been listening for a year.

My fourth-grade class.

Of course, there was another reason for starting school early. It meant I got a free breakfast and, sometimes, lunch. Before that, there were some hungry days at home. This was one of Roosevelt's Depression-era New Deal programs designed to get the economy moving again and help US citizens. The Depression of the 1930s had brought widespread unemployment all over the globe. Economies were lagging, and much of the farm production went begging for a market as no one was buying. While farm surpluses mounted, the prices of farm products cratered to the point that much of the food produced was plowed under because it was selling at prices too low to warrant the expense of harvesting. This happened while many people, black and white, faced starvation.

Farm income of the day provided only a meager subsistence, and sharecroppers were on the bottom of that sparse barrel. Millions of school children across the US were unable to pay for their school lunches, and with limited family resources to provide meals at home, the danger of malnutrition among children had become a national concern. So, President Franklin Delano Roosevelt drove Congress to establish his "Alphabet Soup" programs to, among many other things, buy surplus food at a reduced but reliable price that kept US farms viable. Then the government provided a large part of that food to school children as free lunches, which helped keep them from malnutrition and starvation.

In 1933, FDR cajoled Congress into establishing the Federal Surplus Commodities Corporation, which bought and distributed surplus foodstuffs to the needy, and everyone in our school certainly qualified as needy. By the end of the '30s, nearly six million children across America were receiving free school lunches. Two of them were DV and me. My recollection is that we usually had yellow grits for breakfast, and after breakfast, attendance would drop because a lot of the kids left to meet their parents in the fields so they could work for the rest of the day. At least they started the day with a full belly.

The concept of a one-room schoolhouse is an ancient one, but, even back when I attended, it seemed outdated in every neighborhood in America except rural black ones. The white kids in the Troy school system went to a larger school a half mile down the road where there were separate classrooms for each grade. They also had current textbooks, which we might see two or three years later, full of notes and scribbling as hand-me-downs. Furthermore, the white school was half a mile from the train tracks. When the trains rumbled through town, the white school children could hear their whistles, but their classroom activities weren't completely disrupted. When trains passed our school, on the other hand, the earth trembled and the building shook like the end was upon us. In fact, the first time it happened, I was completely petrified. If DV hadn't been there, I probably would have run out the door screaming. But the combination of knowing he would protect me and never wanting to look scared in front of anyone in my family kept me trembling in my seat until it passed. When it did, all the other children, who had been patiently sitting in their seats, began working right where they had left off. It was like life took a little time-out while the earth shook. The track was only a few yards behind the school, so realistically speaking, trying to communicate or do anything else was futile when those trains thundered past. Like the other kids, I eventually got used to it and just sat quietly in my seat until the train passed and we could hear each other again.

In fact, our school was so close to the railroad tracks that when the trains stopped beside us, hobos would jump off and run to the water faucet beside the building to get a drink. They had to make it back onto the train before it was moving too fast for them to jump aboard. The Depression had put so many people out of work that hoboing was a widespread and accepted way of traveling around and looking for work.

That was my first school, Troy Colored School. It included grades one through seven. All seven grades were housed in one unpainted twenty-by-forty-foot clapboard building perched on cinder block piers twenty yards from the main railroad tracks. I believe it had initially been a freight storage dock and warehouse at a stop where trains loaded and unloaded goods. All seven grades were taught together by a single teacher who was also the janitor, monitor, and everything else. Because some students only came to school for a convenient free breakfast, they didn't graduate. In fact, some of the students were as old as the teacher. One year, the teacher was twenty years old, still in college and not yet certified, but she was the best we had at the time.

At school, water was drawn from an outside spigot and brought inside by the pailful. The building's heat, such as there was, came from a cast-iron pot bellied stove sitting in the middle of the room that burned wood chips and short pieces of wood. The single-seat outhouse was a two-minute walk to the edge of the woods.

When the time came for one grade's lessons, the other students were expected to sit quietly at their desks and do homework or otherwise refrain from disturbing the class being taught. When it was their turn, the class being taught went from their desks to the front of the room, lined up, listened to the lessons, and answered the teacher's questions. That meant the teacher engaged directly with each class for less than an hour each day. It's a wonder we learned anything at all.

During my first year at school, I was bored sitting and listening to the older children throughout the day since I wasn't enrolled and had no work to do. At some point, however, I started paying attention to the teacher and the lessons she taught to all the classes. I found I could learn a lot by following along and doing as much of the work as I could. My mind was too active to resist jumping ahead and, as a result, I was able to do advanced work.

I liked learning from the time I first started school, and I always asked a lot of questions. In fact, I asked too many questions. According to my relatives at home, I was curious about everything.

"I don't know, boy," they'd say.

"But why is it that way, Mama?" (Or Aunt, or Uncle.)

"Just 'cause, boy! Just 'cause!" This was said with much exasperation. "Now get outside and play with your cousins!"

Apparently, I was a lot of trouble at school, too. I didn't know that until I saw one of my former teachers when I went home for a family reunion after I had moved to San Francisco. She told everyone that I had disrupted her classes by questioning everything.

"Once he asked why the sky was blue," she explained to much laughter.

That character trait stayed with me long after grammar school. When I was in high school, I offended Mama by questioning God and the church. I said, "If God is so powerful, why does He let some people have so much while people like us have so little?"

"Shut up, boy!" was the most often repeated answer to that and similar questions.

I attended Troy Colored School through part of the sixth grade, when I moved to Waco in the middle of the school year to live with my mother. We took no transcript of my class work in Troy nor any proof of the grade I was in. My mother and I went to the North Seventh Street Colored Elementary School to get me enrolled. I was still small for my age then and looked younger than I was. At first, I just sat there while the principal and my mother were talking about me as if I wasn't in the room. Neither one had actually seen me in school, and they were both saying things about me that weren't true. I had always been good at math so, after a while, I got up, went to the blackboard behind the principal, and began solving math problems that I thought were advanced work. (I was always confident in my own abilities.) Soon, the *click–click–clack* of chalk on the blackboard got the principal's attention and he turned to see a blackboard filled with my work. I was trying to convince him that I belonged in the eighth grade, not the seventh. It didn't work as he put me in the seventh grade, where I spent half a year before transferring to Moore High School, where I was placed in grade 7A and soon went to the eighth grade.

Because I was good at math, one of the math teachers who taught the grade ahead of me would take me out of my own class to prove to his students that he assigned problems so easy even a student in the grade behind could solve them. That got me into trouble with my classmates more than once because they insisted it was a put-up job and I had been given the answers earlier. The teacher thought it would motivate the other students, but all it seemed to do was get me in hot water with my classmates as "teacher's pet."

When I graduated eighth grade, there was a graduation ceremony with an awards program for exceptional students. The awards weren't announced until the ceremony, and no one besides the school staff knew which students had won awards.

Freddy Mays, my best friend, and I were both in the running for the big one, the Lincoln National Honor Society Award, which honored students for excellence in the areas of scholarship, service, leadership, and character. Aside from getting good grades, I was always helping teachers, often staying after school to do it. And I was also involved in extracurricular activities, which were part of the selection criteria. Even so, I thought Freddy would win because I felt he was much smarter than I was. When they announced that I had won the Lincoln National Honor Society Award, I was called to the front of the stage to accept it and Freddy's mother walked out. Apparently she, too, thought her son should have won.

Both Mother and Mrs. Schmidt, her employer, were there, and they both walked up on stage to congratulate me when the ceremony was over. Mrs. Schmidt was the only white person in the building, and she appeared to be as proud of me as my mother was. They had both taken charge of encouraging me in my education, and that was helpful to me—especially later, when the work got more difficult and I had doubts about continuing.

Soon after graduation, Freddy moved to Denver with his family. I lost contact with him, but much later, after I had moved to San Francisco, I was watching a news magazine program on television, something like *60 Minutes*. The hosts were interviewing someone who looked familiar. When he said he had grown up in Waco, I was sure it was Freddy, though he wasn't going by Freddy Mays then. He was being interviewed as the most renowned pimp in Denver, which was both surprising and not. To be successful at pimping requires a certain level of smarts, and the Freddy I knew certainly had that.

My cousin DV and I were pals from an early age. With all the cousins living within rock-throwing distance of each other on the farm, we made a little group of four or five who always palled around together. The cousins were all friends, but from an early age, it was DV who always had my back. He was a good bit bigger than I was then and stuck up for me on many occasions. Otis, my first cousin, lived nearby and was my age. He, too, was bigger than I was; he and DV turned out to be the fighters in the group. I remember many times when DV's books scattered on the way home from school because he threw off his book bag when a fight started. I hesitate to call us a little gang, although I suppose that is what we were. Our cousin Potsi and I became the mediators in the group.

I had terrible headaches that started early in my life. They were exacerbated by the summer heat and grew even worse when I was dragging a cotton sack between rows of cotton beneath the broiling Texas sun. But I found that aspirin helped, and I wasn't inclined to stop working in front of the others even though there were days when I felt like my head would explode before I reached the end of those infernal rows. One day I felt a headache coming on shortly after I woke up.

"Mama," I called.

"What you want, boy?"

"Ah' have a headache, Mama. You got any aspirin?" I had already checked and knew she didn't.

"No, no aspirin."

"Got any of that menthol tobacco? Ah' hear it helps." I had been rolling my own with whatever tobacco I could get my hands on for a few months by then and knew that it did.

"OK," she said. I officially started rolling my own and smoking at age eight.

Between aspirin and menthol cigarettes, I could control the headaches, for the most part, but they still came on in the worst heat and almost always on hot summer days when I was between cotton rows in the sun.

During the school year, DV and I walked to class every day and met cousins and friends along the way who joined us as we walked past their houses. The school was a three-mile walk down a dirt road that was dusty and hard during sunny days but became a sloppy mess during or after a rain. On one of the first days when I walked to school, I noticed a fence at the top of a little hill. It was at the edge of the road about half a mile from our school. On that day, Otis, Potsi, and others were together.

"What's that up ahead?" I asked DV, pointing toward the fence and the buildings behind it.

"That's the white school," DV said. "That spot next to the fence is where the little white boys throw things at you and call you nigger," he said.

"You must mean they call *you* nigger," Otis said. He was at the age where kids start to act out, and he was touchy about being called names.

"You better quit that foolishness," Potsi said. "You wanna get shot?"

"Ain't no cracker gonna call me nigger," Otis said.

"Where you wanna' be buried?" Potsi sniggered.

As we came to the fence, there was a group of white kids on the other side of it. "Whatcha doin', nigger?" the first one said in our general direction. "Who's the new lil' one?" he asked, tilting his head in my direction.

"That's Lil' Brother," DV said. "He's just startin'."

"Jus' what we need," said a chubby, pasty-faced boy who leaned against the fence, his hands in his pocket. "More jigaboos," he said. "You niggers ain't never gonna learn shit. Too stoopid."

I didn't mind being called a jigaboo because I had never heard it before and didn't know what it meant. But I did mind being called stupid. I was quite proud of going to school a year early, and I felt the anger starting to rise.

"You still in first grade?" DV asked in the boy's direction. "Third year in a row by now, ain't it?" he said.

The chubby one started spouting insults. His face reddened and spittle flew out of his mouth while the others pointed at him and laughed. He reached down, picked up a rock, and flung it over the fence at DV.

Apparently, they had prepared for us because they had gathered a little mound of rocks near the fence, and they all started throwing them at us.

"First grade! First grade! First grade!" DV and the rest of us yelled as we ran down the road, away from the rocks landing behind us.

We were still laughing and out of breath when we reached the schoolhouse.

"You better watch out for that chubby one," DV said to me.

"Why? I didn't do nothin'," I said.

"Might be a fact," DV said. "But, still, Ah' think he blames you."

My school days had begun.

I never again ran into that chubby boy who had been at the fence. But I think I saw him several times when we were walking and one of the buses taking white kids home after school would pass. They would throw things out of the windows at us, and I thought I recognized him. When I heard a bus coming, I would turn to face it, and I always dodged whatever they threw.

One of the games I played when I was young was "conductor" or "porter." Because being a Pullman porter was one of the best jobs a black man could have back then, some of us mimicked doing that work. I would sometimes ride a car's running board and jump off as it stopped, hollering that we had reached our stop and everyone should get off there. I knew hardly anything about Pullman porters back then, but I saw them getting on and off the trains that stopped in Troy when I went there, and they were memorable. They were dignified, well-dressed, and well-spoken. They also seemed worldly to me since their jobs carried them all around the country, a fact they proved by bringing back the *Chicago Defender* or *Pittsburgh Courier,* newspapers that told us how life in the North could be better than that in rural Texas.

In reality, the porters' pay wasn't very high. They often made more in tips since Pullman sleeping cars were, at the time, the luxury or cultured way to travel in the US. Compared to the average income of blacks in Texas, however, the income of a

Pullman porter seemed enormous. I didn't know it then, but one of my mother's first cousins was a Pullman porter. I got to know his very accomplished daughter much later in life when I lived in San Francisco.

The unionization of the Pullman porters happened when I was six years old, after more than ten years of a significant struggle to organize the Pullman Company. Unionization came with all of the usual nastiness companies engaged in to prevent raising wages and improving working conditions. Today, many make the reasonable case that this was the first big step toward the Civil Rights Movement.

The Pullman Company's founder, George Pullman paid another young man (presumably of lower class) to take his place in the Union Army when he was drafted in 1863, like many men did at the time. Then he worked to establish his company in 1867; after the war, it became the luxury standard in rail transportation at a time when rail was becoming the primary means of travel in the US. At first, he hired freedmen because they were well-skilled in service positions and would work for low wages. (Not hard to understand when one has been used to no wages!)

Pullman leased his cars rather than selling them, and passengers would pay a separate fee on top of the standard rail fare to ride in a Pullman car. When a rail line leased a Pullman car, it came equipped with porters, just as it did with standard equipment like sleeping berths and light fixtures. But in the black community, the Pullman porter was considered a presti-gious position because it offered a steady income (which was hard to come by), the experience of interstate travel (including exposure to different ways of life), and work largely free of hard physical labor (which was unusual for the time). It also gave the porters an opportunity to develop their intellect along with their reading, writing, conversation, and other soft skills. They were dignified men who did undignified labor. They were respected in the black community and they dressed, walked, and carried themselves like they were proud to be Pullman porters, which they were.

The porter's work was actually a combination of maid and bellhop for these "hotels on wheels." They cleaned cars, shined shoes, carried baggage, changed linens, made beds, cooked and served meals, and catered to the passengers' every whim, almost as a butler would. And when they were south of the Mason-Dixon line, they were not allowed to be in the same cars they serviced because of Jim Crow laws in the South. For the porters, the glamor left as soon as they reported for work. At their peak in the early twentieth century, Pullman cars accommodated twenty-six million people a year and adopted the moniker "the largest hotel in the world."

The Pullman Company became the largest single employer of blacks in the US. However, porters had to buy their own uniforms, shoe polish, meals, and all other necessary supplies while they worked as many as 400 hours or 11,000 miles a month, often in twenty-hour shifts after doing unpaid prep work. At some point, like on the plantations many had come from, they were all assigned the name of their employer and were eventually called "George" by the white passengers. This demeaning practice continued until their first labor contract contained the provision that it had to stop and all cars had to display a card with the attending porter's name on it.

Pullman's workers had a lot of animosity toward him because of his harsh labor practices and strike-breaking tactics. When he died in 1897, he was buried at night in a lead-lined coffin within an elaborately reinforced steel-and-concrete vault. Several tons of cement were then poured over the vault to prevent his body from being exhumed and desecrated by labor activists. Even so, those who took over company management continued Pullman's harsh approach and anti-labor practices.

From 1909 to 1913, the porters unsuccessfully tried to unionize three times. In response, the company started a union of its own, a "company union." It was a sham, but it distracted the workers for another twelve years. In the 1920s, Pullman employed 20,000 porters, more than any other company in history. One in fifty was a woman working as a maid on the cars. Finally, in 1925, the porters had taken enough and a group of disgruntled workers approached A. Philip Randolph, a prominent Black labor rights advocate, and asked him to help them form a union.

Their demands were:

- A significant pay raise (to earn a decent living without relying on tips)
- Abolishing tipping (which often required accepting demeaning treatment)
- Adequate rest breaks
- Increased pensions
- A name card in each car listing the porter's actual name

The company refused and began firing, spying on, and otherwise retaliating against the organizers and union sympathizers. Everything had to go underground, including secret handshakes and passwords. Porters' wives formed a ladies' auxiliary unit, and it proved to be one of the most critical components of the secret operations.

After ten years of active organizing, in 1935, the Pullman Company recognized the union, the Brotherhood of Sleeping

Car Porters (BSCP)—the world's first all-black union. They won a favorable contract in 1937 after the New Deal created the National Labor Relations Act, which changed the law to make organizing labor unions and negotiating contracts easier. In the process, many blacks learned how to organize in dangerous situations, how to influence people, and how to negotiate—all skills they sorely needed when the Civil Rights Movement exploded. The BSCP was the training ground for E.D. Nixon, who later organized the Alabama Voter's League, led the Birmingham bus boycott, organized the Montgomery Improvement Association, and convinced Martin Luther King to become MIA's first president. The BSCP was also the training ground for C.L. Dellums (uncle of Ron Dellums), who moved from Texas to the Bay Area in 1923 where he became an active and effective union organizer and West Coast Vice President of the BSCP as well as Western Regional Director of the National Association for the Advancement of Colored People (NAACP).

Of course, I was ignorant of all this when I jumped from still-moving running boards yelling "station stop—everybody off." All I knew was that I wanted to be like the manly, good-looking porters I saw getting on and off the trains in Troy in immaculate uniforms, the porters that all the passengers seemed to rely on.

Learning how to get along with other races began early for me. Potsi's comments to Otis about getting shot on my first day of school weren't entirely without merit. Getting into a fight with a white kid could be a dangerous game in that part of Texas in the late '30s. Even black grade schoolers had heard the tales of nearby lynching trees—it seemed every Texas town had one. If a black boy of that time wanted to grow into a man, he learned the rules of racism early and decisively. Simply put, the rules were that whites could call you almost anything they wanted to, and if you fought back, it meant you were "uppity" and retribution could be harsh.

The "rules of race" were defined by the color of your skin. It seemed that lighter-skinned Negroes got the best jobs and jobs inside the homes of whites. Strangely enough, this also applied to interactions within our own race. When I was younger, all of my teachers and most other black professionals that I knew were light-skinned. I have rather dark skin, and in my early teens, all of my girlfriends had a similar skin color. It seemed like people tended to pair off with someone who had a similar skin color. Maybe this was a holdover from slave days (just two generations away), when the masters often selected light-skinned slaves to work inside the house and, for the most part, gave them the best, easiest jobs. This changed as I got older, and it definitely changed when I moved north. It probably disappeared entirely when the "black is beautiful" campaign gained traction in the 1960s and '70s.

This tendency has also been prevalent in all of the European colonial occupations. In India, the British gave lighter-skinned Indians better jobs. There, it actually resulted in a new animosity between groups of different skin color, regardless of caste or other grouping. This animosity lasts today, years after their colonial masters gave their country back. It is another legacy of the evil scourge of racism that has played out throughout history. It is easy to define and recognize "others" when they are identified by a noticeably different skin color.

I attended Troy Colored School until I was eleven, when I dropped out of the sixth grade in 1941 to help my grandmother and the rest of the family work the farm. I stopped going to school in April like most of the other older kids did so I could help out during that year's farming season. But when the crop-tending and cotton-picking was finished in September, I didn't go back. That was an eventful year for me, though I didn't know it. That act of conformity triggered the start of a new and quite unexpected journey that eventually brought me to a judgeship in San Francisco and a life I never could have imagined.

Chapter 5
A Little History

Because historical events in the Southern states laid the foundation for the culture I grew up in, I should give a brief review of the highlights.

To most people, my early life probably seems quite harsh, especially compared with current conditions in the United States, but in the 1930s and '40s, black education and black life were quite different in America, especially in the South, where Jim Crow laws were still brutally active. At the time, we were living through the Depression, and my grandparents, along with many of my classmates, had lived through even harder times—some as slaves. Because someone in every family had known real hardship and everyone had heard stories about what it was like, we were all very appreciative of what we had, meager though it was.

The Civil War had been over for only sixty-six years when I was born, so some of the oldest blacks had lived through it. When those bent and withered elders talked about their old times, we all listened with rapt attention. Even for the very young among us, those stories of not being considered "persons" shook us and made us pay closer attention to things around us, as paltry as they might be. We appreciated what we had then, but we weren't oblivious to our mistreatment and didn't like it.

Before the Civil War changed things, most whites in slave-holding states thought black education was wasteful and even dangerous. The racist white trope was that blacks were stupid and shiftless, unwilling and unable to learn even when given the opportunity. Besides, education wasn't needed for the manual labor slaves were bought and sold for. And many whites thought that educating black slaves would lead to problems like discontent and insurrection. They were probably right. God knows what people will do when they learn how others like them live—especially when they can compare their own lives to their cousins' much better lives in other cultures or even just other states.

Those few of us who could read and write before liberation were likely taught by the dim light of a candle that they snuffed as soon as we finished because it was so dear. Or, they learned in small groups who sneaked away from the fields when the masters weren't watching and who hid while being taught by someone who knew a little more than they did. More than a few slaves suffered harsh penalties—including the lash or even murder—for the crime of trying to learn to read and write. In most slave states, it was illegal for whites to teach blacks to read, and it was also illegal for blacks to learn to read. The punishment varied from state to state but could include imprisonment of up to a year and a fine ranging from $100 to $500 for white teachers, quite a large sum at the time. In North Carolina, the punishment for a free black giving instruction to black slaves was imprisonment and up to thirty-nine lashes. The slaves themselves usually received both lashes and imprisonment, often in solitary confinement while chained to a stake in tiny, claustrophobic "hot boxes" in the boiling Southern sun.

I haven't mentioned much about how my life and circumstances were shaped by the policies of the US government in its intermittent effort to make the races more equal in society, but, because education has been so instrumental in my life, I should. In many ways, the lives of blacks in America, especially Southern blacks, only started in 1865, after the Civil War. Before then, for the most part, we were strictly property in slaveholding states and were mistreated as such without rights or humanity, the record of our lives showing up only in our owners' profit and loss journals. Although teaching blacks to read and write was illegal in most slave states, that was not the case in Texas. However, illiteracy was still brutally enforced as a way to limit and control the slave population.

This changed after the Civil War, but not all at once. When Lincoln was assassinated on April 14, 1865, only five days after Lee's surrender of the largest Confederate army at Appomattox (effectively the end of the war), the vice president assumed that position. Lincoln's successor, Southerner Andrew Johnson, was much less committed to Negro freedom. The Thirteenth Amendment passed in December 1865, outlawing slavery in the United States and requiring Southern states to ratify it as a condition of readmission to the union.

Then, Southern states, most with their prewar legislators, retaliated with so-called Black Codes. These were state laws passed in 1865 and 1866 that had the intent and effect of restricting African Americans' freedom and ensuring a cheap and subservient labor force. Many of the Black Codes were based on former slave laws. They codified white supremacy by restricting blacks' civic participation. The codes deprived them of the right to vote, the right to serve on juries, the right to own or carry weapons, and, in some cases, even the right to rent or lease land. The codes varied from state to state, and in some states, blacks were even forbidden to work in the skilled trades or certain industries. Additionally, the codes usually required blacks to have a labor contract; they defined anyone without such a contract as a vagrant who was subject to arrest and fines. If "vagrants" were unable to pay fines, they were bound out for a term of labor to anyone able to pay the yearly fee (typically ten dollars). Often, this meant they were bound out to their former masters. They were then forced to work for a specified term as prisoners without wages, returning them to another form of slavery. In 1871, the Virginia Supreme Court even ruled that a convicted person was "a slave of the State." Convict leasing was brutal and inhumane. More than 3,500 prisoners died in Texas between 1866 and 1912, the year Texas outlawed convict leasing because the death toll was so high.

The Civil Rights Act of 1866 was passed on April 9 by incensed Northern anti-slavery forces who recognized the South's unwillingness to change even after surrender. It was the nation's first civil rights bill. The Civil Rights Act invalidated the Black Codes and contradicted the 1857 Dred Scott decision that said Negroes could never be citizens. Congress also attempted to protect African Americans' rights by extending the life of the Freedmen's Bureau, which was established in March 1865 to ease the transition from slavery to freedom. But Johnson vetoed the bill. An act to define and guarantee African Americans' basic civil rights met a similar fate, but Republicans overrode the president's vetoes and passed these in spite of Johnson.

The period of Johnson's heavy influence was known as Presidential Reconstruction. It ended on March 2, 1867, when Congress passed the Military Reconstruction Act. This led to the period of Radical Reconstruction that lasted until 1877 when Union troops were pulled out of the South.

Even after they were outlawed, the sentiment of the Black Codes endured and morphed into a new ruling racial order. Support for Reconstruction policies waned after the early 1870s, undermined by nationwide economic issues and the violence of white supremacist organizations such as the Ku Klux Klan. When Reconstruction ended in 1877, freed people had seen little permanent improvement in their economic and social statuses. This set the foundation for the racially discriminatory Jim Crow segregation policies that impoverished generations of African Americans. Many of the provisions of the Black Codes were reenacted in the Jim Crow laws, which were not done away with until Congress passed the Civil Rights Act of 1964.

Black education in Texas is a good example of how this worked, even though Texas is different from the other Deep South states because its slave history involves Spain, Mexico, and the United States. No matter who was in charge, there was always a mix of pro-slavery and anti-slavery activists in Texas. Slavery remained controversial even after Texas won independence from Mexico in 1836; at that time, the colonists owned a total of about 5,000 slaves. Southern slaveholders populated the region in greater numbers, bringing their slaves with them, and when Texas was annexed to the United States as an official slave state in 1845, the number of slaves had grown to 30,000. The period of Anglo-American slavery in Texas officially lasted from 1845 through 1865, when the Civil War ended, and this is why people identify Texas as having a short twenty-year slave history. In reality, slavery went on much longer in most of the state, having started before Texas gained statehood.

According to the 1850 census, the 58,558 African

Americans who lived in Texas represented 27.5 percent of the population. Fewer than 1 percent of them, or 397, were free, of which 217 were believed to be literate. There are no formal statistics on the 58,151 enslaved African Americans, but available data indicate that only a small portion of the slave population had been instructed in the basic rudiments of reading and writing.

By 1860, on the eve of the Civil War, the enslaved population accounted for 30 percent of the state's population (182,566). At that time, one in four Texas families owned slaves. Slaveholdings were typically small, as most enslavers owned fewer than ten people. In 1860, the largest slaveholder in Texas owned a little over 300 slaves, much different from South Carolina, Georgia, Mississippi, and other Southern states where the largest plantations had 3,000 slaves or more.

At the start of the Civil War, Lincoln and others thought it wouldn't last long. Lincoln argued for tempered treatment of prisoners as he thought most Confederate soldiers had been led astray by their leaders and politicians. Many in the North thought Confederate soldiers would realize the error of their ways and not stay on the battlefields once the war started. But after a few of the early battles, they learned better when they realized the Confederate Army and the Southern population, in general, was made up of true believers who held onto their views throughout the war and for many years after as they were confronted by former slaves who demanded to be treated as equals.

By 1863, the Union army had lost many soldiers to the battlefield and even more to disease, and they weren't being replaced by a dwindling Northern recruitment. Abraham Lincoln's 1863 Emancipation Proclamation freed African Americans in rebel states. One of its provisions allowed for slaves to join the Northern army, where their numbers rose to approximately 10 percent of the total near the war's end. In part, Lincoln had sought to remove the means of production from the Southern states' slave economies and create discord among them, further weakening the South. The Proclamation also meant that the war to preserve the Union became, undeniably, a war also about slavery. It encouraged slaves to run away since they would be free if they reached the North, but that was a hard and dangerous path. In spite of that, many left, some joined the Union Army, and over 200,000 former slaves—about 10 percent of all Union soldiers—were fighting for their true emancipation by the end of the war. Their service was often exceptional. In addition to receiving many lesser awards, four Negroes won the Congressional Medal of Honor, the nation's highest military award.

When the war ended, soldiers were mustered out according to their seniority; Negroes, in general, had less seniority. In addition, after many of the plantations were destroyed, they had nowhere to go. Huge discharges happened at the war's end, and most of the discharged soldiers were white. That left a large percentage of the total Negro population in the army, about 30%. Consequently, when the South was occupied after the war, many of the occupation soldiers were Negroes. They often treated the white population poorly for enslaving and mistreating their race for over two hundred years. This didn't help pacify the South, and when the KKK and other resistance groups arose, their reaction to this treatment added to the KKK's barbarity. It would take more than a century for most of the true believers (those who supported the Confederate cause) of the KKK to vanish, and even longer for notable pockets of inbred racism to dwindle into the dustbin of history, where they belong.

When the Civil War ended in 1865, the United States Congress instituted the Freedmen's Bureau. Its primary function was to supervise and coordinate a vast educational enterprise in the former Confederate slave states, including Texas and a few adjacent states. The bureau supervised schools offering classes from the elementary level through college. These schools provided a formal curriculum of arithmetic, reading, writing, history, and geography. In addition, they provided a practical curriculum of civics, politics, home economics, and vocational training. One of these was Wiley College in Marshall, Texas, which I attended.

In January 1866, Texas had only ten day schools and six night schools for black children. These schools employed ten teachers, mostly Northern missionaries, with a total enrollment of 1,041 students, many of whom were adults. Six months later, on July 1, 1866, the Freedmen's Bureau in Texas had ninety schools, including day, night, and Sunday schools that employed forty-three teachers and enrolled 4,590 students.

Because the majority of the Civil War battles were fought further north, Texas suffered only a small part of the horrific destruction the rest of the Confederacy saw, and the war's impact on the economic base was relatively minor. As a result, the Freedmen's Texas schools needed only minimal assistance from Northern states. By the end of 1870, in addition to the Freedmen's Bureau schools, there were twenty-seven Sabbath schools with twenty-eight teachers (twenty-three were black) and 1,350 students. Clearly, Texas's Negro population had no issues with educating itself.

Shortly after the war ended, the Northern Radical Reconstructionists mandated the inclusion of African Americans in state politics across the former Confederacy. This so incensed the white population that, for a time, whites resorted to violence and intimidation in an attempt to resist this change. They were so vehemently opposed to the Freedmen's Bureau that they burned schools and physically intimidated the missionary teachers. While this behavior was not universal, it was widespread across Texas as well as most of the other former slaveholding states. This did begin to change, but very, very gradually.

The first post–Civil War Texas Constitution was adopted in 1866 and provided that the "income derived from the Public School Fund be employed exclusively for the education of white scholastic inhabitants" and that the "legislature may provide for the levying of a tax for educational purposes." African Americans were taxed for "the maintenance of a system of public schools for Africans and their children." Since most Negroes had little income, this acted as a brake on black education.

After the Civil War, the United States Constitution was ratified to include three additional amendments. As previously discussed, the Thirteenth Amendment was passed on December 6, 1865, as the war ended. It abolished slavery "within the United States, or any place subject to their jurisdiction," and Congress required former Confederate states to ratify the Thirteenth Amendment as a condition of regaining federal representation.

Then, on July 9, 1868, the Fourteenth Amendment was ratified. It granted citizenship to all persons "born or naturalized in the United States," including former slaves, and provided all citizens, including former slaves, with "equal protection under the laws." This extended the provisions of the Bill of Rights to all people in all states and overturned the Dred Scott decision, which had excluded African Americans from these benefits. Among other provisions, it granted Congress the power to enforce this amendment, a provision that led to passing other landmark legislation in the twentieth century, including the Civil Rights Act of 1964 and the Voting Rights Act of 1965. Congress required former Confederate states to ratify the Fourteenth Amendment as a condition of regaining federal representation, as had been the case with the Thirteenth.

Finally, the Fifteenth Amendment was ratified February 3, 1870. It prohibited states from disenfranchising voters "on account of race, color, or previous condition of servitude." The amendment had many loopholes, however. It allowed states to institute voter qualifications as long as they applied equally to all races, and many former Confederate states took advantage of this provision, instituting poll taxes and literacy tests, among other qualifications.

These three so-called Reconstruction Amendments were meant to extend new constitutional protections to blacks, giving them protections equal to those of whites. However, the struggle to fully achieve equality would continue into the twentieth century and beyond. The amendments were intended to restructure the United States from a country that, in Abraham Lincoln's words, was "half slave and half free" into one in which the constitutionally guaranteed "blessings of liberty" would be extended to the entire population, including all former slaves and their descendants.

The Civil War gave some four million slaves their freedom, but the process of rebuilding the devastated South during the Reconstruction period (1865-1877) introduced new challenges. There were three distinct points of view regarding the next steps at the war's end. The Reconciliationists' primary goal was to heal the war wounds by helping the nation cope with the death and devastation as quickly as possible—in other words, they wanted both sides to reconcile above all else. The Radical

Republicans and others held the emancipationist view. This group sought full freedom, citizenship, and constitutional equality for African Americans, giving them the same rights as white citizens. However, the white supremacist viewpoint persisted in pockets of the North and throughout the entire South. Those holding this view resisted full emancipation with violence and terror that, in many cases, was even more obvious and brutal than that which had been present during slavery.

Abraham Lincoln's assassination worked in the white supremacists' favor when Vice President Andrew Johnson assumed the presidency. Born in North Carolina, Johnson had been governor of Tennessee before being elected to represent the state as a senator. Despite his connections to two slave states, he was the only sitting senator from the eleven Southern states making up the Confederacy not to resign his seat at secession. For that reason, Lincoln selected him as his running mate in 1864. Lincoln's goal was to have a Southern unionist as a member of the sitting government to facilitate connecting with and reconstructing the devastated South after the war's looming end. Six weeks after he was sworn in and five days after Lee surrendered to Grant at Appomattox, Lincoln was assassinated and Johnson became president.

Unfortunately, Andrew Johnson sided with the Southern states by favoring a quick restoration process in which the South would rejoin the union without any serious measures to ensure African Americans' emancipation and equal rights. His so-called Presidential Reconstruction Plan involved a series of presidential proclamations that directed the seceded states to hold immediate conventions and elections to reform their governments with few other requirements. Predictably, the Southern states elected many of their former leaders, who then passed Black Codes depriving blacks of many of their newly won civil liberties. Congressional Republicans refused to seat many of these new Southern legislators and passed national legislation to void the presidential proclamations and overrule the South's recalcitrance. Johnson then overrode them, and the cycle repeated for months. Johnson even opposed the Fourteenth Amendment, which gave citizenship to all former slaves. Congress finally passed the Reconstruction Acts over Johnson's presidential veto. The Reconstruction Acts divided the South into five military districts, put them all under martial law, and stationed Northern troops within the districts to enforce the law. The Southern states were also required to hold constitutional conventions with very different rules from pre-Civil War rules.. In these conventions, African Americans could vote for or become delegates while former Confederates could not. Each state was required to ratify the Fourteenth Amendment to be restored to the Union.

Finally, the conflict came to a head and Johnson was impeached by the House of Representatives. After an impeachment trial that lasted almost three months, he was acquitted by the Senate—by one vote—and avoided being removed from office. There were accusations of bribery that were probably true; these bribes, though never proven, likely saved him. However, Johnson lost the 1868 Democratic presidential nomination to Horatio Seymour, who was defeated in the 1868 general election by Republican Ulysses S. Grant. Grant made it known that he would not ride to the inauguration in the same carriage as Johnson, a long-standing custom in the transfer of power, so Johnson refused to go to the inauguration at all. With Grant, African Americans finally had a friend in the White House again.

Grant had graduated from West Point and was a national hero after the war. He was the nation's first four-star general and became the youngest president-elect to date at age forty-six. As president, he protected former slaves' civil rights while also supporting pardons for former Confederate leaders. He did this to bring the Confederate states back into the Union while still protecting slaves' true emancipation, which he had seen so many Union soldiers die for.

Northern outrage over the Black Codes and other reactionary policies had eroded support for Presidential Reconstruction and led the more radical wing of the Republican Party to triumph. The next phase of Reconstruction, known as Radical Reconstruction, began in 1867 and enfranchised blacks by giving them a voice in government for the first time in US history. During Radical Reconstruction, significant numbers of African Americans were elected to Southern state legislatures and even to the US Congress; more than 1,500 African American officeholders were elected during and just after Reconstruction.

Among other perceived dangers, the Southern white population was petrified of what might happen to them should African Americans become a true political power in the South. More than half a million blacks became Southern voters in the 1870s. In Mississippi and South Carolina, the black population outnumbered the white population, and there were a number of other Southern states with a black population nearing 50 percent. As they registered to vote and gleefully exercised that newfound right in large numbers, blacks began to elect governments that really did reflect their needs. For a brief time, blacks and whites served side-by-side in Southern legislatures and, during Reconstruction, 700 African American men served in elected public office, among them two United States Senators and fourteen members of the United States House of Representatives. Another 1,300

African American men and women held appointed government jobs.

In less than a decade, however, reactionary forces led by the Ku Klux Klan would reverse the changes wrought by Radical Reconstruction. It was a violent backlash that lasted over several decades and restored white supremacy in the South. On average, the period of biracial Republican state governments lasted just four-and-a-half years.

During the entire Reconstruction period (1865–1877), soldiers from the Northern army, many of them black, were stationed throughout the South to enforce these and other laws protecting the black population. Hated by white Southerners, these soldiers weren't able to stop all mistreatment of African Americans. But they did manage to enforce most of the laws that the Radical Reconstructionists in Congress had passed to protect African Americans. By the end of Reconstruction, when they left the South, they had managed to somewhat tamp down the KKK and other violent hate groups.

In the South, biracial, Republican-controlled Reconstruction state governments were regularly accused of inefficiency and corruption. Although they were hardly perfect, they did bring about significant improvements in the lives of former slaves. For the first time, black men and women enjoyed freedom of speech and movement, education for their children, the right to a fair trial, the right to travel without restriction, and all the other privileges and protections of American citizenship. Furthermore, more than half a million black men gained the right to vote during Reconstruction. But beginning in 1873, a series of Supreme Court decisions limited federal support of Reconstruction-era laws, and the 1873 financial panic and subsequent depression further stressed Reconstruction aims. This financial panic triggered the first global depression brought about by industrial capitalism. It was the longest recorded financial downturn in modern history until the stock market crash in October 1929 brought on the Great Depression. The 1873 economic collapse was significant across the entire United States and gave recalcitrant Southerners even more reason to object to the Radical Reconstruction policies. It also triggered the North to reconsider all associated Reconstruction costs.

Property owners in the South demanded that taxes be cut and state budgets and expenditures be reined in. Southern penitentiaries were also closed and convicts were leased to private contractors. Spending on medical care, orphans, and public education was sharply reduced, and black schools were especially hard-hit. By the time the 1876 election came around, Northern troops had been stationed in the South for over ten years. Northerners were tired of this and wanted their sons home. Besides, it was expensive, and the depression had been walloping everyone for three years by then. The 1876 election was the most contested in US history, marred by both black and white ad hoc militias and significant bloodshed on both sides. Three Southern states, Florida, Mississippi, and South Carolina, returned two official ballot results, one Democrat and one Republican. In the end, the Compromise of 1877 gave political control of the South to the racist Democrats and removed federal troops from the old Confederacy. It also gave Democrats control of the US House.

In the compromise, Southern Democrats promised to protect blacks' civil and political rights. Predictably, they did not keep their promises. Subsequent removal of federal troops from the South ended federal influence in Southern affairs and resulted in the widespread disenfranchisement of black voters. From the late 1870s on, Southern legislatures passed a series of laws requiring that whites be separated from "persons of color" on public transportation and in schools, parks, restaurants, theaters, and other locations. Known as the Jim Crow laws (after a popular minstrel act that was developed in the antebellum years), these segregationist statutes governed life in the South through the middle of the next century. They didn't end until after the hard-won successes of the 1960s Civil Rights Movement began to take hold.

Physical violence and intimidation played a big part in this. Beginning in 1868, the Ku Klux Klan and organizations like it, such as the Red Shirts in North and South Carolina, arose to physically intimidate the Southern black population and stop them from voting.

In South Carolina, the Red Shirts gained traction during the 1876 state and national elections in opposition to Radical Republicans. These armed paramilitary groups supported the Democratic Party and adopted an official battle plan:

Every Democrat must feel honor bound to control the vote of at least one Negro, by intimidation, purchase, keeping him away.

We must attend every Radical meeting. Democrats must go in as large numbers as they can, and well-armed, behave at first with great courtesy and as soon as their speakers begin tell them that they are liars and are only trying to mislead the ignorant Negroes.

In speeches to Negroes you must remember that they can only be influenced by their fears, superstitions and cupidity. Treat them so as to show them you are the superior race and that their natural position is that of subordination to the white man.

Never threaten a man individually. If he deserves to be threatened, the necessities of the times require that he should die. A dead Radical is very harmless—a threatened Radical is often troublesome, sometimes dangerous, and always vindictive.

The Journey

Every club must be uniformed in a red shirt and they must be sure and wear it upon all public meetings and particularly on the day of election.

Bloody intimidation campaigns were ubiquitous throughout the South, escalating rapidly after US troops were removed by newly elected President Rutherford B. Hayes in 1877. Until the gains made in the '60s during the Civil Rights Movement voting results across the South indicated universal fraud and, along with violent voter discouragement, resulted in massive declines in black turnout.

Brutal bands of racist whites engaged in all sorts of racial and political terrorism, including surrounding polling places with armed men, burning black churches, attacking teachers, and beating or killing freedmen who didn't show proper deference to whites. Blacks fought back with rifles, rebuilt schools and churches, and generally refused to give up the hard-won independence that had come with emancipation, even in the face of widespread lynchings. Beginning in about 1890, an African American was lynched, burned alive, or mutilated in the Southern states every week for the next fifty years.

Though we fought to keep our rights after the Civil War, resistance in the face of continuous intimidation and violent retribution could not last forever. The resistance continued at varying levels. At the same time, governments introduced poll taxes, literacy tests, civics tests, and other ridiculous voting requirements like proof of residency and property ownership. As a result, the percentage of eligible Southern blacks who were registered voters dwindled from 90 percent during Reconstruction's heyday in the early 1870s to, by one historical account, 3 percent in 1940. (In 1870, women were not yet able to vote, so the 90 percent statistic reflects men only.)

Reconstruction governments disappeared immediately upon the removal of US troops and, in some states, it was more than ninety years until another Republican governor was elected. It didn't really begin to change until the mid-twentieth century when the modern Civil Rights Movement started throughout the South. Then, in 1965, the administration of President Lyndon B. Johnson, a Democrat, passed the Voting Rights Act. The Republicans formed their racist Southern Strategy in response, effectively causing the Democrat and Republican parties to switch sides regarding their support of black voting rights. (In other words, the Republicans were opposed beginning in 1965 and the Democrats were in favor.)

W.E.B. Du Bois wrote a thorough study of the Reconstruction period in his 1935 classic *Black Reconstruction in America*. More recently, Henry Louis Gates Jr. published *Stony the Road: Reconstruction, White Supremacy, and the Rise of Jim Crow* with Penguin Press in 2019. This book thoroughly examines Reconstruction and its continuing fallout from a more modern viewpoint. The book is summarized in Adam Gopnik's article "The Takeback," which appeared in *The New Yorker's* April 8, 2019, print edition. (In the online edition, the piece is entitled "How the South Won the Civil War.")

When I was growing up, I often asked my aunts and uncles if they voted. They all told me they did not, and when I asked why, they told me that they didn't want to pay the poll tax, which was $1.25 at the time—more than a day's wages. In Texas, citizens were required to pay the poll tax in February if they wanted to vote in November; that was before the growing season, at a time when we lived on credit and every nickel was dear. Most people I knew would have had to borrow money to pay the tax, and in Texas, loans and gifts for the payment of poll taxes were against the law. It was also illegal to pay someone else's tax.

When I moved to Waco, I had another experience with poll taxes. I was about fifteen years old, World War II had recently ended, and my mother had just married my second stepfather, whom I called Mr. Robert. It was a sunny day in November and Mr. Robert went downtown to vote. He had served in the army during the war, was wounded in Germany, and was awarded the Purple Heart. He was patriotic and enjoyed participating in civic duties like voting and serving on juries. That day, he returned home hotter than a two-dollar pistol. When I asked why, he said the registrar would not let him vote—the registrar claimed he hadn't paid the $1.50 poll tax which had increased in price in the years since my aunts and uncles told me they hadn't been able to pay it.

I can still hear him even now: "Ah' know damn well that Ah' paid that stupid tax. Ah' made a special trip downtown back in February. Paid it from the penny jar that I put the day's leftover change into just for such an occasion. But that evil white man had me 'cause I didn't have mah receipt. Who the hell keeps a receipt for nine months?! Ah'll get him next time, tho. Ah' won't forget that receipt next election. Ah' saw too many friends fight for that right in Germany! That cracker won't stop me from votin' again, no sir!"

This was another way the Southern white power structure disenfranchised blacks after Reconstruction. Reducing the roles of black voters cut into the Republicans' voting strength and shifted power to the Democratic Party, which at the time was made up of plantation owners, bankers, merchants, railroads, and their supporters. Voter disenfranchisement began in Texas in 1890 as a way to keep poor whites and blacks from voting. Texas institutionalized the poll tax by adding it to the Texas

Constitution in 1902 to stop the few Negro voters who hadn't been scared off by real or threatened violence. In 1963, there was a big push by state civil rights advocates to repeal the tax, and this push was supported by many local leaders, newspapers, civic organizations, and national leaders, including Martin Luther King Jr. and John F. Kennedy. But the good people of Texas voted to keep the law for many reasons, including the huge number of poor people who weren't able to vote against it because they couldn't afford to pay the poll tax. One statewide poll showed that only 38 percent of eligible black voters across the state voted, with the final tally being 243,445 for and 330,008 against repealing the tax.

The federal government enacted the Twenty-Fourth Amendment to the US Constitution in 1964, prohibiting a poll tax nationwide for national elections. Most Southern states challenged the amendment; it wasn't until two years later, when the US Supreme Court ruled the tax unconstitutional, that the Texas Constitution issued an amendment to repeal the poll tax that had been disenfranchising poor citizens across Texas, including most blacks, for sixty-four years. (Texas didn't "post-ratify" the Twenty-Fourth Amendment until 2009.)

We moved to Michigan in 1948, a couple of years after Mr. Robert was denied the right to vote in his home state because he hadn't kept the receipt when he paid the poll tax. He would not have had that problem in Michigan.

The history of black education in Texas is similar to education in the rest of the South. The Texas Reconstruction legislature of 1870 eliminated segregation on paper and gave the state a single educational system in which all children shared. But in 1873 and 1875, the Texas state legislature repealed most of the laws from the Reconstruction period and, again, Texas took two steps back like the rest of the former slaveholding states.

The Journey

Under the Constitution of 1876, Texas reestablished racial segregation but made "impartial" provisions for each race. For the first time, African Americans in Texas had a functioning school system. Between 1873 and 1893, African Americans from across the state met at black state conventions to express their opinions, define their needs, and shape educational policies. In 1884, the first meeting of the Colored Teachers Association was held in Austin.

The Texas State Board of Education conducted its first survey of black schools in 1921. At that time, 6,369 pupils were enrolled for secondary work, the majority in city high schools. By 1925, there were 150 institutions in the state offering one or more years of high school work for African Americans, including fourteen city high schools, six or more country high schools, and high school departments in every junior and senior college. In the 1920s and '30s, the average length of the school term for black children was only about four days shorter than that for white children. We were clearly making progress. However, during the same period, Texas spent an average of only $3.39 a day to educate African American students—about a third less than it spent for white students—and black teachers were paid significantly less than white teachers ($91.60 a month versus $121.03). This was the approximate state of affairs in 1936 when I entered that one-room schoolhouse beside the railroad tracks of Troy. As you can see, statistics alone don't tell the entire story, but they do bolster the facts.

The next wave of significant improvements to the Southern educational system, including the Texas state public school system, started in the late 1950s as an offshoot of the larger Civil Rights Movement. By then, I was long gone.

Chapter 6
Life at Mama's

For the seven years before 1943, the year when my mother was finally able to support me on her own in Waco, I lived with my grandmother and various other relatives, mostly on the farm in Bell County. During that period, we moved four or five times, living in a different house each time.

I remember all of these as Mama's houses. There were invariably three rooms for between five and nine people at any one time depending on the vicissitudes of the sons, daughters, aunts, and uncles. Mama's house was always a house of refuge in hard or difficult times. But we all made the most of it, and I never thought of living with her as a hardship. Mama's house was simply home, and our lives weren't much different from those of the other Negroes we knew in Bell County. Living there ingrained two things in me: you can always rely on family when times are hard, and you always do what you can to help when members of your family are having hard times.

Though we bought (or took on credit to buy) staples from

Mr. Thackston at his general store, we still had to hunt and fish in the fields, woods, streams, and creeks nearby to complete our diet, such as it was. The small streams and creeks dried up in the summer heat, and so did the food that lived in them, but Big Elm Creek never dried up and was always only a short walk of between a half mile and two miles from home. There we caught crawfish, catfish, and perch year-round on willow poles or poles made from any other strong tree branch from which we stripped the bark and cut off the knobs. Once, someone built a new cow pond. DV and I sat there for months holding our poles waiting for the fish to show up. We finally gave up and went back to Big Elm Creek, still oblivious to how fish actually came to be in isolated bodies of water. The fish we caught in the creek were mostly small, although what we considered minimum eating size is probably different from what you think now. DV once caught a five-pound catfish in a pond over on Mr. Gill's property. Grandma Rose breaded it in cornmeal and spices and fried it for a very tasty meal that all of us enjoyed.

We hunted year-round with rifles and shotguns, mostly for rabbits and squirrels. DV and his stepfather, LE, my Uncle Jace, and others, kept dogs that they used for hunting. The dogs could catch jackrabbits and, as retrievers, were trained not to eat what they caught or what we had shot—they knew to bring the game back and drop it at their owners' feet. The older rabbits were occasionally so tough would have to boil them for what seemed like days to make them edible. Jackrabbits often yielded five pounds of meat after skinning and gutting, but racing for their lives between the scrub brush on those Texas plains could build up a large and tough set of muscles. The best ones were the adolescents with huge hind legs that hadn't yet toughened up. We fought over those legs as the best part of the "rab." Whether tough or tender, a five-pounder or a two-pounder, we ate all of it and savored every bite.

Greyhounds were the favored dog breed in those parts because they were so fast and could change directions instantly to keep up with rabbits. Uncle Jace was known as one of the best greyhound trainers in Bell County. His dogs could catch a jackrabbit within fifty yards of scaring it up—and they usually did. Uncle Jace and Aunt Anna had thirteen children . . . yes, thirteen! That was a large family even for our neck of the woods. We said he needed every dog he could get, catching all the jackrabbits they could scare up, to feed all those hungry mouths.

We also ate cottontails and swamp rabs. The cottontails didn't have as much meat as jackrabbits, but they were tenderer and tastier. The swamp rabs were a little bigger and didn't have white tails, and they were also pretty tender and good eating. Cottontails were always my favorite.

Early on, DV and I hunted squirrels with slingshots that we cut from the V-shaped branch of any tree we could find. As odd as it sounds, we both got pretty good at knocking squirrels out of trees from twenty or thirty feet away. Sometimes, someone would kill an opossum and Mama would make baked opossum with sweet potatoes. Everyone raved about it . . . except me. I couldn't bring myself to eat an animal that was so mean and ugly. I thought anything that looked and acted like that must have shoe-leather-tough meat. I never tried it—I was too stubborn. I never ate raccoons, either.

Somebody gave me a BB gun when I was eight or nine years old, and I learned to use it well enough to kill birds. We got a few pigeons and other birds to eat that way. Then, when I was about ten, someone gave me a .22 rifle. I once used it to kill a skunk, which promptly sprayed everything within twenty feet the moment I shot it. Thank goodness it was downwind and a couple of miles from our house because that biting skunk smell permeated everything within a quarter of a mile until someone buried it weeks later.

As was the case for most country people, guns were part of our way of life. Everyone used them regularly for hunting, so they were not unusual in any way. Someone tried to give me a pistol when I was six or seven. Uncle Jack fired into the air on New Year's Eve, but Rosie confiscated it before I ever saw it. Pistols weren't for hunting, and she didn't want me to have any part of them.

In addition to cooking the game we hunted, Rosie made preserves from wild blackberries, peaches, and plums that we picked—mostly from the property we lived on. We also raised one or two hogs, which we slaughtered when the weather started getting cool. We used them to make sausage, cracklings, hog's head cheese, pig's feet, and anything else we thought of. We even ate the ears and snout. In fact, we ate everything but the hooves, eyeballs, and blood. We did boil the hooves and made medicinal tea from the water—we drank it for measles, coughs, and other ailments. We also smoked, cooked, and canned the meat and then stored it in a smokehouse if we had one at the time. Sausages were stored in five-gallon cans of fat because the fat kept the meat from spoiling. We didn't make sausages every winter because we didn't have hogs every year, but whenever "hog-killing time" came around, we shared the meat with our family members, friends, and neighbors, who always reciprocated.

We raised fifteen or twenty chickens when there was a chicken coop behind the house. When we moved in, the landowners would bring them to us to take care of and to gather their eggs. We kept some of the eggs as payment, but most of them went to the white landowners. We also raised chicks and killed some of the adults for chicken dinners from time to time.

When I was nine or ten, the house we lived in had four rooms, including the kitchen and an enclosed porch. It was cold during the winter, so we brought the young chicks onto the enclosed porch where there was a kerosene lantern to keep them warm. The chicks knocked the lantern over, the house burned down, we lost what few possessions we had, and the landowner lost his house. At least no one was hurt or killed.

After the fire, we moved to another house on the same landowner's property. It had three rooms plus the kitchen, and six of us lived there at the time. One of the rooms was an extra bedroom with a second bed that DV, Duke, and I slept in. One afternoon, I was lying on the bed trying to get rid of one of my splitting headaches when I saw a snake crawling over the rafters. I jumped out of bed and ran into Mama's room to rest. That night, I made a pallet. I kept sleeping on the floor until we moved from that house, leaving the bed and the extra room to DV and Duke. For months, my aunts made fun of me.

"Aw, Lil' Brother, you know you didn't see nothin'," they would say. "You are just a mama's boy. You jes' wan'ta be close to Mama." But I knew what I saw. I never slept in that room again.

I have never liked snakes.

One of our jobs was to feed the landowner's animals, and though we never owned cows ourselves, we would feed and milk a landowner's cows when he had them. We churned some of the milk for butter and shared both milk and butter with the owners.

We always had a small, three-foot-tall, wood-fed potbellied stove for heat, and when our woodpile dwindled, either Uncle Jace or LE, Aunt Ceola's husband and DV's stepfather, would hook two mules to a wagon and draft as many of us children as they could corral to go logging with them.

From about the time I was ten, the logging crew usually included me and DV along with Uncle Jace's three sons: Restine (Potsi), Junior, and Otis (Duke). DV and I thought Uncle Jace was a slave driver, and it seemed to us children that he pushed us unmercifully. Of course, that was probably because we were young and the work was really hard. We had to crosscut large trees and then crosscut or axe the trunks and branches into logs for firewood small enough to fit into Mama's little heater, the house's only heat source. Jace usually found the best trees in the bottoms or the gullies, and we would cut and carry or drag logs up the hills all day long until the wagon was full. Those were tough days that both DV and I were glad to see the end of.

When we cut logs, the wood wasn't all for our family. Uncle Jace was always hustling to sell wood to the white families to help support his family. We worked for many of the white families in Bell County who owned land in the area. This was during and right after the Depression, and no one in Central Texas, black or white, had much money, so cooperation was necessary for survival.

My first awareness of the dangers of race relations came when I was about four years old. I was young, but the memory of it is as fresh as if it were yesterday. Mother was working as a domestic for one of the local families. They had a little girl about a year older than I was, and the two of us were outside in their dusty yard playing games that children make up at that age. As I recall, the girl was making up the games and I was following along, doing what she said to do. Suddenly, I heard the screen door hit the side of the house, followed immediately by Mother grabbing me by the shoulders and snatching me from my friend's embrace. She lifted me up so my face was directly opposite hers. Our noses were almost touching and she was trembling, her countenance as serious as I had ever seen it. At first, she could hardly speak, but she finally got the words out. "Lil' Brother! What do you think you are doing?!" Her appearance and demeanor were so extreme that it frightened me.

"We . . . we're playing house," I said.

"Why are you two hugging each other?!"

"Betsy is the mother and Ah'm the daddy," I said, thoroughly confused and getting more frightened by the moment. "Ah' just came home from work," I said.

"Whose idea was this game?" she asked.

"Betsy's, Mother. It was Betsy's game," I said.

"Well, you two stop huggin' each other, Lil Brother! You hear me?! You two just stop that huggin'!" she said as she shook me.

"Betsy was doing the huggin', Mother," I said.

"Never mind who started it," she said. "Just stop it!"

Soon she calmed down and put me back down on the ground.

"You understand, too, don't you, Betsy? Whatever game you are playing, you two just stop that huggin'."

"OK," Betsy said, hanging her head.

Because of the way Mother acted, we both knew we had done something wrong, but we didn't know exactly why it was wrong.

"In fact," Mother said, "why don't you come inside with me, John? You can stay out here and play by yourself for a while, Betsy."

"Yes, ma'am," Betsy said, still confused.

Once we were inside, Mother sat down and leaned over,

pulling me close to her. She was still shaking, and we were once again face-to-face.

"Lil' Brother, don't you ever go huggin' a white girl again," she said sternly.

"But why, Mother?" I asked.

"Just because!" she said forcefully. "That's jus' one of the things you don't ever do, son. Ever . . . ever . . . ever! Understand? Colored folks just don't go huggin' little white girls, that's all," she said with finality. "It . . . it's dangerous," she said shaking me for emphasis. "Even if it's her idea. Especially if it's her idea!"

She was still trembling when she let me go. My shoulders and arms hurt where she had been squeezing, and I was still scared of what had happened. She had never acted like that with me before.

Later, when I was back outside with Betsy, I wouldn't let her get too close to me. The words "it's dangerous!" kept running through my head, and although I still didn't know why or how, the effect of Mother's upset made me wary of even getting close to a little white girl again. It was years before I understood what my mother meant, but I sure did believe what she said about it being dangerous. I didn't get close to a white girl again until I was much older.

DV and all my cousins were constant companions when I was growing up in Mama's house. DV was a very good artist, and he began fashioning small animals out of clay when we were very young. Unfortunately, while I was encouraged to excel in school and go on to higher education, he had no similar encouragement for his artistic abilities. If he had, I believe he could have gone far as an artist. But as it was, he dropped out of school in the seventh grade and got his GED much later, when he was in the army. The educational encouragement that I got from my mother made me focus even more and work even harder in school. And just as DV protected me outside of school, I helped him in school. Although I always thought his memory was better than mine, he never loved school and learning as much as I did.

Although DV looked out for me, there was one danger he could not protect me from—retribution from the property owners we worked for. But I distinctly remember two instances when Mama stood as a barrier between us and them.

My earliest problem with a landowner occurred when I was eight or nine years old. Mama told me to go outside to the water spigot to fill a bucket for her to use inside. In the winter, it was common for the outside spigots to freeze, and I had seen Mama Rosie tap on a frozen spigot repeatedly until she broke enough ice for it to pass through the spigot and release the water behind it. So, I began tapping on the handle like I had seen Rosie do. I must have gotten impatient because I eventually hit the spigot so hard the handle broke off.

A few days later, the landlord knocked on the door when he came around to fix it. When Rosie answered the door, he said, "What happened to the handle on the spigot, Rose?"

"Oh, the boy hit it too hard trying to get water out of it when it was frozen," she said.

I had come to the door and was standing behind her, listening to the conversation. When he saw me, he said, "Little Brother, you know you'll have to pick me a hundred pounds of cotton next summer to pay for that broken spigot."

I thought a hundred pounds of cotton was an awful lot for such a little handle, but I didn't say anything. After he left, I asked about it.

"Mama, will I really have to pick a hundred pounds for the broken handle?"

"Just never mind that, boy. He was just trying to scare you about it to keep you from doing it again," she said. "By the time next summer comes 'round, he will have forgot all about that spigot. Besides, I would never let that happen to y'all."

I remember one other time when I had to answer to a landowner for a child's mistake. I was nine or ten, and DV and I had moved to a small house in Troy with Mama. It was just after the holidays and we had both gotten bicycles for Christmas, a gift our parents had undoubtedly struggled to pay for. Mine was a Western Flyer. One of our friends had gotten a bike, too. One afternoon, all three of us rode our new bikes the three miles out to the "country," where we used to live, to show off to our friends there. The road was raised above the level of the fields on both sides, and we stopped to look at some horses in a pasture off to the left.

"Let's ride down there and pet the horses," our friend said.

Neither DV nor I wanted to ride down the steep bank to where the horses were, but our friend was adamant.

"Oh, come on!" he said. "You afraid to ride down that lil' hill?"

"Those are Mr. D. Majors's horses," I said. "I don't wanna' mess with anything of his." He was a particularly mean landowner, and he was always gruff with us kids.

But our friend was undeterred and took off down the hill towards the horses. He lost control of his bike as he went skidding and bouncing down the hill and ran into the fence right in front of one of the horses. Our friend fell off the bike and landed hard, yelling and screaming from fright. This so startled one of the horses that he bolted and tried to jump the barbed wire fence. He didn't quite clear the top, and the barbed wire cut his belly as he went over. He landed hard and took off across an open field until he was out of sight.

Riding back home, I said to DV, "Ah' guess we better tell Mama about tha' horse."

"No way," DV said. "That's a whippin' offense."

"We weren't the ones caused tha' horse ta' spook," I said. "Besides, Mr. Majors is bound to find out who did it and ask about it."

We argued for some time while we rode home. When we got back, I told her about it.

"Jimmy was the one who scared the horse," I said. "DV and I didn't have anything to do with it."

"OK, boys," Rosie said. "Jus' let that be a lesson to you to not try and do things with those bicycles that you don't know how to do."

Sure enough, Mr. Majors knocked on our door a few days later and demanded that we pay for the vet bill to sew up the horse. Someone had seen us riding our bicycles that day and he figured it out.

"Rose, those boys are just gonna have to find the ten dollars to pay the vet bill," he said.

"Well, Mr. Majors," she replied, "they told me about it as soon as they got back. They said it wasn't them but their friend that spooked your horse, and I believe them."

They argued for a few minutes until Mr. Majors left in a huff and headed for our friend's house for his pound of flesh.

We never heard anything else about it, so our friend's parents must have paid him. Mama Rose could always tell when we'd lied to her, and she would always stand up for us if she thought we were in the right.

We played all sorts of games growing up, but only those that did not require money. We never had expensive toys, but we made do with those we did have. One of our favorite games was marbles. Both DV and I got pretty good with our taws and gathered a nice collection of aggies that we won from the kids we played with. We kept our marbles in a little jar that we hid under the house, where DV also kept a stash of the animal figures he made with clay he'd mined from a creek bank. After he had finished forming them, he would leave them to bake in the sun. They would dry and harden so we could play with them without destroying them. DV was quite a good artist, and his horses, cows, sheep, and other animals were very recognizable. By the time I was ten, when the house burned down, we had a big collection of both marbles and DV's clay figures. The fire melted and totally destroyed both our marbles and DV's animals, along with all of our clothes and what few possessions we had.

We played another game, "hoops," with old car tires. We spent many hours using sticks to roll or trundle the tire beside us, having races to prove who could make it go fastest or furthest using only our hands or the stick to propel it. I always lost the races because I was so small, but what I lacked in speed, I made up for with tricks. I was better than anyone at using my knees to make my tire turn left or right, or quickly stop. Most of the games we played, both among ourselves and with the grown-ups, were very physical. As farmers, our work was almost 100 percent physical, as it has been for our race since our ancestors were brought here on slave ships. There was a lot of "show me your muscles" and such from the adults when they were kidding us, and pitting two of us against each other in a wrestling match was common. As the smallest, I don't ever remember winning a wrestling match, but I participated in them until I left Mama's.

On Saturdays, Mama Rose sometimes liked to go to town, where she might drink a beer or two. She often took us with her to Lugo's Italian Restaurant, where she would put salt in her beer to go with a bowl of chili. She would buy us a strawberry soda with our chili, and we would all eat at a table in the kitchen. Sometimes she bought us an ice cream, too. Both DV and I really looked forward to those trips. Once in town, we followed the practices we'd learned: always show deference to whites and never do anything to insult the white people who passed us, especially white women.

On one of those Saturday trips, Mama Rose took us on a side trip that I wouldn't soon forget.

"But the store's that way," DV said.

"Come this way with me, boys. Ah' want to show you somethin' that I think you two little hellions need to see," she said. Apparently we were of the age where young boys begin to get too big for their britches. She led us down the street and around a corner to where the jailhouse was located.

"What're we headin' there for?" we both asked.

"You'll see," Mama said.

We went into the small building and the sheriff greeted her. It appeared she had arranged it with him earlier. He showed us past the booking counter into a small, dark hallway that led to the cells.

As we came to the cells, we were greeted by three young black boys. They looked to be about ten to twelve years old, our age. They had been caught stealing figs from one of the local farmers, who had them arrested. The boys were all behind bars and lined up next to each other at the front of their cell, holding onto the bars with both hands. They had forlorn looks on their faces.

Mama didn't say anything, and neither did anyone else. But as we left the building a few minutes later, she did address the sheriff, whom she seemed to know.

"Thank you, Sheriff Jones," she said.

"Any time, Rose. I'll always have room for those two if they get out of line," he said, nodding in our direction.

"Don't think that's necessary jus' yet, Sheriff," she said. "But I'll keep it in mind."

We walked on to the ice cream store in silence, where Mama bought us our usuals—a single scoop of strawberry for DV and a single scoop of vanilla for me. Sitting on the curb outside, eating our ice cream in silence, it seemed to taste even better than usual as we felt the warm summer sun on our skin and enjoyed our freedom. But for the next twenty years, I thought about that side trip each time I was presented with an option that was clearly outside the law. Mama's lessons were always thoughtful and well delivered with a long shelf life. I never ate figs again.

While I don't remember anyone having "the talk" with me growing up, adults were continuously warning us that "white people will kill you." While no one explained the KKK to me, adults would sometimes say "You want the KKK to come and drag you off to a hanging tree?" They often talked about hanging trees in different towns, and by the time I was in high school, I was well-versed in how to stay alive as a black boy in Texas. It wasn't until I was twelve that I met a white family with whom I didn't have to act as if I were stupid, like I didn't understand much that they said. This was the Schmidt family—Mrs. Schmidt was the one who attended my eighth-grade graduation.

The families in Bell County's black community all knew each other, and we helped each other when we could. For example, there was an old man that we knew as Puddin'. His real name was John Mathis, and he was the first homeless person I ever knew. We all knew him, and he was friendly and considerate. He would sleep in one house for a few days, often on the floor, and then move on to another one. While he was there, he would contribute to the chores, the family would feed him, and no one seemed to begrudge him his circumstances. He stayed with us many times and was like an uncle to us young children. Many of us even called him Uncle Puddin'. When it was cotton-picking season, there were times when a crew went through a field so fast that they left some of the smaller or harder-to-pick bolls on the stalks. That didn't happen very often, but when it did, Puddin' would come by the house with a proposition.

"Y'all want to make some extr' money?" he would say.

Now, I was always looking for work and ways to make money, even when I was young, so I was always keen to go with him. DV wasn't usually so keen, but he normally joined us, too, working hard once he got into it. So, Puddin' and his little crew of four or five children would work through the scraggliest cotton leavings you ever saw. The few bolls that were there were usually tough and hard to pick, but we were diligent and hungry, and we normally got every last one. And DV and I might make an extra ten cents or so for our trouble.

During the Depression, some of our neighbors went to work for the Civil Conservation Corps (CCC), though no one in our family did. That was a public works relief program that operated between 1933 and 1942 when the war created millions of jobs that improved the economy for everyone. The CCC was only for unmarried men between the ages of eighteen and twenty-eight. It was a major part of FDR's New Deal, and it provided unskilled manual labor jobs related to the conservation and development of natural resources in rural lands owned by federal, state, and local governments. It was designed to help poor families during the Great Depression by providing jobs for young men. Through the course of its nine years in operation, three million young men participated in the CCC. It provided shelter, clothing, food, and a wage of thirty dollars a month, twenty-five of which had to be sent home to their families. That was about $570 in 2017 dollars, and it was much more than they could have earned on the farm. That money kept a lot of my neighbors from starvation's door.

The CCC built bridges, roads, dams, and other public works projects, and it was the most popular of all the New Deal programs. Besides the direct advantages it gave to those who participated, it also increased public awareness and appreciation of the outdoors and the nation's natural resources. The CCC proved the continued need for a comprehensive, carefully planned national program to protect and develop natural resources.

There was a mattress program for the poor, too. Uncle Jace (the uncle with all the children) got mattresses free by going to the factory to help make them. When he brought the mattresses home, his family put them on the floor since they didn't have bed frames. At least no one had to sleep on a hard floor anymore.

Everyone on the farm wore overalls, and we usually had several pairs in various states of wear. Some were more rags than anything else, and those were reserved for the dirtiest jobs so we didn't ruin our "good" overalls and could make them last. We also had one set of "church goin' clothes," a pair of regular cotton pants and a white shirt—always a white shirt—for church. If things were good, we had a "dress coat," a tie, and a hat for church. Even the children wore hats . . . everyone did. Of course, most of these were given to us by the white families we worked for because we needed the little money we had for food, so they were often worn and not exactly the right size. I also saw many shoes on people of all ages, especially work shoes, with the sides or toes cut out—although the shoes were too small, they were all the person had. In the summer, we might go barefoot if the soil in the field hadn't dried up so much that it was full of hard dirt clods that hurt our feet. We also were careful to wear shoes in the middle of summer, when the sun would make the soil so hot it would burn your feet to walk on it.

Things changed for us after Pearl Harbor was bombed on Sunday, December 7, 1941. Because we didn't have a radio, we didn't hear about it until we went to town the next Saturday. The entire town was abuzz with news of the attack, our declaration of war, and what that would mean for us. I was ten then, and while the war changed life dramatically for most Americans, we were spared at first; farmers were exempt from the draft because farming was in the national interest. However, the local draft board was, of course, run by white men, which offered another avenue for whites to control Negroes. In about 1942, Uncle Jack was approached to change jobs and work for one of the local farmers that he really didn't like. He refused, and two weeks later, he got his induction orders in the mail. Once again, we were reminded of how small-town power worked and who held it.

Uncle Jack was a big man, all muscle from doing farm work since childhood. Like Uncle Jace, he was quite accomplished with his fists, so instead of sending him to the front lines in Europe, the army made him an MP (military police). He spent his service putting drunks and unruly servicemen into the brig on stateside bases. He claimed he never had to use his baton or his pistol. According to Uncle Jack, he just knocked them silly if they were close, and if they were out of reach, he knocked them down by throwing something at them. Uncle Jack was never afraid of letting the exact truth get in the way of a good story. Then again, he had always been very accurate when throwing a ball at home, so maybe it was true.

Beyond Uncle Jack's service, the war affected us in a myriad of ways. For example, every American was issued a series of ration books. They contained removable stamps that permitted people to buy certain rationed items, like sugar, meat, cooking oil, and canned goods. A person could not buy a rationed item without also giving the merchant the right ration stamp, and everything that affected war production was rationed. We were also given stamps for many other things. For instance, we each received stamps for two pairs of shoes a year—but since we only needed one pair, we traded or sold our extra stamps.

There were hundreds of details in poor people's lives that were changed by the war. As an example, farmers got extra gas for their tractors, and since tractors were left in the fields overnight, people would siphon gas from them to put in their own cars.

From the time I was ten or twelve, I was always looking for ways to help my mother with the expenses, even though I was young and small. I saw how hard she worked for what little money she had, and I felt guilty having her pay for everything I needed. I guess that stemmed from the way we'd handled money at Mama's house. There, everyone worked hard and chipped in with handling the finances. We all knew what everyone else made, and we all talked about pulling our own weight. So, from the time I was five years old, I was proud of being able to say that I was contributing. Also, I was acutely aware that I was living with Mama because my mother couldn't afford to have me live with her. My feelings about pulling my own weight didn't change when I began living with my mother.

When Aunt Ann got married and moved in with her new husband, she began working in the restaurant where he worked, leaving a vacancy for a domestic at the Schmidt household in

Waco. My mother filled that vacancy and began making enough money for me to live with her again.

The Schmidts were a local Jewish family—the first Jews I knew—and Mr. Schmidt had a printing business in downtown Waco. We lived in servants' quarters there, a small, one-room apartment with a bathroom above the Schmidts' garage, which we accessed by walking upstairs and across the garage's tin roof to the door. Mother and I ate in the Schmidts' kitchen and both slept in a single bed in the servants' quarters until I had a growth spurt when I was fifteen and got too big to sleep two in a bed. Mother

Ann Banks, the author's aunt.
She was mother to two sons,
Wayne and Ray.

bought a fold-up cot with a wooden frame, and I slept on that until we moved to Saginaw in 1948.

I seldom saw a pair of coveralls after I moved to Waco. From then on, it was regular pants and a shirt with a nice jacket and a hat for going to town.

Since the neighborhood was all white, I often played with white kids. In fact, I became good friends with the Schmidts' son, Bobby. For some reason I never knew, the Schmidts were devoid of the racism that infected most people in the area. Maybe they had moved to Texas from the North or from another country, but their lack of racism served as a dramatic counterpoint to the ingrained and often subconscious racism around them.

Once, when we kids were clearing a vacant lot to play base-

ball on, I was waist-deep in weeds with the other kids when someone's mother came out with bug repellent spray to keep us from being bitten by the hundreds of bugs that infested the area. She carefully sprayed all the white kids, but not me. Bobby, who was never shy about speaking up, asked her why she hadn't sprayed me.

"Because insects don't bite colored people," she said as she turned and headed home with the half-full can of insect spray.

That night, when I was scratching all the red bites on my legs and arms, I thought about why she had done that. There was no good answer aside from the pervasive racism that enveloped us all. She might not have thought about it, or she might have been quite intentional and deliberate, but the effect was the same. It was as if she was saying I wasn't good enough to waste bug spray on. I didn't say anything about it, but Bobby was incensed and insisted we never go there to play again. Having experienced similar things for years, I was less affected by it. Of course, I didn't like it, but that was just the way of the world for blacks growing up in the Deep South, and I didn't like wasting time and energy on something I couldn't change. Although I couldn't do anything, I thought about it a lot because I wanted to understand what was happening to me and my people—and why.

The Schmidt family encouraged me to express myself, and I didn't have to play the part of the dumb black boy with them like I'd been doing with other whites for years. They encouraged me to not be afraid, to show that I understood things, and to show that I wasn't stupid. They fed me with books and encouraged me to read-read-read.

Their older daughter was in college, majoring in sociology, and she seemed quite interested in my history and my opinion of things. She asked me cogent questions about my experiences and what I thought about things. She listened and often followed up with even more probing questions. It sometimes seemed like I was the subject of a history or sociology project, but I always believed she was genuinely interested. It was refreshing to be asked my opinion about various issues . . . especially by a white person.

The entire Schmidt family was supportive, and they all encouraged me to learn. They are another of my lucky stars. It's amazing how people and events from your childhood affect the way you grow up and what you grow into. Without their help and encouragement, I undoubtedly would have never had the courage and chutzpah to excel and move forward in my education.

Mother didn't own a car, so we took a Waco city bus whenever we went downtown. They usually came about every twenty minutes, and if you weren't ready to get on when the bus stopped, the driver would pull away and leave you behind. The "colored section" was the rear four rows, and that is where we sat unless the white section up front was already full. In that case, someone in the colored section would have to give their seat to a white person. If the bus filled up with whites, we had to stand. We only had a problem once, and that was when a white man arrived at the bus door just after Mother did.

"Out of the way, girlie!" he said, pulling her off the bus steps. "Let a white man on first!" He hissed as he stepped past her. Blacks weren't supposed to get on until all whites had boarded, but she hadn't seen him.

I could tell Mother was really steamed, and for a second or two, I was afraid she would talk back to him. She'd always had a quick temper, and she didn't always control it. But the anger washed over her face and she waited until he'd placed his nickel in the fare box and started back to his seat before she led me onto the bus. It seemed like every little thing was designed to reinforce the subservience of the black race.

I turned thirteen after I moved to Waco, and I got a job working at a shoeshine stand after school with four other boys. There was plenty of business. In 1942, the army had built a new base about sixty miles outside of Waco, halfway to Austin. Initially, its 108,000 acres were used to test tanks and tank destroyers, practice armored tactics, and generally train tankers before sending them overseas. It opened in August of that year with billeting for over 6,000 officers and more than 82,000 enlisted men. By 1943, when I moved to Waco, it was even larger. On weekends, many of those men came to Waco or Troy, and many of them got their shoes shined. A lot of young black boys worked as shoeshiners. Along with cutting grass, that was one of the most available jobs open to us. I became very proficient with a rag and could make it sing, snap, and pop on command, earning an extra nickel or dime by performing for the soldiers as I worked on their shoes. The soldiers generally paid more for a shoeshine, tipped better, and seemed to appreciate our rag skills more than the local whites. It seemed to us shoeshine boys that white people, in general, liked to see us dance—and even though it felt demeaning at times, we weren't above performing for an extra five- or ten-cent tip while we did our work. I would even practice at home to the songs on the radio, shining my own shoes to a high gloss. When those same tunes came on the radio at work, I'd break into a dance. I was always hustling for money.

"Boy, that nigger sure can dance!" was as insulting with a five-cent tip as it was without it, but it left me five cents richer, and it did add up. I had seen a motor scooter that I wanted to buy, and it cost ninety dollars. I figured that with an extra ten cents a shine, I could buy it in a month, so I became the best dancing shoeshine boy in Waco.

I worked in two shoeshine parlors: one for whites in Waco and one for blacks in Temple. One day, I was finishing my shift at the white shoeshine parlor when the manager told us to stay after work. Soon a short, muscular, tough-looking man in a cheap brown suit walked in and told us all to stand against the back wall while he asked us some questions. It seems they thought one of us shoeshine boys had stolen a fan from a shelf in the back room. The man in the brown suit was a detective, and he spent the next forty-five minutes grilling us about it and trying to get someone to confess. He was one tough detective—he acted and talked like it, and the whole thing scared the daylights out of me. No one confessed, and he finally let us go with the admonition, "Ah' know one of you niggers stole that fan, and Ah'm gonna find out who it was and put him in jail." All this for a two-dollar fan. For all I know, someone else stole it—there were a lot of people going in and out of that storeroom. But they were all sure "one of the niggers did it." I never did make enough money for that scooter, but it wasn't for a lack of trying.

Willie Brown, my former law partner and still my best friend, also shined shoes. He worked in Minneola, Texas, where he grew up. He tells a story to make the point about how poor he was growing up and how mean and disrespectful some of the white residents were. The story goes that he shined shoes on Saturdays, and one Saturday, a customer gave him a nickel tip but flipped it into a nearby spittoon out of meanness. Willie claims he was so poor that he fished that nickel out of the spittoon. Now, I have no reason to doubt most of the story, because I experienced much the same thing in Waco, but I have never believed the part about the spittoon. Willie Brown is too proud to have gone near that spittoon, no matter how poor he was. Still, it does make an accurate point about the meanness some people in the South showed us. I know I wouldn't have gone near a spittoon, and I was country poor—even poorer than Willie. He was town poor, a step up from country poor. But like Uncle Jack, Willie has never let the absolute truth get in the way of a good story.

Chapter 7
The Longest Swim

As the end of my first year in high school approached, the weather turned scorching. It was clear that summer was going to deliver a sweltering extreme even for Texas. "Over a hundred in the shade" was a common phrase that described all but the humidity quite well. It was regularly over 90 percent, and that made the heat all but unendurable.

A black housing project had recently been built in Waco and the city reluctantly built a small swimming pool beside it. So, after school one sizzling day, I went to check it out with my best friends, James and Freddy.

As we walked across the asphalt parking lot next to the pool, James said, "Bet Ah' could fry an egg on the hood of that car!"

"Bet Ah' could fry one on the sidewalk!" I said.

"Bet Ah' could do both," said Freddy. "It's hotter 'an a stolen tamale!"

After we got there, we were leaning on the fence around the pool, watching the other kids splash each other and cavort around in all that cool water, when James said, "Tomorrow I'm goin' swimmin'." There was a wide, dark sweat stripe down the back of his shirt where it was stuck to his back.

"You crazy," Freddy said. "Ah' know you can't swim."

"So what?" James said. "You see any grown people to tell me to leave? So what if Ah' can't swim. Ah'm gonna stay in tha' shallow end. You two too scared to go with me?"

"Ah' ain't scared!" replied Freddy.

"Me neither!" I said.

None of us could swim. But watching those other kids playing in all that cool water was just too enticing. I went home and asked Mother if I could go.

"James and Freddy are going swimming in the new pool next to the projects tomorrow, Mother. Can I go with them?"

"Swimmin'?! Are you out of your mind, John Edward? You don't even know how to swim!" she said.

"We'll stay in the shallow end, Mother. An' besides, James says he can teach me to swim. Ahl'll never learn if Ah' never try!"

We argued about it all evening. I came up with reason after reason why she should let me go, but she refused every time. We were still sharing the double bed, the only bed in our apartment, and every time she rejected one of my arguments, I would snort and jerk myself over to the edge of the bed, trying to find a dry spot to rest on where my sweat hadn't soaked the mattress. We didn't have air conditioning.

I really gave her the business about it. I had already told my friends I was going and didn't want to be embarrassed by backing out. Finally, we went to sleep still arguing even after the lights were out. She must not have gotten much sleep that night because she went downtown the next morning and bought a folding cot for me to sleep on.

The fact that none of us could swim was common. At that

time, there were very few public pools in the South available to blacks. Ever since the first swimming pool was built in the United States, pools have been a particular bone of contention in the fight for civil rights because the interaction is so intimate and social. Where I grew up, learning to swim involved braving exposure to snakes and facing the danger of brown, turbid, and swiftly flowing water from a nearby river. Not the safest of environments.

The earliest public pools in the US were built in large Northern cities during the late nineteenth and early twentieth centuries to serve mostly poor and working-class boys, both black and white, who swam together. Back then, swimmers were separated by sex. These pools were built to help get them clean since many lower-class domiciles lacked running water and bathing facilities. The arrangement of these pools revealed the class prejudices of the time.

For example, in 1910, there was a proposal to build a large municipal pool in New York's Central Park, which generated intense opposition from the city's middle and upper classes. They were concerned it would attract large numbers of immigrant and working-class kids to their oasis of genteel recreation.

During the 1920s and '30s, large resort-like public pools were built around the country, allowing men and women to use them together for the first time. This gender integration brought about racial integration, and the white population objected to having their women in such close proximity to black men in these visually and physically intimate spaces. During the years between the wars, Northern pools often became segregated through physical intimidation. A famous situation occurred at Pittsburgh's Highland Park Pool in 1931, for example; white swimmers frequently attacked black swimmers—sometimes with rocks and clubs—to prevent them from entering the pool.

The police actually encouraged these attacks and often arrested the black victims for "inciting to riot." This only illustrates the racial hatred and naivete that immigrants from Ireland, Italy, Western Europe, and other racially homogeneous areas brought with them. Some of this came from their original cultures, but some also came from their naivete, making them easy targets for the active segregationists of the time.

After World War II, public pools were desegregated across the country. However, whites usually abandoned public pools rather than share them with blacks. In the North, they were often sold to organizations that could make them private since discrimination was still legal for private clubs. In 1962, several years after Pittsburgh's municipal pools were desegregated, a sign posted outside a city pool still used exclusively by whites read, "No dogs or niggers allowed." In the North, public pools may have been racially desegregated, but that did not mean blacks and whites started swimming together. Apparently, the irony of formerly widespread signs—such as "No dogs or Irish allowed" and "No dogs or wops or spics allowed"—was lost on them.

The same type of trouble had no chance to arise at public pools in the South because public officials openly mandated racial segregation, explicitly barring blacks from entering "whites-only" pools. When the Civil Rights Movement passed federal anti-discrimination laws that applied to the South, many local governments filled municipal pools with dirt and paved over them rather than allow us to use them, too.

As the Civil Rights Movement developed in the 1950s, public pools became frequent battlefields in the South. In 1957, a few years after I graduated from Wiley College in Marshall, Texas, the NAACP represented a young man suing the local government there, trying to force the integration of a brand-new swimming pool. Before the trial was over, the judge made it clear the city would lose. Citizens then voted 1,758 to 89 to have the city sell all its recreational facilities rather than integrate them. The pool that was the subject of the suit was sold to a local Lions Club, which was thereafter able to legally operate it as a whites-only private facility.

There are still examples from across the country showing that things haven't changed much in some areas. In 2009, for example, sixty-five black and Latino campers from North Philadelphia's Creative Steps day camp used the pool at the private Valley Swim Club, located in a nearby suburb, after the day camp paid $1,950 so its campers could swim for ninety minutes once a week throughout the summer. As campers entered the water for the first time, club members began pulling their children out while asking aloud what all these black and Latino kids were doing there. A few days later, the Valley Swim Club canceled its agreement with Creative Steps. When asked to explain, the club president said, "There was concern that a lot of kids would change the complexion . . . and the atmosphere of the club." What he should have said is, "Club members are so racist they think letting their kids swim in the same pool with blacks will somehow infect either their bodies or their thinking with something they believe to be unwholesome."

Why do pools bring out the worst behavior in people? Pools are visually and socially intimate. Swimmers gaze upon one another's nearly naked bodies, lie in the sun next to one another, navigate crowded water, and flirt. This type of contact and interaction piques social anxieties and exposes the lack of trust and understanding between people of different social classes, different cultures, and different backgrounds like nothing else.

That small pool in Waco was the first public pool any of us boys had ever seen that was both close to home and open to blacks. That, on top of being a place of refuge from the heat of the Texas sun, made it so attractive to us. And we all very much wanted to learn to swim. For a swimmer, the fear engendered in a non-swimmer by any body of water deeper than one's knees is hard to imagine. And adolescent boys hate to be controlled by anything, especially their fears.

The next day Freddy and James wore their bathing suits to school underneath their clothes. Neither one had asked their mothers for permission to go swimming. And I regretted asking mine all day. After school, we walked to the pool, and they went in while I stayed out in the boiling sun watching them have fun in all that cool water. Eventually, I walked home disgusted that Mother would deny me something that looked so fun and inviting. I was frustrated, and by the time I got home, my temper was almost as hot as the afternoon was. As soon as I got there, I began giving Mother the business about being old enough to do things and telling her what it was like to watch my friends splashing in that blue water. This continued through supper.

We always ate in the Schmidts' kitchen after Mother cooked and served them their dinner in the dining room. There was no phone in the servants' quarters, so that night, before we went back to our room, Mother called one of her friends from their phone.

"Hello, Jane. My boy keeps badgerin' me about going swimmin' at that new swimmin' pool next to tha' projects and I wondered if they give swimmin' lessons there," she said.

She had turned to look at me as she talked, and suddenly her face went pale.

"The little Jackson boy?" she said. "How awful! His parents must be heartbroken."

After she hung up the phone, she was quiet for a moment.

"What was that about?" I asked. "Did I hear you say somethin' about James?"

"Yes. That's why I didn't want you to go swimmin', John Edward."

"Why?"

"He drowned," she said. "He's dead."

I sat down hard on one of the kitchen chairs, speechless. None of my friends had ever died before and I was trying to get my head around the idea of James not being at school the next day—or any other day.

Mother watched me for about a minute before she said, "Uh-huh . . . Ah' told you . . . you didn't want to listen, but Ah' told you. That boy would still be alive today if he had just listened to 'is mother."

The rest of the evening was as devoid of argument as the one before had been filled with it. We went to bed quietly that night. But for years after, she used that sad day as an example when she wanted to give me the business when I did something she'd told me not to do.

A few months later, there was a trial and I was called to testify. This was to be my first experience in a courtroom. I was just being called as a witness, but it was still a frightening experience. Even at that age, I knew who held power in the courts, and it sure wasn't black people. The jail was behind the courthouse in the same building, and there were always policemen going in and out. I wasn't just scared—I was petrified.

Mother and I dressed up in our good clothes and took the bus downtown to the courthouse. She sat with me on the bench outside the courtroom until a deputy came out and called for "a John Dearman." I went into the courtroom behind him while Mother followed the arrows marked "colored" to the upstairs balcony where blacks were allowed to sit.

It was as close as she could get even though her son was in the witness box. Mr. and Mrs. Jackson were sitting at the plaintiffs' table on the right with their white lawyer. I passed them as the court clerk directed me to the witness box next to the judge. They were suing the county because there was no lifeguard on duty when their son drowned.

It seemed the county had built a public pool grudgingly—because they had to. However, the county didn't feel it was necessary to provide a lifeguard despite being well aware that most blacks in the area either couldn't swim at all or could swim just enough to get themselves in real trouble.

The author at age thirteen. Around the time he had to testify in court.

I took the stand. The clerk had me put my hand on a Bible that was reserved for Negroes, which he held in front of me. He said, "Do you solemnly swear that the testimony you are about to give in the case now on trial is the truth, the whole truth, and nothing but the truth, so help you God?"

I was thirteen or fourteen years old, alone at the front of a courtroom filled with important-looking white people and several policemen, with my hand on a Bible. I was petrified. I took a deep breath, trying to stop the shaking, and said, "Yes, sir."

Apparently, that wasn't exactly what I was supposed to say, but the judge nodded to the clerk that it was adequate. The clerk sat down, leaving me alone.

Then the judge asked me some questions. "Now, Johnny"— no one ever called me Johnny—"you have been brought here as a witness for the plaintiff and you will be asked to answer some questions. You have been sworn in. Do you know what taking that oath means?"

"Ah think so."

"Do you know what perjury is?"

"Yes, sir. It means lyin', sir," I said. I had been coached by the Jacksons' attorney the day before, and that was something we had talked about.

"Do you know what the penalty for perjury in court is?" The judge smiled.

He had a nice smile. *This isn't going to be so bad*, I thought.

"If you lie, you could spend five years in prison," he said with exactly the same smile. Now it looked like one the devil might have as he showed you the door to hell.

Five years in jail, I thought. *They didn't tell me that!*

"But Ah' am goin' ta' tell tha' truth," I said.

"Yes, but if you don't, you could go to jail for a looong time!" he said.

He already said that, I thought.

"But Ah' already said Ah'm goin' ta' tell tha' truth, sir," I said.

"You're a smart one, aren't you?" he said. His smile was gone.

"Ah' . . . Ah' guess so, sir," I said.

He leaned down over me and said, "Well, don't try to fool us. We are pretty smart, too." His smile was gone when he said it.

"OK . . . sir," I said. "Ah' sure won't, sir."

The Jacksons' lawyer wanted me to be respectful. He had told me to end all sentences with "sir" when I was in court. Now I was petrified.

"The nice man sittin' with the Jacksons is their lawyer," he said. "He is goin' ta' ask you some questions, and then the county's lawyer, sittin' at the other table, is also going to ask you some questions. Just don't forget what could happen if you tell a lie to either one of them," he said.

"Yes, sir," I said. "Ah' won't, sir."

The Jacksons' lawyer asked me a number of questions about what I had seen the day James drowned. They wanted to know if I had seen any lifeguards on duty when James was in the water. I knew what he was going to ask, so that part was pretty easy. The lawyer was nice to me and didn't ask anything we hadn't gone over the day before.

This isn't so bad, I thought. *What was I worried about?*

Then the county's lawyer started in on me and I spent a most uncomfortable half hour repeating the same thing over and over in different ways as he tried his best to trip me up. But I was telling them the exact truth about what I had seen. Either the county had not assigned a lifeguard to the pool or the one they had assigned wasn't there. Because I was telling the truth, I didn't have to keep straight what I was making up. I just remembered exactly what I had seen and didn't get flustered when the lawyer twisted my words, trying to make me contradict what I had already said. The Jacksons' lawyer had prepared me for this when we role-played, and he'd acted aggressive and nasty to me like he said the county lawyer would. He was right about the way the other lawyer would act. I kept my cool throughout and stepped down off the stand feeling pretty good about myself.

The Jacksons won the lawsuit, but I never heard how much they were awarded—how much the county valued the life of a young black boy back then. I hope it was a bundle, but I doubt it.

Across the South, Jim Crow laws kept blacks out of public swimming pools and off the most desirable beaches and lakeside swimming spots. Some communities built "colored pools," but there was no race mixing where black boys or men could be in the same location as white women in bathing suits. In the 1930s, the Works Progress Administration built "colored pools" and white pools and promoted swimming among both racial groups. But the number of "colored pools," the size of those pools, and the opportunities for blacks to swim were far from equal to those of whites. Still, some of us took advantage of the few opportunities we had to learn to swim—like future civil rights leaders Dr. Martin Luther King Jr. and Andrew Young. Young was even on the swimming team at Howard University, a black college.

It wasn't until 1964 that the Waco Community Relations Committee succeeded in desegregating the city's park and recreation facilities.

All except swimming pools.

Chapter 8
Anything for a Dollar

As the war wound on, I saw newsreels at the movies of the atrocities both the Germans and Japanese were doing to "our boys." Like everyone else, I began to develop a real hatred for both Japanese and Germans. I also developed a desire to enlist and help the war effort. My girl-friend's brother was a few years older than we were. He had enlisted in the army, and I saw how much she respected him for that. Even though the war was over, my fifteen-year-old mind decided that enlisting might be a good way to impress both her and other girls, so I thought I would at least find out the details. When I looked into it, I found that the military offered to pay for college with military service (four years' school for three years' service), which would solve my dilemma of how to pay for a college education. That was when I got serious about joining up. I thought the minimum age for enlistment was sixteen, so when I turned sixteen, I went to the Waco navy recruitment office with Theodore Martin, a good friend of mine who was my age and had similar ideas of travel and adventure. We were also both from single-parent families and felt like parasites for not contributing more to help our mothers. We thought we could send part of our military pay home to help out.

It was early 1947, and the recruitment officer told us sixteen was too young to enlist without parental approval. So, I carried the enlistment form to my mother, naively sure she would sign. To my surprise, she refused to sign and then convinced me to accept her decision. That was one of the earliest examples of my mother's advanced ability to manipulate me. I didn't see it at the time, but looking back after I had children of my own, I began to appreciate her skills in that area.

This was about the time I started working after school setting pins in the local bowling alley. The alley had twelve lanes, and each of us six pinsetters would simultaneously work two adjacent lanes. After the bowler had bowled his frame, I would jump down from a ledge between lanes, roll the ball back, and reset the pins to ready them for the next frame. There was usually plenty of time for the pinsetter to work two lanes because they seldom finished a frame at the same time.

There was a lot of jumping around, but I was young, thin, and spry and it was not a hard job for me . . . except for the times, usually on Friday or Saturday nights, when the soldiers would come to town and get drunk. It wasn't always the soldiers, but maybe I remember them most because they were the best at the game the drunks often played: Who can throw the hardest?

There was an alley between lanes so a pinsetter could walk between them, and the view from the bowler's end was of my legs from the knee down. Sometimes I would stand between the lanes in this alley so I could move more easily from one lane to another, but when the drunks challenged each other to throw the ball the hardest, I took a few steps back—a really hard throw might send pins through the alley and into the adjacent lane. They only hit me a couple of times, but I still remember the bruises they left. In general, however, the soldiers weren't as vicious as the locals in trying to hit us with the pins or the ball. If they were really drunk, they would sometimes slide all the way down the alley on their butts to where we set the pins and give us a quarter tip for "being such a good boy." "Here, boy," they would say. "Here's a quarter for helpin' me whup ma' buddies."

Usually, this was after they had spent some time slinging the balls down the lane as hard as they could. I'd take the tip, but I'd usually mutter under my breath, "Sure, you drunk white prick, I'll take your tip. After you tried to kill me, I get a quarter, you cheap white bastard!" The other pinsetters, for whom my remarks were meant, had a good laugh over it.

The other pinsetters and I made up a game where we would see who could insult the drunks the most when they slid down the alleys on their backsides to tip us. Of course, we were careful not to let them hear us or we could have suffered severe consequences.

When I heard a ball hit the lane at the far end and start rolling toward me, that was my cue to get the heck out of the way. This maneuver was usually followed by "Boy, that nigger sure can move!"

This is when I learned never to turn my back to a drunk Southern white man. You just never knew what they would do.

Many of the soldiers tipped better too—but they seemed to tip even more when they tried to hit me and couldn't. I was paid two cents a game but might be tipped several nickels on good nights. Tips were collected at the cash register and evenly split at the end of the shift, except when the bowlers slid down the lanes to tip us directly.

"Here, boy. Take this nickel. You really did good for me. Go buy yourself a strawberry ice cream."

Sometimes the mean drunks would insult us in between slinging the balls down the lanes. "Havin' opossum for supper tonight, boy?" was a favorite, usually followed by uproarious laughter. That was one of many questions that didn't require an answer.

That summer, I stopped setting pins when I got a job at the Waco bus depot. I was hired for the late-night shift at the cafe to clean up for a dollar a night. One night, I was cleaning up after we had closed when a late bus came in. A man who was waiting for his connecting bus came into the cafe and looked around at the empty tables.

"Can I get something to eat?" he asked the waitress.

"Not now. We're closed," she said. "The cook has gone home."

The man saw me cleaning up in the kitchen. "What about him?" he said, pointing in my direction. "I'll bet he could make something for me."

"Oh, he's just tha' clean-up boy," she said.

"I'll bet he can make me a sandwich," he said. "Hey, boy! Think you could make me a fried egg sandwich?"

"Ah'm not the cook," I replied.

"How about if I paid you for the sandwich plus an extra dime for you?" I looked at the waitress and she just shrugged.

I had previously worked at a restaurant in Temple for a few months as a dishwasher and busboy. I even waited tables for a while there, but I had never cooked.

"Well, sure, Ah' could do that." That's how I became the unofficial after-hours short-order cook. DV's mother had been a short-order cook after the growing season on the farm and I had watched her work. Besides, Mother was teaching me to do everything she did, and one of those things was cooking. Of course, I could make him a fried egg sandwich. I wasn't paid a dime every time, but the patrons were so glad to get a midnight sandwich that they usually tipped very well. That job paid less per hour than pinsetting, but I brought home a lot more from the tips. As always, I was hustling for money and putting almost all of it into the bank. Mother thought of my bank account as my college fund, but my teenage wisdom was starting to have other ideas. The money was beginning to add up, and once I passed my sixteenth birthday, the legal driving age in Texas, my plans for my fast-growing nest egg cycled between buying some flashy new clothes and going in on buying a car with my friend Theodore.

Theodore and I had been trying to buy a car for several months. Like many boys growing up in Waco, he and I were serious car buffs. We found a broken-down 1935 Ford Model A with a rumble seat for sale for seventy-five dollars. It was a four-cylinder flathead coupe that had a ragged interior and rust spots in various places. It was sitting on cinderblocks behind Johnson's Used Cars and didn't have a battery so we couldn't start it, but Mr. Johnson assured us it ran beautifully. Unfortunately, we both had very good imaginations, and we thought it was the most beautiful thing we had ever seen.

Cars with rumble seats were the rage for teenagers then—a couple could sit in the rumble seat in back and the folks in the front couldn't always see what they were doing. We thought we would be complete chick magnets if we could just manage to buy that car.

Mother resisted the idea of her sixteen-year-old having a car of his own. She didn't even own a car. As far as I could tell, she spent all her money on clothes for herself (she loved nice clothes and always looked nice), clothes for me (she never wanted me going around in worn or ratty-looking clothes), and my educational costs and college fund.

A few days after I'd gone to the navy recruitment office, I was pressing Mother again about the car. As a consolation for her not signing the recruitment form, she said, "John, I'll make you a deal. If you'll stay in school until you graduate, you can join the military then, and I'll even let you buy that old car with Theodore now."

That sounded good to me, but when Theodore and I went to inspect the car again, we found so many things wrong with it that we changed our minds. It seemed Mr. Johnson had an even more active imagination than we did. If Theodore and I pooled our money, we could buy an old car—just not one that would run, that we knew how to fix, or that we could afford to fix.

Theodore's mother had signed his recruitment form, so he began getting ready to go to the navy when the car didn't materialize. However, his mother also wanted him to graduate first, so he finally agreed and didn't join until after graduation. By that time, I had moved to Michigan, lost interest in the service, and was planning on going to college. Later, when Theodore got out of the navy, he went on to college on the GI Bill and became a teacher. I believe he did that until he retired.

Since the car purchase had dropped through, Mother agreed to let me buy the zoot suit I had been staring at in a clothing store window for months. Zoot suits were all the rage at the time, especially for African Americans, Latinos, Italian Americans, and Filipino Americans. The zoot suit is a high-waisted men's suit with wide legs, tight cuffs, and pegged trousers. They have long coats with wide lapels and wide, thickly padded shoulders. They are very distinctive, and we wore them with sharp collared shirts (usually a dark color), a wide tie, big hats that had wide brims, and a long watch chain that dipped to below the knee.

My zoot suit was bright blue, and the hat was the same color with a wide, flat brim and a long dark-blue feather secured in a band that matched the suit. I wore a dark-blue shirt and a wide blue tie that also matched the suit. I didn't have a watch, but I did sport the chain, a big-linked silver one that reached almost to my calf. I also wore dark lace-up shoes that had thin, squared-off toes. I think I paid fifteen dollars for the whole thing, and I was really stylin' when I wore it to parties. I put the rest of my car money back into my college fund.

Not long after I bought the zoot suit, I thought again of the hugging incident with the young white girl. I had left my job at the bus station for what I thought was a better one at a hotel in Waco, making extra money in the afternoons after high school let out. I was hired to serve at parties, deliver room service, and do odd jobs like cleaning up around the building at fifty cents a day for the two or three hours I worked after school.

At sixteen, I was excited to have a regular job so I could bring in extra money to help my mother. We were still living with the Schmidt family, and I was proud to finally make regular contributions to our income.

One afternoon, I was taking a load of trash down to the alley behind the hotel. I stepped into the service elevator, which was operated by hand. That day, it was the hotel manager's pretty blonde teenage daughter at the controls. She was my age and was in the same grade as me at the white school. She had started working after school a few weeks earlier, about the same time I had. I was pretty sure she didn't really need the money, but apparently her father was teaching her how the hotel business worked. She'd seemed entirely too friendly from the moment we met, but until then, I had managed to avoid her most of the time.

"Oh, hello, John!" she said as I stepped into the elevator car.

The service elevator was rather large, and when I walked in, I slid into a corner, behind the trash bags.

"Have I done something to offend you?" she asked. "It seems you have to go somewhere else every time I come into the room."

"No, ma'am," I said. "I just have a lot of work to do, that's all."

"Ma'am?" She paused. "Why, John, it's Lola. You should call me by my actual name, don't you think?"

Decidedly not, I thought.

"Well . . . well, sure, Lola," I said. The elevator seemed to be getting smaller and moving slowly—very, very slowly.

Lola stepped around the trash bags and sidled up close to me.

"You do want to get to know me, don't you, John?" she said softly.

Uh-oh, I thought.

She reached across me and pressed the "STOP" button as the elevator crept past the fifth floor.

"Seems like we never have an opportunity to be alone," she said.

The phrase "hanging tree" flashed through my mind as I stepped around the trash bags and quickly pulled out the "STOP" button, starting the elevator back on its very unhurried way to the ground floor.

"I . . . I've got an awful lot of work to do today, Lola. Better to keep after it," I said. *Before you manage to get your father after me with a pitchfork and a rope*, I thought.

If she thought I was avoiding her before that elevator ride, she must have thought we were on two different planets afterwards.

The Journey

When I think about that elevator ride even now, I still get a nervous feeling in the pit of my stomach. That was in 1947, and race relations were being tested by soldiers returning from the war in Europe, where they had gotten used to being treated very differently by the people there. There were regular confrontations, and they didn't usually end well for blacks. It wouldn't have been a good time for me to test conditions.

When school let out for the summer, I started working longer hours. Summers in Waco can be scorching, and I appreciated that the hotel was air-conditioned. The minimum wage was forty cents an hour at that time. But Mother was working as a domestic, and domestics weren't required to be paid minimum wage. She made five dollars a week on top of our meals and our room over the garage. At the hotel, I was paid by the job, not by the hour. For example, parties lasted about three hours, and I helped set up and break down, so I worked about four hours for a little over a dollar. I don't remember exactly how much I took home each week, but I only worked part-time and I never made more than Mother did. I recall taking home three or four dollars a week—always less than five dollars.

I had suggested to Theodore that he could get a job at the hotel, too, and he did. A few weeks later, Theodore came to work excited to tell me something.

"Hey, Dearman, there's a new apartment house going up over on Market Street. Ah' checked and they are payin' forty cents an hour for laborers. They are hirin', too!" he said.

"Dang," I said. "That's a lot more than we're gettin' here. You wanna' stop by after work and see if we can get on?"

Theodore agreed, and we started our new careers in construction a week later. It was June and the temperature in Waco was often over ninety degrees. Most of our work was outside, and it usually involved lugging heavy material from one place to another or digging trenches for something or other in that sweltering heat with no breeze. After two days, Theodore and I were dripping wet with sweat, sitting under a shade tree we had walked a hundred yards to find. We were dusty, dirty, and exhausted while we ate our lunch.

He looked at me and said, "Remember last week when we were sittin' in that nice hotel ballroom eatin' an ice cream after lunch?"

"Uh-huh."

"Remember how cool that air conditioning was?"

"Yeah, Ah' do."

The next day, we were back at the hotel, where we gratefully picked up our meager checks each week. We were thankful we hadn't burned any bridges when we left and were grateful we had air conditioning to look forward to all summer. That's the only time I remember a job getting the better of me . . . and it really whipped me. It had been that hot when I worked in the fields, but I was used to it then. We'd also set our own pace and took breaks as we needed them. I just wasn't used to that kind of work at that pace in that kind of heat. I would remember it for many years as I worked hard jobs that were much less miserable than that one.

We moved to Michigan five months later, where the heat from the factory furnaces was also hot, but in a different way. It was only really bad right near the furnaces, and we had regular breaks out of the heat. I would never again have to confront trying to work in Texas's searing summer heat.

Chapter 9
Moving North - 1947

In 1947, I was sixteen years old and going into my sophomore year at Moore High School, an all-black high school in Waco. My mother still worked as the Schmidts' maid, and she and I were still living in the servants' quarters above the Schmidts' garage. Mrs. Schmidt was the perfect model of kindness, generosity, and equality—the first white person to treat me that way. On April 15 of that year, Jackie Robinson became the first African American to play Major League Baseball. Suddenly, our pantheon of sports heroes doubled as Joe Louis was joined by another exceptional talent. We hung on every pitch Jackie took a swing at because each one meant so much more to us than a simple spinning baseball. Each stolen base, each hit, each on-base, and each run driven in or scored meant we could compete. And we could win.

The white myth of black inferiority was being publicly shattered every day on the level playing field of the Major League Baseball diamond. At the same time, the world was being introduced to an elegant black couple with class and style: Jackie and his wife Rachel, a registered nurse and accomplished individual in her own right. Our race was coming out of the shadows and exhibiting truths we had always known: we were capable of fitting in, contributing, and even excelling—something most of us had believed for a long time. At the same time, we clearly saw that sports were a way out of the smothering poverty we had grown up with. None of this was lost on me.

That summer, I had my growth spurt. I know it must have taken longer than one summer for it to happen, but it felt to me like I had gone into summer at five foot nine and 140 pounds and ended it at six foot one and 155. When I went back to school, the football coach approached me.

"Well, well, Dearman, you have really grown. Looks to me like you are ready to join the football team."

I went home that day excited at the prospect of playing football and proud that the coach was recruiting me. But Mother had other ideas.

Her first reaction was, "John Edward, I don't want you to play football . . . you'll get hurt."

I knew she was just trying to keep me safe, but teenagers generally think they are invincible, and I was no exception. Besides, I had begun taking an interest in girls, and playing football was an obvious way to attract them. Mother and I went around and around for a few days until she finally relented and I started football practice. As luck would have it, I injured my foot two weeks later, and playing football made it worse, so I had to drop football just after the season started. It turned out that I have flat feet, and all the running and jumping caused extreme pain in my heels after a few days. The inside of my foot swelled up, and the pain was something like that caused by plantar fasciitis. It prevented me from running.

Mother just looked at me sideways and said, "I knew you'd get hurt!"

We moved to Michigan that October, and once again, I wanted to play football. But school and football practice had already started when we got there. This elicited a little sigh of relief from my mother. She was still worried about me getting hurt or having my goals (really, her goals for me) diluted by interests outside of schoolwork. She was keeping her eye on the ball of education for me. For my part, I was disappointed—I saw sports as a way to have fun, fit in at a new school, and attract girls. I also saw it as a possible way out of poverty, the memories of which had shaped my childhood and dogged me still.

In college, I again had the desire to play, so I went to practice and sat in the stands to watch for an afternoon. It seemed like all the players were huge—certainly much bigger and stronger than I was. Even after working at the foundry in Saginaw, I was still skinny and much less muscular than the football players. But I wanted to play football anyway and decided to go to college at Wiley, a historically black college in Texas that was well-known as a football power. They had won the championship in their conference for several years, and the football players took it quite seriously. They spent a lot of time in the weight room. It seemed there was a big difference between high school and college football. So, I went back to the dorm and reconsidered. That was the last time I thought seriously about playing football.

Before Jackie Robinson broke into the majors, Satchel Paige and Joe Louis were the big role models for Negro youth. We had very few living heroes then, and those Negroes who spent little or no time in school knew very little of our other historical heroes. Those of us who had attended school and read history knew of Frederick Douglass and others, of course, but if you didn't read history, you had no way of learning about those exceptional men.

A few years after we moved to Saginaw, I had the pleasure of meeting Joe Louis through his manager, John Roxborough, the black owner of the insurance agency where Mother worked. By that time, I stood six foot one. I was relatively muscular, and my hands were large even for that height. But when I went to shake Mr. Louis's hand, he held out an appendage that seemed to be the size of a baseball mitt. His hand swallowed mine. He stood about six foot two, and it was said he only needed six inches to knock out a man. After that handshake, I understood why. My hand disappeared in his, and he shook it—and me—like I was a rag doll.

Before we moved to Saginaw, Mom and Mrs. Schmidt had kept up the drumbeat of education-education-education for me. They had introduced me to a tiny flame—the possibility of going to college, no small thing given that none of my family members had even finished high school. In fact, at the time, seventh grade was the highest grade anyone in my family had completed. At the same time, my love of learning began to grow, and I started to believe what they were saying as my grades proved I could be a good student.

When I was sixteen, I started taking the Waco city bus through the Baylor University campus, looking out the window at the white kids wearing bobby socks and letter sweaters. They all seemed to be having the time of their lives. It still seemed a far reach to me—a distant dream of possibility on the other side of a bus window. But I was beginning to believe there might be some way I could attend college.

In 1948, the Supreme Court struck down the practice of legal redlining—excluding blacks from entire neighborhoods with whites-only housing. But it would still be years before it was enforced in the Southern states, including Texas. That same year, the Democratic Party, pushed by the Young Democrats, adopted a civil rights platform for the first time. The entire block of Southern states walked out of the Democratic Convention en masse and established the Dixiecrat Party. Segregation was the new party's primary raison d'être and put Strom Thurmond up for president. We hoped this scourge of overt and brutal racism was the last gasp of a dying culture. Reality proved much different; racism would morph into a more covert but no less brutal version of itself that lessened only in small, hard-earned steps over the next fifty years. It would continue in smaller pockets for even longer.

But this was happening beyond my awareness. My life changed forever that year when my mother, new stepfather, and I moved to Saginaw in October 1947. We left our family, our friends, and the racist barriers of Texas to join another great migration of blacks out of the South, this time looking for decent jobs in the auto and steel industries of the North. We were following my stepfather's sister and her husband, who had moved there several years earlier and had sung the praises of decent pay and a better life ever since.

Life in Saginaw would be very different from life in Texas. For the first few months, we shared a three-bedroom, one-bath house with two other families, and I slept on a cot in my parents' bedroom. Next, we moved into a two-bedroom apartment in the projects. We lived there until my parents saved enough to buy a small two-bedroom house with a small apartment on the second level basement that they could rent out. I finally had my own room. I was in heaven!

My mother did what she knew, and as soon as she could, she went to work as a maid for a local doctor. My stepfather found work in the GM plant and was paid many times the hourly wage he would have earned back in Texas. In Texas, all I remember him doing is yard work at a local country club. This was a man who had served his country in World War II, was wounded in battle, and was awarded a Purple Heart—but all he could do was yard work! He came home from the war with an M1 rifle and an American flag. He proudly gave me the flag, and I later donated it to Moore High School, the segregated school I attended until we moved north.

It's too bad Uncle Jace never managed to join us in Saginaw. With all those kids, he sure could have used the extra money he would have made.

In Michigan, I attended Saginaw High School, my first integrated school. I was seventeen when I entered my junior year there in October 1948. Soon, having white friends my own age didn't seem so dangerous or extraordinary. Though it did take some time to fit in. For one thing, my Deep South accent from rural Texas was like a foreign language to many of the kids who had only known a Northern accent for their entire lives.

During the first few weeks, I listened but didn't comment, just getting the lay of the land. Finally, I raised my hand in class for the first time and made a rather long comment about the subject of the day. When I finished, I sat down feeling reasonably proud of myself. I thought the teacher and my classmates were impressed with how bright the new boy must be. There was a very long silence, after which a kid sitting near me raised his hand. The teacher recognized him and the kid stood up with a puzzled look on his face. "What did he say?"

I realized I had more work to do.

This was the first big move of my life, and both the culture and surroundings were different from what I had grown up with in Texas. Saginaw's population was just over 90,000, only a little bigger than Waco's 80,000. But Saginaw was a Northern industrial city whereas Waco was located in an agricultural area of Texas. The pace of life was faster in Saginaw, and there was more mixing of races. The cultures were very different, too. Saginaw was more direct, with less racial violence simmering just below the surface. In Saginaw, there were ten whites for every black, and most minorities —including my family—lived on the northeast side of the city.

At first, I was very shy in school, essentially because I was new and hadn't made any friends yet. I was especially shy around white girls, although they seemed friendly enough and were always friendlier than the boys. At the end of my first school year there, I convinced Mother to send me back to Waco for the summer to live with Robert's father's brother, my step-uncle, Thomas Evans. I wanted to attend a remedial class in Algebra and Trigonometry since I hadn't done as well in math as I wanted to at my new school.

After I returned to school for my senior year, the students protested an issue involving the school and civil rights, and everyone boycotted school for one day. I was on the front page of the local paper in a picture of the group marching down the street. Since I was one of the biggest boys, they had me at the front holding one end of the banner. That banner went across the whole street, and the protest got a lot of attention. It was my first taste of taking part in a civil rights protest. It would not be my last.

One of my teachers, Miss Bertovick, was the first to mention law school to me when I was nearing the end of my senior year. A few years earlier, Mother had decided I could—and should—be a doctor. She still had her eyes on a medical career for me when Miss Bertovick made her recommendation. I had completed all my required subjects by January 1950. Shortly before the semester ended, Miss Bertovick asked me about going to college.

"What's going to be your major?" she asked.

"I'm not sure I'm goin', Mrs. Bertovick. I'm plannin' on working at Grey Iron at least for a while."

"Did you ever think about the law?"

"No ma'am. It never occurred to me."

"Well, I think you would like it and would do well, too. You might consider it. We have a class in commercial law that starts soon. Since you've taken all of your required courses, why don't you take that class and see if you like it?"

So, I took the commercial law course, did well, and found that the law interested me. That one class, which was suggested by one teacher who took an extra interest in her students and who went further than required in teaching them, changed my life. Another of my lucky stars!

Chapter 10
Wiley College

June 1950 was a very eventful month in my life. Robert Coy Evans Jr., my brother, was born June 29, 1950. I was nineteen. At the time, my stepdad (Robert Jr.'s father) and I were working the graveyard shift at the Chevrolet Grey Iron plant in Saginaw cleaning up and doing maintenance work. That morning, Uncle Jack—who had also moved to Saginaw and worked at the Grey Iron plant—met us at the gate and told us my brother had arrived. We all piled into his 1946 Chevrolet sedan. He drove me home and then took my stepdad to the hospital to see his new son, my brother.

I had completed my high school requirements in January and started work immediately at the Grey Iron plant, in addition to taking some elective courses. I proudly marched with my class in the June 1950 graduation ceremony, which Mother and Uncle Jack attended. To say my mother was proud as a peacock is an understatement. Her work and guidance had paid off! I was the first in the family to graduate from high school, and there were congratulations all around. I heard from all my relatives and friends back in Texas, and no one had anything to say except "congratulations" and "well done." Mr. and Mrs. Schmidt were as proud as if it were their own son graduating. I was grateful and glad for the accomplishment, but the thought of college still nagged at me. So did my mother. She became as determined to see her firstborn become a college graduate as she had been to get me through high school.

On June 25 of that year, North Korea invaded South Korea and the Korean War began. The US was building up its military forces for the war, so within two months of graduating, I got my draft notice in the mail. That immediately got me into high gear to get into college; I could see nothing good happening for me if I went to war, and college students got deferments.

When I received my notice, I was making $125 a week at Grey Iron. I was taking home more than $100 a week, and as hard as factory work was, it wasn't nearly as hard as the farm work I had experienced in Texas. I enjoyed having a pocket full of money for the first time in my life. It allowed me to do all the things a young man of that time was able to do. But, to be honest, I didn't do much with the money that might be called "kicking up my heels." I don't know what the other young men did with their money, but all I did was buy a few clothes. I saved most of it. After all, I had a college education to pay for!

The year before, when I was eighteen, I had tried to join the airforce. Somehow, I had gotten it into my mind that I wanted to become a pilot. The sergeant at the recruitment office listened politely before telling me that only officers could become pilots, and I had to be a college graduate just to be considered for flight school. That experience had soured me on the military. Between that and the racist tableaus I'd seen in Waco involving soldiers from Camp Hood, I was sure I didn't want to risk my life for a racist organization that would treat me so badly if I did return alive.

Still, I tried four times in my life to join the service. This was the second time. The first was when Mother refused to sign the navy's age waiver when I was sixteen.The third time was in March 1954 (just before my 26th birthday). I was in my third year of law school. I knew that I was going to be drafted immediately after law school. In my mind going in as an officer would be better than going in as a recruit. I went to the recruiting office and asked if I could enlist and get into the officer training school. They said yes. Prior to that meeting my step father had told me that being a second lieutenant wasn't good enough and a Master Sergeant had more authority. So, I asked the officer if I could be a first lieutenant. He said no because that would be against army regulations. I told the recruiter I was going to go home and think about it. Over the weekend President Eisenhower issued an executive order saying those who had been given an educational deferment would not be drafted after graduation if they were 26 years old or older unless it was a time of an emergency. Since I would be 26 years old upon graduation, I went back to the recruiter and said, 'Are you sure you can't give me a first lieutenant position?'

The recruiter responded, " I'm sorry we can't do that."

I said, "Then I won't be enlisting."

The recruiter said, "Then you will be drafted."

I said, "Didn't you see the President's Executive Order? I'll be 26 and won't be drafted."

The fourth would be in 1961, at age thirty, when I was living in San Francisco. I had just passed the bar exam but hadn't yet joined Willie Brown, my future partner, in our own law firm . I got a call from the army recruitment office in the Presidio, a local army post, to ask if I wanted to enlist. The recruiter told me that if I joined, I would start as a captain in the Judge Advocate General's Corps, where I would join other attorneys in applying military law. I asked the recruiter if I could get the position of major, rather than captain. "Well, sir," I said, "I don't think I could get along as a captain. I do have a wife to support."

"Oh?" the recruiter said.

"Yes, but if I could start as a major, I think that would work." I didn't realize I was asking them to go against the established military hierarchy and the rules of enlistment they had been using for the last several hundred years.

"I don't think we could do that, Mr. Dearman," he replied. And that was the end of that.

A few months later, I was invited to be on the board of the Red Cross and attended a Red Cross Board of Directors meeting. There were numerous celebrities at the meeting, including Shirley Temple Black, who had been lending her talents to the Red Cross since 1936 when she first made a public service announcement for them as a child star. There were also several retired army officers as well as many active-duty officers. I was introduced to one of the retired officers, who turned out to be the same man I had talked to months earlier when I had suggested starting as a major. I told him they had missed out on a good man. He and I had a good laugh over the circumstances.

When I finished high school, I thought I would work at Grey Iron for six months or a year, during which time I might save enough to pay for a year or two of college. But, after getting my love letter from Uncle Sam, I immediately called Helen Green, a friend from middle school, who was enrolled at Bishop College in Marshall, Texas. I thought she might have some ideas for me. She told me it was too late to apply at most colleges, but I might be able to get into Wiley College, a Negro college also located in Marshall that had a good reputation among blacks in the South.

In the '30s, Melvin Tolson, a teacher at Wiley, had built an award-winning debate team that became a renowned pioneer in interracial collegiate debates. In 1930, the team debated white law students from the University of Michigan in Chicago. Then, in 1931, it participated against University of Oklahoma in the South's first known interracial collegiate debate. The Wiley debate team rarely lost, and during their national tour in 1935, they won against the University of Southern California debate team. That was long before my interest in Wiley, but we all knew about the school's debate team.

Marshall is located in East Texas, about 150 miles east of Dallas, ninety miles south of Texarkana, and twenty miles from the Louisiana state line. Wiley was founded there in 1873 by Bishop Isaac Wiley of the Methodist Episcopal Church and chartered by the Freedmen's Aid Society in 1882. The Freedmen's Aid Society was founded in 1861 by the American Missionary Association, a group supported chiefly by Congregational, Presbyterian, and Methodist churches in the North. They realized the important role education would play for integrating newly freed blacks into a racist white society. After the Civil War, they arranged for teachers from the North to set up schools in the South and teach freedmen and their children. Overall, they founded more than 500 schools and colleges for freedmen in the South. Wiley was one of them. It was the first black college in Texas and one of the first black colleges west of the Mississippi. It was established to provide education to newly freed men and women in preparation for their new lives as a free people. The college also has a notable history of service.

There is a long list of outstanding Wiley graduates who

have done much through the years to further the lives of black people. Among the most famous at the time was James L. Farmer Jr., one of the founders of the Congress of Racial Equality (CORE) in 1942. Herman Marion Sweatt, a recent graduate, was a plaintiff in the US Supreme Court Case that integrated the University of Texas Law School through a decision handed down on June 5, 1950, just before I applied to Wiley.

That case had made headlines around the country, and I thought a school that produced people like that would be one I would like to attend. Besides, it may have been my only option because I'd waited so long to apply.

Wiley College also generated other significant firsts for blacks, but I wasn't aware of them at the time. I just knew that I needed to get into school right away. After a very depressing night of thinking about my options, I wrote a letter to Wiley and attached my high school transcript. I pleaded my case, asking to get in for the semester starting in September of that year, just six weeks away—a very long shot, indeed, and I was applying late.

A week later, I got a letter with the Wiley logo on it. With trembling hands, I tore it open as Mother watched. I had been admitted! We were both ecstatic. Now, we just had to figure out how to pay for it!

In 1947, James Farmer's CORE had organized what it called the Journey of Reconciliation. Eight white men and eight blacks (including Bayard Rustin of the American Friends Service Committee) had ridden public transportation across Virginia, North Carolina, Tennessee, and Kentucky, all states with segregation laws. Blacks sat in front and whites in back, sometimes side by side, always in violation of segregation laws, to test the states' adherence to the 1946 Supreme Court ruling saying segregation in interstate travel is unconstitutional. The

Southern states were refusing to enforce the court's decision, and CORE wanted to make an issue of it. Farmer and the others chose states in the Upper South for the Journey of Reconciliation because the risk of violence in the Deep South was much greater. They suffered several arrests along the way, with the most notable in North Carolina. At the detention hearing, the judge said, "It's about time you Jews from New York learned that you can't come down here bringing your niggers with you to upset the customs of the South. Just to teach you a lesson, I gave your black boys thirty days [on a chain gang], and I give you ninety."

A few days after I got my acceptance letter from Wiley, Mother packed some sandwiches and food for the trip to Marshall in a big paper bag, along with magazines to break the boredom. With some savings from work (I had worked nonstop for 8 months prior to this), and the help of my mother, I had just barely enough money to pay for the first year of school. I took a seat at the front of the bus when I boarded a Greyhound bound for Marshall, Texas. When we got to St. Louis, on the west bank of the Mississippi River, just short of the Kentucky state line, the driver clipped a "Coloreds Only" sign to the handrail on the top edge of an aisle seat two rows from the back and announced, "Blacks to the rear of the bus." From then on, the two rearmost rows became the "colored section"—unless whites filled up the front of the bus, and then additional white passengers would be given the option of sitting in the "colored section." Our only option was to sit in the colored section, but at least they didn't put us off the bus. The "colored section" could grow if it needed to, as long as there were empty rows in front. The driver just moved the sign forward until it reached a partially filled white row. If the bus was full, those not on yet would have to wait for the next bus. There was no standing—everyone had to have a seat. As the bus picked up more people, the driver moved the sign forward or back as necessary to enlarge or shrink the sections and accommodate the passengers' racial makeup. If the moving sign put someone in the wrong section, they had to move to the right one. It must have seemed bizarre to people who were unaccustomed to it.

But at least the interstate buses didn't have two doors like many local buses did. On those, the front door was for whites only and the back one was for blacks. If there was no ticket machine at the back door, or if it was broken, we had to get in the front door, pay our fare, exit, and walk to the back door to get on for good. If it was raining, we just got wet—rules are rules.

And blacks never entered a door in front of a white person. Never, ever.

In total, my ride was over 1,500 miles long, all on secondary roads. It took over three days and nights because the bus stopped every few hours to pick up and drop off riders, take meal stops, and allow passengers to use the bathroom. (At that time, buses didn't have toilets.) Besides that, the speed limit on most of the roads we traveled was forty-five or fifty miles per hour—the Interstate Highway System did not start building freeways until 1956, and the freeway system wasn't substantially complete and in widespread use until the late '70s. To date, it is the largest and longest public works project in US history.

I started that long bus ride in the industrial North in the twentieth century and ended in the Deep South, which felt, in many ways, like it was still in the nineteenth century. I knew what was coming when I boarded the bus, and I had accepted going back if that's what it took to get a deferment and go to college.

The Journey

When I left Saginaw, I was eating at the lunch counters, tables, and booths in the front of restaurants like everyone else. That changed when we stopped in St. Louis and the driver installed the "colored section" sign. In the 1950s South, blacks and whites could not ride together in the same rail car, sit in the same waiting room or theater, attend the same school, or eat in the same restaurant. The races even had different Bibles to swear on in most courtrooms. We could pay for the food at most restaurants, but we could only eat it at tables in the kitchen, in a corner of a storeroom, at an outdoor picnic table, or on a curb outside after picking it up at a window off the kitchen. We were denied access to beaches, swimming pools, parks, picnic areas, and many hospitals, though most hospitals had a separate entrance and waiting room for us. Rosa Parks and everything that followed came later. Her famous and impactful bus ride was in December of 1955, five years after mine.

As we drove deeper into the South, there were more and more open fields and more cotton fields, some stretching as far as the eye could see. We passed several chain gangs wearing thick, rough cotton uniforms of wide horizontal black-and-white stripes. Shackles sometimes chained prisoners together, and those I saw were doing road maintenance with shovels and picks, toiling in the blistering August heat. One or two guards were nearby, sometimes on horseback, carrying shotguns and whips.

At that time, chain gangs were another form of slavery without even the dubious softening of paternalism. Men on chain gangs had no rights, and individuals—or even the entire gang—might be rented out to private contractors for ten dollars a year, often to perform construction labor that included road and railroad building and maintenance as well as government building construction. Those with short sentences for minor offenses were put together with hardened criminals. They were often shackled during the day and chained together at night, bound to an iron post. Living conditions were horrific. There was no medical care, and the gangs' poor diets brought scurvy back to the South. Punishments included whippings and time in the "sweatbox," a tiny corrugated tin box where they were chained in solitary confinement and left to bake in the blazing Southern sun for days at a time. By 1950, when I took that bus ride, there were both white and black gangs, and white prisoners sometimes served as guards for the blacks. This inhuman institution wasn't discontinued completely until the 1970s, and you often saw prisoners working by the roadside in Southern states in the '50s. It wasn't a happy sight.

Watching a gang working in the scorching summer sun, I thought about the Journey of Reconciliation participants' fates just four years before. I reflected on how different the last two years had been for me, and how unlike them the next four were going to be. But I'd grown up in the South and had become accustomed to its ways long ago. I knew I would be able to survive. Besides, I was finally going to college!

The week before I left Saginaw, I ran into two of my former black classmates from Saginaw High. They were both heading South, too, as they had been accepted to Bishop College—the black college my cousin attended, also located in Marshall. They were full of bravado about how they would deal with racists below the Mason-Dixon, but as I walked home after we said our goodbyes, I thought about how hard it was going to be for the two of them to adjust to life in the South. They had both grown up in Saginaw and had never been to the South, so they didn't really know what awaited them. Although I had had a year-and-a-half respite in the North, I had grown up in the Deep South and knew the culture and customs, including the lines a black man could never cross and the extreme and dangerous reactions he might expect should he cross them. I was close to my long-sought dream now and was quite determined not to let Southern racism interfere. After I finished my first semester, I came home to Saginaw and inquired about my former classmates to find they had both dropped out of school. They couldn't take being treated like second-class citizens and encountering regular insults or threats when they crossed lines they didn't know existed.

That's not very smart, I thought. *After all, what did they expect? Didn't they believe the news reports? They must not have wanted it very badly.*

That news further steeled my spine about getting my college degree. I wasn't about to be stopped by behavior tamer than what I had already lived through. When I returned to Wiley, I was even more determined to graduate.

I didn't know it then, but Wiley would prove to be another of my lucky stars. I had saved enough from my job in the Grey Iron plant to get me through the first year. I also worked at Grey Iron for three summers, which helped cover much of my tuition. My family also helped to pay for my schooling, but the amount they paid was small enough that it didn't stress them too much. (That would come later, when they paid for law school.) I also had scholarship jobs at Wiley; the college had been founded on the principle of social responsibility and was dedicated to improving the lot of the black race, which included helping students pay their tuition.

Many of my classmates were also on scholarships of one kind or another. From its inception, Wiley's charter was to help improve black people's skills so they would better fit in a mixed-race society as free people. As a result, Wiley did everything it could to help me and my classmates learn our subjects and get through school.

When I arrived at Wiley, they assigned me to a dorm room for two on the top floor of Coe Hall. I lived in that room for the entirety of my freshman year. One summer night shortly after arriving, I heard something making a racket in the rafters of my room. It turned out to be a couple of bats that had gotten in through the rotten sashes around the windows where they made their homes. I hate bats, and I hardly slept that night. The next day, I reported it to Dean Coleman. It turned out that I wasn't alone in my fear of bats, and the critters were a bit of a problem for the school. Soon, Dean Coleman offered twenty-five cents for each bat we caught or killed. I quickly perfected my skills and became Coe Hall's champion bat killer. There was a good reason for that. A week after I discovered my first bat, I awoke one night to feel something crawling up my leg inside my pajamas. I rolled out of bed and tore those pajamas off so fast you would have thought they were on fire, only to find a bat crawling up my leg. After that experience, I hated bats even more. It was the last time I wore pajamas at Wiley.

Wiley's history includes many twists and turns, much like those of the Southern states themselves after the Civil War. The original Ku Klux Klan had died out in the late 1870s, as Reconstruction was ending, but a new one arose in 1915. Its epicenter was Stone Mountain, Georgia. It was started by William Simmons, a Methodist minister who was inspired by D.W. Griffith's film *The Birth of a Nation*. During World War I, blacks stationed in Europe, and particularly in France, had experienced a much less prejudiced culture, and when they came home, they longed for a more accepting America. The conflicts that arose helped fuel the rise of the KKK.

The KKK's appeal spread to the North and West and

peaked in the mid-1920s. The KKK held considerable influence then, especially in the South, where they had a national membership of four million or more and members served in state politics, state legislatures, and Congress. KKK members were also elected to governorships in several states.

Even with the rise of the KKK in 1915, and many Southern blacks migrating north, Wiley College continued to expand and thrive. That school didn't let much of anything get in the way of its mission.

I felt much more comfortable at Wiley than I had in high school, probably because it was a black school and I was back in Texas where, even though the racism and bigotry were harsh, things were familiar. I knew the boundaries well and made fewer mistakes in that regard. Shortly after my arrival freshman year, I pledged a fraternity, Omega Psi Phi (Theta Chapter). The pledge rituals involved some minor hazing, like walking a gauntlet where the brothers whacked the pledges with paddles as they passed and drinking a disgusting mixture of beer, hot sauce, and other foul substances. I got through my pledge time and was admitted. The president took a liking to me. He nominated me to serve as president the next year, and I was elected. I kept that position through the remainder of my time at Wiley.

One of the first changes I made was to stop the worst parts of the hazing. They were demeaning practices that served little benefit and were generally hated by everyone. Before me, hazing was something the brothers just accepted without question as part of fraternity tradition and history. Maybe ridding the place of the hated pledge rituals is what kept me in the president's role, or maybe no one else wanted it. But I wanted it. I had long before developed the habit of saying "I'll do it" when some task came up that no one else wanted. I suppose that came from wanting to be accepted on the farm, and I continued the habit throughout my life. It has often gotten me into situations I regretted, but I have never regretted the habit. It makes people rely on you, and that is a very good reputation to have. I also developed the habit of trying to improve the things I was involved with. I have never regretted that, either. (Regarding the pledge rituals, I would guess no one had asked "why?" before I did.)

Just like that superb debate team had been the outstanding public face of Wiley in the '30s, the a cappella choir was its face during my time there. It was known around the South and had won numerous singing competitions. I joined soon after starting my freshman year and participated during all four years.

Since we couldn't afford a radio or newspapers when I lived on the farm, we often sang for entertainment. We critiqued each other's singing and competed by singing alone and together in little a cappella groups (though we had never heard the term "a cappella"). We often sang in the fields, too, as it made the time go by faster and lightened the load. And, of course, everyone sang at church, where we had a choir director to give us lessons. I also continued to sing in the choir when I moved to Waco. By the time I arrived at Wiley, I probably had thousands of hours of practice and had become a pretty good bass.

In my freshman year, four of us began an a cappella barbershop quartet that we named The Four Clefs. We were all members of the Wiley a cappella choir, and the four of us were very good together. Soon, the school was sending us to singing gigs all around the South and charging performance fees for them. I would introduce us: "Charles Herndon, tenor, from Muscogee, Oklahoma; Raymond Williams, baritone, from Houston, Texas; Tyler Edwards, alto, from Marshall, Texas; I'm John Dearman, also bass, and I'm from Saginaw, Michigan. We are The Four Clefs."

The school took care of all the money (and by "took care of" I mean "kept"), but we usually got free meals along with notoriety and excitement, which we liked, and we felt good contributing to the school. Once, we were traveling to a performance and stopped for dinner at a roadside restaurant. We were sitting at a table in the back of the kitchen eating dinner when one of the waitresses noticed our matching outfits and asked what they were for. We told her we were a singing group, and before we knew it, we were singing "Blue Moon," "Swing Low Sweet Chariot," and another tune I don't remember while strolling through the tables in front like crooners. We didn't get paid for that, but we did get a long ovation from the diners and an exceptionally fine dinner at no cost.

We were on the local radio in Marshall many times, and in August 1951, we were invited to compete on *Ted Mack and the Original Amateur Hour*, a stepping stone to the entertainment profession—the *Ed Sullivan Show* or *American Idol* of our day. Unfortunately, our tenor and baritone were both drafted in June and sent to Korea, so we missed our September date with Ted Mack in Shreveport. It remains unclear to me why they got drafted and were not deferred. In any event, we filled their spots after a few months, and I ended up continuing to travel around the South with the new group.

Some years later, I saw our original tenor performing on television. He was still in uniform and appeared on *The Ed Sullivan Show* by himself. He did well, although I never heard about him again. I don't know if he had a career in music on his own, but our original group was good enough to have had one.

During my second year at Wiley, I became the mailman for my four-story dorm. There were about sixty-five dorm rooms in Coe Hall, and it took more time than one would imagine. That job paid my room and board for the rest of my time at Wiley.

And, outside of my summer jobs, mostly at Grey Iron, it was my only paid job while I was in college. I continued as the mailman until I graduated and only had to earn enough additional money to pay for books and tuition, along with some party money.

During my last two years at Wiley, I partnered with my friend Nelson D. Wade (Ned) to organize a poker game that was played in his room almost every weekend. (I had a preacher in mine.) We discovered we were both good at the game, and the winnings added to our meager bank accounts. We both made a good bit of money playing poker (maybe ten dollars each game when we won), but, of course, I never told Mother about that. I did feel good about not having to ask her for any real money during my time at Wiley, although she did insist on sending me twenty dollars a month like clockwork, and I gratefully accepted. At the time, twenty dollars was still quite dear to her, but she never complained nor begrudged me for it.

My second year was the year of decision regarding Mother's plan for me to go on to med school and become a doctor. When I took some pre-med courses, I discovered that I didn't like them and wasn't very good at that subject, so I changed my major to social sciences. Of course, I didn't tell Mother about that, either. Back then, the highest aspiration most blacks could have was to be a doctor, a dentist, or a teacher. I knew Mother just wanted me to be the best I could be, but none of those occupations appealed to me.

My roommate for three years, Richard Stewart, was studying for the ministry. As odd as it sounds, he was from a part of Texas where the accent was so thick that even those of us from other parts of Texas could not understand him. When I first met him, I asked him where he was from. He answered "Angleton, Texas," but in his deep, deep Texas accent and slow drawl, I thought he said, "Ain't gonna tell you." After asking him to repeat it several times, I replied, "OK. I don't care anyway!" He thought I was very rude, but we soon got that ironed out, and I learned to translate his speech so that kind of thing didn't happen again. I spoke slowly, but he spoke even slower and with a drawl so deep you couldn't see the bottom.

I was in the habit of sitting on the edge of my bed when I came back from poker games on the weekends to think through what had happened and how I could have played my hands better. One night after I returned late from a poker game, I was sitting on the side of the bed collecting my thoughts in the dark. I must have been talking to myself because I woke Richard up. He thought I was praying, so he got down on his knees beside his bed as if saying goodnight prayers. At first, I thought he was going to pray for me. But instead, when he woke up completely and realized where he was, he began making arguments about how gambling was a sin and not very smart besides.

"You know, this gambling just isn't right. In any game of chance, your chance of losing is greater than that of winning."

This was particularly unusual because I was about a year older than him and he had never before given me advice.

"Well, I won," I said.

"Oh," he replied. "But you won't always win."

We were both quiet for some time, each thinking how to win our point.

After a little time, I said, "In fact, I was thinking about giving you a couple bucks out of my winnings to take your girl to the movies. Is that all right?"

Richard thought for a few moments before replying. "Yes, OK. I guess that would be all right."

"But you'll have to stop preaching at me to stop playing," I said.

"If you feel that strongly about it," he said.

After that, I occasionally gave him some of my winnings and he never tried to talk me out of playing poker again. I don't mean to say Richard wasn't serious in his faith. I guess he just thought that I wasn't so great a sinner if I gave away some of the ill-gotten gains.

Richard dropped out of Wiley before he graduated, probably because of money troubles—all of us were very poor there. A few years later, he re-enrolled at Southern Methodist University (SMU) as an ROTC member, and he was one of the first blacks to graduate from that college. Cecil Williams from San Francisco was one of his classmates. Many people know him as Reverend Cecil Williams of United Methodist Glide Memorial Church fame in San Francisco. He became one of the most effective community leaders and organizers in San Francisco in the last half of the twentieth century.

Maybe Richard used his ROTC money to help pay his way through SMU and needed to fulfill a commitment, but in any case, he went into the military as a chaplain during the Vietnam War era, and I don't envy him the situations he must have found himself in there. He made a career of it and retired after twenty years in the army. We have stayed in touch intermittently and get together every time he passes through San Francisco to catch up and relive old times. He still doesn't preach to me about gambling.

When I started at Wiley in 1950, the Civil Rights Movement was but a nascent movement. It had made some limited progress by 1954, when I graduated. Still, 1952 was the first year since 1881 without a lynching in the US. The *Brown v. Board of Education* Supreme Court ruling stating that sanctioned segregation of public schools was unconstitutional didn't come down until May 17, 1954, and the Rosa Parks "incident" didn't happen until December 1, 1955. Each of these events is variously cited as the start of the modern Civil Rights Movement, and neither happened until well after I left Wiley. And the Montgomery bus boycott associated with the Rosa Parks action, led by a young Baptist minister, Martin Luther King Jr., wasn't won until December 21, 1956.

Still, while I was at Wiley, students scoured the newspapers, paid attention to the news, and were keenly aware of each gain our race made, big or small. During my second year, in 1952, some of us formed a group with the purpose of finding ways to help the movement. Most were small local actions, like on- and off-campus demonstrations, but we all pledged to do something to make a significant contribution to the Civil Rights Movement after graduation. After many long nights discussing our options, we all decided to focus on integrating the federal government because we saw that as both a place where change could be initiated and where it might succeed.

During school, I saw a number of *Movietone News* shorts that played before movie features and were essentially advertisements for the FBI. Additionally, the weekly radio program *The FBI in Peace and War* was my favorite show, and I listened to it almost every week. Being an FBI agent seemed like a significant job, and I viewed it through the romantic lens of FBI propaganda, like many of us did. So, I committed to the group to integrate the FBI as the first black special agent as my goal in service to civil rights.

I had heard how racist J. Edgar Hoover was, but he was still the head of the organization, so I wrote him a letter in 1952 applying for a job. He replied thanking me for my interest in the Bureau but told me that I couldn't be considered unless I had graduated law school and passed the bar in at least one state. I was still interested—it sounded exciting, and being a trailblazer for blacks in the Bureau was attractive. I didn't tell Mother until

I was actually applying to law school in 1954, and then she wasn't too happy about it. But she soon warmed to the idea and accepted it. I think "lawyer" was just below "doctor" on her hierarchy of acceptable professional jobs for her son. My, had her sights grown since her initial determination to get me through high school!

Chapter 11
Wayne State University Law School

As college graduation approached, I began looking at law schools because of the FBI requirements, and because I realized I could get further educational deferments by staying in school. I still entertained the idea of being the FBI's first black special agent, and I wanted to fulfill my commitment to my friends at Wiley. Wayne University Law School (now Wayne State) in downtown Detroit was almost automatic for me. It had a good reputation and a history of admitting blacks. Beyond that, it was only ninety miles from Saginaw, and, most important of all, I would pay in-state tuition since my family lived in Michigan. This made it cheaper than most other law schools by a long way. I applied and was admitted.

My biggest problem would be paying for it. Even in-state tuition at Wayne State was a lot more expensive than the out-of-state tuition I had been paying at Wiley. Delivering mail for my dormitory had gotten me free room and board, but I wouldn't have that option at Wayne State. Also, living expenses in downtown Detroit were much higher than those in small-town Texas. I would need more help from my parents to pay for it. It would be a stretch.

There were a lot of obstacles, and I was still insecure about "making it" in law school. Sure, I had graduated from college with a decent grade point average, but it was a black college and the tired white trope that black schools were all second-rate still rattled around in my brain whenever I felt insecure. I had heard it so many times I couldn't escape it, no matter how much I wanted to.

I would need as much money as I could get, so when I graduated from Wiley, I went to work at Grey Iron for the summer. I was still mulling law school over in my mind and thinking I might stay at Grey Iron for a year or two to save money for tuition so I wouldn't have to burden my parents so much. Coincidentally, I remembered a white lawyer I had met through the local undertaker. Everybody in the black community knew the undertaker, and Mother had introduced me to him at a social function. This lawyer was with him, and the undertaker introduced us. So, I called Peter Cincenilli. He was a white lawyer in Saginaw who was very friendly and seemed to be quite successful. "Mr. Cincenilli," I said. "I was thinking about going to law school. Do you think I could cut it at Wayne State? I graduated from a black school in Texas and I am worried that I am not prepared for law school."

"What were your grades, John?" he asked

"I did OK. A little above average. Probably a solid B+."

"Well, you go ahead with law school, John," he said. "Don't worry about the black school thing one bit. Anyone who keeps a B+ average can get through law school."

"You think, sir?"

"Absolutely. You'll have to work, but if you put in the hours, you'll be just fine."

He seemed to take a personal interest in me, too. He asked how I was doing at law school every time we met when I came home from Wayne State. He even took me with him to court a few times so I could see what it was like.

Before that, I'd been inside a courtroom twice before. The first time was when I testified after my friend drowned. The second was during my junior year at Wiley. Somehow, I had met Judge Wolf, a white judge in Saginaw, when I was home for the summer. When I mentioned that I was considering law school, he invited me to his court, where I sat with him for several sessions in 1953. He also seemed to take a special interest in me and encouraged me to pursue law school.

Many years later, my wife and I were standing in line at Tadich Grill on California Street in San Francisco and she struck up a conversation with the couple behind us. They mentioned being from Saginaw, Michigan, and were in San Francisco on vacation. I told them I used to live in Saginaw and asked their names. The woman told me her maiden name was Wolf, and she turned out to be Judge Wolf's daughter. This was after I had become a judge. I was very glad to tell her how much her father had meant to me in guiding me to go to law school way back then. Peter Cincenilli and Judge Wolf were definitely two of my lucky stars. Without their encouragement, I could have easily let my insecurities make me turn away from what seemed, at the time, like an almost insurmountable task.

I started at Wayne University Law School in September 1954. They say law school scares you to death the first year, works you to death the second, and bores you to death the third. However, I was scared to death the first time I walked onto campus, and that didn't end until graduation. It did soften a bit in the second and third years since I'd passed all my first-year classes and even had the second-highest grade in first-year Torts.

Still, I thought that, with my background, just being there was a miracle, so my lack of confidence was palpable from the beginning. Then, through friends, I met another lucky star, James Jackson, a black second-year law student. He helped me by reinforcing Mr. Cincenilli's comments. I told him that I lacked confidence in my academic abilities because I had mainly gone to black-only schools. He, too, asked about my grades. When I told him my GPA, he said, "If you got into law school, that means you can do the work. You don't have anything to worry about. If you have any problems, talk to me."

The author, Dante Cosentino, and Charles Jackson,
Wayne State Law School friends.

I also met James's brother, Charles Jackson, who went to medical school and became a surgeon. We lost contact after I graduated from law school, but in 1966 or 1967, Charles drove up to my law office in San Francisco in a red Triumph convertible. By then, he was a surgery intern at Kaiser Hospital. We renewed our acquaintance, which has continued to this day.

I officiated the marriage ceremony for him and his wife Fran, and later he became a top surgeon at San Francisco's Kaiser Hospital. As a matter of fact, he performed surgery on me.

During that first year of law school, I worried about everything. I still worried that going to a black school for my undergraduate education had not sufficiently prepared me. Frankly, I was kind of shocked I had actually graduated from college. Remember, I was one of the first in my extended family to even graduate from high school. Then, I had the gall to go to and graduate from college. *Even if it was a black school*, I thought. So, into my second year, I still had a nagging fear that I didn't belong.

There were over 100 students in my class the first year, but only seventy-one remained at graduation. In 1957, the year I graduated, there were over 400 total students enrolled. When I first arrived, I discovered that about a quarter of the students were Jewish. I had heard that Jewish students were very smart, and I thought, *How can I compete with them?* The first thing I did was join a couple of study groups whose membership turned out to be more than half Jewish. One thing I discovered right away was that they all worked very hard. I thought, *OK, I can do that.* I had always been a hard worker. Some of those study group friends remain good friends to this day, and I have stayed in touch with many for over sixty years now. Most of them tell me the one thing they remember most about me is that I always carried around a big pile of books. The thing I remember most is how many hours I spent studying those books. I might not be the smartest guy in the room, but I am usually among the hardest working . . . and, at the time, I was scared of flunking out, which motivated me every day.

I was buried in law books during my first year at Wayne

State, petrified I wouldn't measure up and I was wasting my parents' money. But I was still there by the second year, and I had proved to myself that I could do the work. I felt more secure and made more time to do things outside of class. One of those things was outside reading about the law and famous lawyers.

A young lawyer needs role models, especially if he is a young man whose experience and exposure are as far from the law and lawyers as mine was. By the end of my second year, I had three legal heroes. They were (and still are) my role models in the law: Clarence Darrow, Vincent Hallinan, and Melvin Belli. They influenced my philosophy of the law and its practice at a time when I was just beginning to learn what could be done within the confines of the law. I was also learning how to stretch those boundaries, how judges and juries are influenced, how to win cases for your clients, and how to use the law to impact and change society.

These three exceptional legal minds all had four things in common: their preparation was thorough and complete; they were aggressive and unrelenting in court; they used emotion as one of their primary tools for convincing juries in the fact-based US legal system; and their method was to turn any defense into a vigorous offense—making the defense a prosecution, usually of some larger social ill or wrong of which their cases were a result or their client an example.

Torts was always one of my favorite subjects and areas of the law, and it was the one A grade I scored during my first semester. My Torts instructor had gone to Hastings Law School in San Francisco. He told us, "People think differently in different parts of the country. When you are studying opinions, pay attention to the dissenting opinions as well as the majority ones. If you read a dissenting opinion, it almost invariably will come from California. They will most likely look at things from the individual's point of view. They are particularly aware of the underdog out there. If they can level the playing field within the limits of the law, they will."

My instructor knew Melvin Belli from his time in San Francisco, and he arranged for Belli to come to Detroit and talk to the class as a guest lecturer. I had been drawn to him for his unique methods and his total commitment to his clients. During the class talk, Mr. Belli gave several examples of how to influence a jury, and he told us one that I have always remembered.

He said, "I was trying a case once wherein a middle-aged woman was suing a plastic surgeon for malpractice for botching her breast implant operation. It occurred to me that the jury, especially the men, would not really grasp the situation. So, I made a motion to have the plaintiff show them how the doctor had butchered her. This man had sold the operation to her by promising to 'give you the breasts of an eighteen-year-old.' He hadn't, and it was obvious when you saw the result. So, I arranged to have her in the jury room with a wrap around her to cover her breasts with one of the court matrons to assist her. Of course, the other side was there, as was the judge, and I had the jurors come in one by one where the woman would expose her breasts to them to show them the result. As she did, she started to cry. Each tear that splashed off those breasts sounded like a cash register to me. She won her case and was awarded over a million dollars. That trial was won the moment I convinced the judge to allow that very unorthodox way of explaining things. Trials turn on myriad possibilities. Sometimes it is the sum total of a lot of small things, and other times it is the very unorthodox or unexpected single incident. It's important to not limit your thinking about how to influence a jury and what tactics to use. Be creative and fearless in representing your client!"

I had the pleasure of having Mr. Belli appear before me

when I became a judge in later years. Even at his advanced age, his preparation and delivery were impressive. His mind was still sharp and his devotion to his clients had not dimmed with age. I chose well when I put him on my list of legal heroes, especially when I was still representing clients.

Another of my legal heroes, Clarence Darrow, was considered one of the greatest trial lawyers in American history. He died in 1938, seven years after I was born, but the intervening years had not diminished his standing in the legal community, which recognized him for his oratory skills, his courtroom skills, and his total commitment to his clients. Aside from his lawyering skills, I was drawn to him for his record of taking on and winning unwinnable cases and for his defense of the poor—especially his defense of blacks. He was particularly fearless when a case challenged a basic principle to which he subscribed.

Born in 1857 in a small Ohio town, his parents were poor abolitionists and his mother was an advocate of women's rights. Their house was a stop on the Underground Railroad, and he learned about the lives of enslaved Negroes from the escapees who stayed with them on their way to a better life in Canada or the Northern US. He experienced an unvarnished view of a brutal system at a young age. He never forgot it.

His father imbued in young Clarence a serious love of reading and learning. He was encouraged to read dense works by Voltaire, Thomas Payne, and other iconoclasts who wrote about ideas and the nature of man—heady subjects for a young man but a great foundation for sparking curiosity about life. His father also taught him about the most active abolitionists of the time; additionally, he learned from the men themselves when they stayed in the Darrow house. He wrote in his 1904 book, *Farmington,* a barely fictionalized autobiographical novel, "As a little child, I heard my father tell of Frederick Douglass, Parker Pillsbury, Sojourner Truth, Wendell Phillips, and the rest of that advance army of reformers, black and white, who went up and down the land arousing the dulled conscience of the people to a sense of justice to the slave. They used to make my father's home their stopping-place, and any sort of vacant room was the forum where they told of the black man's wrongs."

Darrow attended law school for only one year before passing the bar, mostly the result of what he learned while working in a law firm to support himself. After he passed the bar, he began his career practicing common civil law in a small Ohio town. However, he moved his young family to Chicago in 1887 to pursue challenging and interesting cases that paid more. He was only thirty-two in 1889 when, after establishing a reputation as one of the best young attorneys in Chicago, the city's mayor appointed him as Corporation Counsel for the City of Chicago. Then, in 1890, he was hired away from the city by the Chicago and Northwestern Railway as their assistant general attorney. He made plenty of money representing the powerful railroad, but after watching the railroad wield an unequal application of power, he was quite unhappy with his role in the process. When Pullman Company's workers went on strike in 1894, Darrow made a huge financial sacrifice by switching sides to defend them against the railroad. Initially, he represented the leader of the American Railway Union, Eugene V. Debs, who was being prosecuted by the federal government for leading the Pullman strike. He saved Debs in one trial but could not keep him from being jailed in a second, which ended with Darrow arguing before the US Supreme Court.

From then on, he defended both the weak and the strong, but never the strong against the weak. He was primarily known as a defender of the underdog, the despised, the oppressed, and the inarticulate. During his time, he was known as the foremost champion of personal liberty and raged against the concentration of wealth and power that accompanied the nation's industrialization. A trademark was his extraordinary and lengthy closing statements, which he packed with philosophy, poetry, and enough emotion to make men cry.

I was particularly attracted to his defense of unions and unionists. My mother's first cousin had been a Pullman porter in the late 1930s and 1940s, and he told me a lot about what the unions were doing for working people. Aside from him and the other Pullman porters I saw around the train station, I never knew anyone who belonged to a union while I was in Texas, so I personally saw and experienced how powerless non-union workers were and the extent to which they were at their employers' mercy.

But when I moved to Michigan and went to work in the automobile industry, I automatically joined a union. Unions had established themselves there many years earlier, and Michigan was a "union state." I really learned about the power of the United Auto Workers union (UAW) when I got a steel sliver in my eye one night while I was sorting scrap iron and putting it into the furnaces. In that job, we sorted scrap iron from rail cars, loaded pieces into carts, pushed them over to huge vats for melting in the furnace, and dumped them into the vats. One afternoon, a sliver of metal flew into my eye when I was dumping a load of scrap iron. It was quite painful and I couldn't use my eye, so I went to the company doctor at the factory. A nurse looked at it, put a bandage-like patch over it, and sent me back to work. She said, "It'll work itself out in a day or two. You go on back to work." It was like what they would have done back in Texas.

When I returned to work, one of my coworkers told the

shop steward about it. I think the foreman was complaining about me working so slowly. The shop steward came to see me and told me to quit work, go home, and go to a "real doctor" as soon as I could, using my very good union insurance to cover the cost. The doctor took the steel sliver out of my eye, then told me to go home and see him again after a few days, whenever I could use my eye without pain. So, I enjoyed my two weeks off with pay for a workplace injury, all the while thinking about how different it would have been back in Texas. It only took that one incident to make me a union supporter for life. It was thrilling to read how Clarence Darrow had defended unions at their inception, and it was also shocking to learn how tough and often bloody that fight had been. To think that one man, a defense lawyer, had been so instrumental in helping improve working people's lives was both aspirational and inspiring. I was beginning to learn that the boundaries of lawyering were much wider than I had thought.

After the Debs cases, Darrow defended strikers, labor leaders, and anarchists. By the turn of the century, he was a celebrity of the radical left, having earned a reputation as one of the country's first labor lawyers at a time when unions were first beginning to gain power—a time when outrage against the miserable conditions endured by working people was first beginning to gain traction.

In arbitration hearings representing striking miners during the Pennsylvania anthracite coal strike in 1902 and 1903, Darrow's cross-examinations focused the nation on the arduous and dangerous working conditions in the mines. He also drew attention to the mine owners' common practice of using child labor. Then, in 1906 and 1907, Darrow successfully defended William D. "Big Bill" Haywood, leader of the newly formed Industrial Workers of the World, against a charge of plotting to murder the former governor of Idaho. After Haywood's acquittal, Darrow took on the defense of the McNamara brothers, two labor leaders charged with dynamiting the *Los Angeles Times* building. Darrow left the practice of labor law when the brothers unexpectedly switched their pleas to guilty during their 1911 trial and he was accused of attempting to bribe a juror. Although he was charged with misconduct, Darrow was found innocent of all charges. It took the jury thirty-five minutes to acquit him.

As a consequence of the bribery charges, however, most labor unions dropped Darrow from their list of preferred attorneys. This effectively put him out of business as a labor lawyer, and he switched to civil and criminal cases. He took criminal cases mostly because he had become convinced that the criminal justice system could ruin people's lives if they were not adequately represented. In addition, he was ardently opposed to the death penalty. Darrow tried more than 100 murder cases in Chicago, saving many from the gallows. He only lost one. But his most famous cases came at the end of his career.

In 1924, Darrow defended Leopold and Loeb, two Chicago teenagers from very wealthy families who were charged with murdering another Chicago teenager. Before Darrow took the case, the boys had already confessed to the murder and the death penalty looked certain. So, Loeb's parents hired Darrow to keep them from the death penalty.

After thoroughly studying the evidence, Darrow had both boys plead guilty. This meant the case wouldn't be heard by a jury that was unlikely to show mercy. Instead, Leopold and Loeb would be sentenced by a single judge. Darrow saved the boys from the gallows by delivering a persuasive, powerful twelve-hour summation. In it, Darrow attacked the death penalty as atavistic, saying, "It roots back to the beast and the jungle . . . If the state in which I live is not kinder, more humane, and more considerate than the mad act of these two boys, I am sorry I have lived so long."

Darrow reminded the judge how little Leopold and Loeb would have to look forward to in the long days, months, and years ahead. "In all the endless road you tread there's nothing but the night," he said. When Darrow finally ended his appeal, according to one newspaper account, tears were streaming down the faces of the judge and many courtroom spectators. The two boys were given life sentences.

In 1925, Darrow defended high school teacher John T. Scopes when he was accused of violating Tennessee state law by teaching Charles Darwin's theory of evolution. It was perhaps his most famous case, which became known as the Scopes Monkey Trial. It allowed Darrow to argue against William Jennings Bryan, the best-known orator of the time. While Darrow lost the trial, the ruling was reversed on appeal, and it helped bolster the evolution side of the creationism vs. evolution debate. That debate in US textbooks continues to this day.

Then, in late 1925, Darrow defended Dr. Ossian Sweet, who, along with ten of his family members and friends, was charged with murder after a mob attacked his Detroit home. The trial caught the nation's attention and remained front page news from 1925 through 1926. This trial, and the re-trial of Ossian Sweet's younger brother, Henry, exposed racial tensions in Northern cities in the years following the Great Migration of blacks out of the racist South to the supposedly more tolerant North. The fact that it had happened in Detroit, a few miles from my new home, particularly drew my interest.

From 1915 to 1925, Detroit underwent a radical transformation driven mainly by the exploding auto industry. During that time, the number of blacks living there grew from 7,000 to 82,000, and the number of Southern whites also exploded. Of course, they brought their racist ways with them. The KKK was seeing a resurgence across the country, and Detroit was a hotbed of turmoil. So, in 1925, the KKK mounted a campaign to dominate Detroit, the fourth-largest city in the US and the symbol of the rise of industrialism. The KKK burned crosses, marched in white hoods and robes, and held organizing rallies of up to 10,000 people that summer, especially on Detroit's working-class east side. The Detroit Police Department was known to be racist at that time, even sending recruiters to the South. In 1924–25, over forty blacks were killed by the Detroit Police Department, but none of the deaths were investigated.

In the spring and summer of 1925, there were a number of ugly, violent incidents where whites in all-white neighborhoods reacted when a black family rented or bought a house and attempted to move in. The KKK capitalized on this when, on July 11, it held a 10,000-person rally where thousands listened and cheered for a speaker who advocated a law that would compel "Negroes" to live only in certain neighborhoods. Another announced, "When the nigger shows his head, the white must shoot."

That was the situation when a black doctor, Ossian Sweet, bought a home in an all-white neighborhood. He chose this home because options in black neighborhoods were generally older and substandard; he wanted better accommodations for his wife and daughter. He thought there would be minimal upset because he purchased the home from an interracial couple that had been accepted by the neighborhood. But that couple had built the house years earlier, when there were fewer tensions in Detroit. Unfortunately, the neighbors thought both members of the couple were white because they had very light complexions. The Sweets did not.

Dr. Sweet asked a few friends and extended family members to move in for a time, hoping their numbers would protect his family. He also bought guns and ammunition for self-defense.

The day after moving in, everyone went to work. When they came home, there was a large crowd milling about on the street in front of the house, where the Detroit Police Department had stationed several officers. The crowd grew larger and more agitated until it numbered between five hundred and a thousand that evening and began resembling a mob. Dr. Sweet and his family had seen mobs attack and lynch blacks in Florida, where they were born. They didn't intend to be victims of similar violence. The mob's rhetoric grew louder, uglier, and more threatening until rocks and bottles were thrown against the house "like hail in a thunderstorm." That lasted until ten o'clock p.m. when several rocks shattered their windows. Shots rang out, a man in the street was wounded, and a man on a neighbor's porch was killed. The police arrested all eleven of the home's occupants, charging each with murder.

The facts of the case were clear: Dr. Sweet and the others in the house had come armed and the shots had come from the house. All eleven of those in the house were tried together to be judged by an all-white jury. The state would call seventy witnesses. The outcome looked bleak.

But the NAACP convinced Darrow to take the case. W.E.B. Du Bois said Darrow "was absolutely lacking in racial consciousness and one of the few white folks with whom I felt completely free to discuss matters of race and class." Darrow was assisted by the noted civil libertarian Arthur Garfield Hays, prominent local attorney Walter Nelson, and a working staff of anonymous local Negro lawyers who stayed in the background so as not to further inflame the situation.

In his closing, Darrow argued, "If I thought any of you had any opinion about the guilt of my clients, I wouldn't worry, because that might be changed. What I'm worried about is prejudice. They are harder to change. They come with your mother's milk and stick like the color of the skin. I know that if these defendants had been a white group defending themselves from a colored mob, they never would have been arrested or tried. My clients are charged with murder, but they are really charged with being black."

After forty-six hours of heated debate, the jury told the judge they were hopelessly deadlocked and he declared a mistrial on November 27, 1925.

The state quickly began planning for a second trial, and Darrow moved that each defendant be tried separately. The state decided to try Ossian Sweet's younger brother first. He had already admitted firing shots out the front window in the general direction of the man who was killed.

The second trial went much like the first until it was time for summations. Darrow's lasted nearly eight hours. He called it "one of the strongest and most satisfactory arguments that I have ever delivered." He almost closed twice before returning to something he thought important, the history of the black race:

> I was born in America. I could have left it if I had wanted to go away.
>
> Some other men, reading about this land of freedom that we brag about on the Fourth of July, came voluntarily to America. These men, the defendants, are here because they could not help it. Their ancestors were captured in the jungles and on the plains of Africa, captured as you capture wild beasts, torn from

their homes and their kindred; loaded into slave ships, packed like sardines in a box, half of them dying on the ocean passage; some jumping into the sea in their frenzy, when they had a chance to choose death in place of slavery. They were captured and brought here. They could not help it. They were bought and sold as slaves, to work without pay, because they were black.

Four hours after entering the jury room, twelve white men exited and pronounced a verdict of not guilty.

Darrow's closing is included in practically every published anthology of great speeches that changed the world. The judge said hearing it was the greatest experience of his life; he also said he doubted if he would ever hear anything like it again. As the verdict was read, tears rolled down Darrow's cheeks, his client's cheeks, and several jurors' cheeks. A year later, all charges were dropped for the remaining ten defendants. In his motion, the prosecutor said, "It is significant that since the trial of this case, there has not been a single so-called interracial clash in the City of Detroit and a noticeably improved spirit of tolerance and forbearance has arisen between the colored and white groups in this city."

Darrow had, again, changed history.

There is a part of that closing that returned to me again and again as I had the honor of serving the City and County of San Francisco as a judge in its courts for thirty-two years (1977–2009) until I retired. After I retired, I continued to work for five years in an almost full-time capacity by filling in for judges who were out for some reason or another, primarily in the mental health and drug courts. Recalling guidance from my legal heroes helped me nearly every day.

Darrow had begun his closing with this:

The kindness and the consideration of the Court is such as to make it easy for everybody, and I have seldom found as courteous, gentlemanly and kindly opponents as I have had in this case. I appreciate their friendship. Lawyers are apt to look at cases from different standpoints, and I sometimes find it difficult to understand how a lawyer on the other side can think as he thinks and say what he says. I, being an extremely reasonable man and entirely free from all kinds of prejudices myself, find this hard to comprehend.

That spoke to me as I managed my courtroom through the years and did my best to provide fair, honest, and equal treatment of all parties. I did not always succeed perfectly, but, keeping Darrow's words in mind, I was fortunate to succeed most of the time.

Darrow had become a lion in the courtrooms he so respected. As charismatic as he was fierce, he was always on the offensive, he was always his clients' champion, and he won cases that were thought to be unwinnable. In the hands of normal attorneys, they were. When Darrow died in 1938, he left a large part of his estate to the NAACP.

In addition to Darrow and Belli, the third of my legal heroes was Vincent Hallinan from San Francisco. I first learned of him when he ran for president in 1952 while he was in prison. He selected Carlotta Bass, a black woman, as his running mate. I was a sophomore at Wiley at the time and it was the talk of the campus since she was the first black woman and only the fourth black person ever to run for national office. We all speculated about what type of white person it would take to add her to his ticket.

Hallinan ran for president from McNeil Island Prison in Washington state and his wife, Vivian, managed the campaign from San Francisco. He was serving an eighteen-month sentence for contempt of court in his defense of Harry Bridges of the International Longshoremen's Association. Hallinan reported to prison in early April 1952 and was released for good behavior on August 17 of the same year. The whole thing was in the news regularly and became the source of many late-night discussions in the dorms.

A few years later, when I was in law school, I learned more about him and realized he was a great lawyer, elevating him into my small pantheon of legal heroes. Hallinan came from a long tradition of rebels. His father had belonged to a revolutionary organization that fought for an independent Ireland, and his activities in their cause forced him to flee Ireland for San Francisco. There, he became an active member and organizer of the union representing cable car conductors. Consequently, when Vincent left home headed for college, he already had a deep appreciation of the underdog, the powerless, and the role of unions in protecting working people.

Hallinan was very bright and had boundless energy. While attending St. Ignatius College (now the University of San Francisco), he edited the college magazine, played on the basketball team, was captain of the football team, and was the school's champion boxer. He also found time to collect money and guns for rebels in Ireland and India. Likewise, he was energetic throughout his long life, even making it into *Ripley's Believe It or Not!* for playing rugby with the San Francisco Bats, a semi-pro team, at the age of seventy-three.

Hallinan put himself through college by working in a law firm and passed the bar on his first try in 1919, two years before graduating from law school. He became the youngest trial lawyer in San Francisco. Sixty years later, he would become its oldest. In between, he earned a reputation as the most combative lawyer in town, eschewing almost nothing in defense of his clients. His early successes in personal injury actions against the powerful local railway changed the jury selection process in the entire state, making it fair for the ordinary citizen for the first time. He was fearless, often railing against the corrupt San Francisco Police Department and its legal system, both of which he forced into reforms. He often settled disputes out of court by using his fists—twenty-eight times by his count. He once sued the Catholic Church for fraud, challenging them to prove the existence of God, Heaven, and Hell. He subpoenaed the Pope in the process.

Spectators sometimes waited all night for a seat at one of his trials, resulting, at times, in a full courtroom by six o'clock a.m. His preparation was thorough and meticulous, and his powerful closing statements left both himself and the courtroom in tears at times. He would try anything, but his lasting contribution to trial strategy was his revolutionary enlargement of the opening statement, transforming the traditionally short and subdued opening statement to the jury into a passionate and detailed outline of his entire defense. Rather than wait until summation, after the prosecution's damage was done, his goal was to make the jury want to immediately decide in favor of his client.

Hallinan was a skillful and colorful lawyer who often represented "the little guy" against large, powerful corporations and even the government. Reading about his unique and interesting cases gave me some understanding of and respect for what we called the "San Francisco way" of doing law. After I moved to San Francisco, my family became good friends with his, and getting to know him personally gave me an even greater respect for him as a good man, a solid citizen, and a great lawyer.

I became attracted to California early in law school. When I moved there and met my wife, Ina, it turned out she had gone to high school with one of the Hallinan boys. After I became a judge, I had the privilege of managing cases that both Hallinan and Belli brought before the bench. Of course, unless it was a jury trial, I recused myself to avoid any appearance of impropriety.

But before all of that, I had to finish law school. The workload was so severe at Wayne State during the first two years, I didn't have much free time in which to work. But I did take on short-term jobs during school vacations and longer breaks. One that I remember was at the Better Business Bureau (BBB) of Detroit. Television was still new at the time and there had been a spate of fraud scams involving TV repair shops charging for unnecessary work. I didn't have a television, so the BBB gave me one to use that had been checked over thoroughly and was determined to be without problems. Back then, all televisions had a deep chassis filled with tubes. The BBB told me to loosen one of the tubes and call a specific repair shop to complain that something was wrong with my new TV set. They sent a repairman out to my dorm; he removed the back of the set and checked the internals thoroughly, making a big fuss over using his measuring instruments.

There was a lot of "Oh, my," "God, how did *that* happen," and "*tsk, tsk, tsk*" before he solemnly gave me the bad news that my set was shot. There was way too much wrong to fix it; repairing all the issues would cost more than a new set. Of course, he quoted me a high price that he immediately reduced to the "student discount." He even said he would take my "useless" set with him so I wouldn't have to junk it myself. The BBB had given me a recorder that caught all his shenanigans on tape. I turned the tape over to them and they went after the repair shop for fraud. I never heard anything more about it, but they must have had a good case.

After taking a Tax Law course, I tried doing taxes for other students. However, I stopped that almost immediately when I realized I didn't know enough to do it fairly and competently.

I had been a "snappy" dresser ever since my zoot suit days in high school, and I usually spent any extra money on clothes. One Christmas, I got a job in Detroit at the department store where I shopped. They gave me the job of "boxer," which required me to box up customers' merchandise so they could take it home. Some of the customers (particularly blacks) seemed to appreciate the way I dressed and asked my opinion. So, for a few weeks, I sold more merchandise than the salesmen did even though I made no commission. Then, my supervisor told me he had received complaints from the white salesmen that I was taking their commissions and I would have to stop. I did, but not before wondering how many black sales the store was giving up by not having any black salesmen.

It was a considerable hardship for my mother and stepfather to pay for most of law school. I only worked during my last year because I was too scared of flunking out to work during the first two. On top of paying for law school, my parents had bought their house for $12,500 the same year I entered, so they were also paying for that. My stepdad usually bought a new car every other year, and one year he wanted a Buick, not his usual Chevrolet. He went car shopping over Christmas break during my second year at Wayne, and since I was at home, I went to the auto dealership with him one Saturday. When we got home with his new Buick, Mother went over the figures and calculated the costs of paying the mortgage, raising a four-year-old son, putting me through law school . . . and paying for a new car. Monday morning, he took the Buick back and retrieved his used Chevrolet, which he would continue to drive for a few more years—at least until after I graduated.

The Journey

My family was struggling to pay for school but had never mentioned a word about their hardships to me. In fact, they continued sending me twenty dollars every week without fail the whole time I was in law school and never said anything but encouraging words to me—never mentioning the money. I worked every summer, usually in the Grey Iron plant, and I saved every penny for school. In addition, my parents began to take in boarders during my first year and, eventually, every vacant space in our house was rented. So, when I went home for Christmas during my last year of law school, Mother had tears in her eyes as she said my room was not available for me because it, too, had been rented. She had avoided telling me how strapped they were until she could avoid it no longer. That night, I slept on the floor in front of the heating vent without complaint, but it reminded me so much of hard times during Texas winters on the farm that I made an excuse about forgetting something I had to do back at Wayne. That year, I was one of the few students who spent Christmas in a Wayne Law School dorm.

It gets cold in Detroit, so in the winter, everyone wears several layers. Many of us law students also carried a stack of law books in our briefcases, so we'd leave both with the hat check girl at the storage room between the cafeteria and a study hall. During my senior year, I would strike up a conversation with Jeanne, the hat check girl, every day. Soon, we got to know each other. She was a pretty, smart, white sophomore who was majoring in marketing. After a few months, we started going out. She had grown up in a white middle-class suburb just outside of Detroit, and her family was quite conservative.

We had been dating for about six months and thought of ourselves as a couple until she went home one weekend. She was having dinner with her family and her mother was trying to find out more about the new boy she had been dating but not talking about.

"So, what's this mystery man's name, Jeanne?" her mother asked. She knew Jeanne was less likely to evade answering her with her father there.

"Oh, Mom," Jeanne said. "If you must know, his name is John."

"What's his last name, Jeanne?" her father asked. He usually called her Sweetie, so Jeanne knew he was serious.

"Dearman, Dad. His last name is Dearman."

Her mother frowned. "Sounds Jewish," she said in a serious tone.

Jeanne didn't answer. For several minutes, they ate in an uncomfortable silence.

Then her father said, "Is he Jewish, Jeanne?"

"No, Dad. He isn't Jewish!" Jeanne hoped to avoid the inevitable with a forceful answer and a silent follow-up.

The tension built over a few more minutes of silence. Then her father said, "So, he's a white boy with a Jewish name, is he?"

"Why does his name matter so much, Dad?" Jeanne said. "Why does his religion matter so much, Dad?" She was still trying to dodge what was becoming the elephant in the room.

"I'm starting to think his religion isn't what matters here at all," her father said. "So, what is it, Jeanne? If he isn't a white boy with a Jewish name . . . is he even white?"

The knot in Jeanne's stomach had become unbearable. She couldn't lie to her father and mother anymore. She bit her lip for an eternity and finally said, "No, Dad, he's a black boy who's going to law school and I like him very much."

Her father rose without fanfare and walked toward the front door. He stopped at the closet on the way and pulled on a thick jacket. As he took his keys from the small bowl beside the door, he pulled on his trapper hat and yanked the ear flaps down tight.

"Have you lost your mind?" he said to Jeanne. "We still have to live here. Can you imagine a family reunion?"

There was a pregnant pause that seemed to last eons.

"I assume he lives in the law school dorm?" her father asked. After a few seconds' silence, he said, "Thought so." He slammed the door behind him as he walked towards his car.

Jeanne managed to call and warn me her father was angry and on his way to "have a talk" with me.

Like the rest of their neighborhood, her father wasn't a fan of black civil rights. Apparently, going out with a Jewish man would have been bad enough, but going out with a black man was anathema.

Anti-miscegenation laws had made sex, cohabitation, and interracial marriage between white and non-white people illegal in some parts of the US since the seventeenth century, before the US or the states themselves were established. In some areas, this included Native Americans, Asians, and others, but primarily, it was between blacks and whites. These were state laws, never national.

In 1967, the US Supreme Court finally struck down the ban on interracial marriages nationwide in *Loving v. Virginia*. There had been a brief period after the Civil War when these felony laws were struck down in the South, but all the Southern states reverted toward the end of Reconstruction. Anti-miscegenation laws were repealed or overturned in many states after World War II, but never in the South. Nine states never had any laws of this type, eleven repealed their state laws in 1887 or earlier, and fourteen repealed their state laws between 1948 and 1967. However, the sixteen Southern states did not repeal until the US Supreme Court did it for them in 1967.

Although Michigan had repealed its law in 1883, that did not mean the sentiment had disappeared throughout the state. Jeanne's father's reaction to our relationship gave me a lesson on the true nature of discrimination in conservative middle-class white society in the Northeast in 1958. In Texas, I hadn't experienced how Jews were discriminated against since there weren't many living there. The only Jews I had ever known were the Schmidts and those few I knew from school, and they didn't seem prejudiced at all. But the Northeastern WASP community was quite different. Racism there was less obvious than in Texas, but no less pervasive. I had no desire to learn its intricacies up close, so when I heard Jeanne's father's car screech to a stop outside my dorm, I went to visit a friend who lived on the floor above me.

Jeanne was quite liberal, or at least she seemed to be. She was very supportive of black civil rights and even participated in some of the marches from Wayne University with me. I knew the younger generation was confronting their parents' mores all around America—challenging the old ways. In the late '50s, some young whites rebelled or experimented by having a black boyfriend or girlfriend, but Jeanne always seemed genuinely attracted to me, as I was to her. Race just hadn't been an issue between us. We had never even talked about it. Her father, on the other hand, had quite different ideas of what was acceptable for his only child.

When he returned home, he and his wife forbade Jeanne from seeing me. She and I both thought that was the prudent course of action given their feelings. But our young hormones had other ideas, and we kept seeing each other until 1958, when Jeanne left school after her junior year. We stayed together after I graduated but broke up when she left Detroit to become a stewardess with TWA. We lost touch, and six months later, I moved to San Francisco.

Jeanne had a long career flying around the world with TWA. In 1979, I met her for lunch in San Francisco. She told me she had two children, both boys, and was living in Southern California. She had been happily married to her airline pilot husband for many years. They had flown up to San Francisco together that day for a pilots' meeting he had to attend. Somehow, she had read of my appointment to the bench in a local Southern California paper, so she called and arranged the meeting. She was still as beautiful and engaging as I remembered, and we laughed quite a bit over recollections of our time together and the naïveté of two young people in the '50s, so long ago.

Chapter 12

After Law School

I stayed in Detroit after graduation and lived in a rented room downtown just off campus. During that time, I attended frequent meetings of the Young Democrats and the NAACP. They were both lively organizations with black and white members discussing how to integrate the South, how they could participate, and how to improve race relations in Detroit. I had studied for the bar exam during my last year in law school and passed the Michigan bar in March 1957.

Two months after I graduated in May 1957, I went to work for Jessie P. Slaton, a woman attorney in Detroit. Technically, I didn't work for her—I did legal research in exchange for a desk and space in her office, which gave me an address for the law practice I was struggling to start. Jessie maintained the office although she wasn't working full-time as an attorney. In addition to being a member of the Michigan Bar, she also had a certificate in special education and worked full-time as a special ed teacher in the Detroit School District. She carried on her law practice after she finished a full day's work for the school district.

I wasn't having much luck recruiting clients and made more money working for Mrs. Slaton's husband, George, at his parking lot next door to her office. It was large and centrally located downtown, so it made a fair amount of money. He had trained Joe Louis a few years before I met George. Later, John Roxborough, the local black businessman my mother worked for, stole Joe from him when he became Joe's manager and replaced George with another trainer. George was quite bitter about it and complained loudly and often, especially after he'd downed a few drinks—which happened frequently.

During this time, I also looked for work with existing black law firms in both Detroit and Saginaw, but the few that existed weren't hiring. At the time, white firms in the East just didn't hire black lawyers. In fact, prejudice was prevalent throughout the whole East Coast legal world at that time.

For example, Ruth Bader Ginsberg, who would become a Supreme Court Justice in 1993, graduated at the top of her class at Cornell University in 1954. In 1956, she was one of only nine women in her Harvard Law School class of 500, and she was on the *Harvard Law Review*. When her husband took a job at a law firm in New York, she transferred to Columbia Law School and tied for first in her class when she graduated in 1959. Despite her stellar academic record, she also had a hard time finding a job in law. She was unable to find a job anywhere in New York City. At the time, many firms had signs for applicants that read "men only," and many others would not hire Jews. "White-shoe" law firms were aghast that someone with three strikes against her (a woman, a Jew, and a mother) would think she was qualified to work beside them. Unable to find work in private practice, she accepted a courtship with the US District Court for the Southern District of New York; after two years, she began working on Columbia Law's Project on International Procedure. Later, the American Civil Liberties Union (ACLU) hired her to argue cases before the Supreme Court, and she went on to many other honors. But in 1959, she wasn't qualified to work in a private law firm anywhere in New York!

After finding that many doors to legal offices were closed to me, I took a series of other jobs to pay the bills while I looked for employment in the legal profession. At the same time, I was trying without success to build a practice of my own.

One of my early jobs was collecting for a loan office, Household Finance. My job was to harass their late payers by letter, over the phone, or in person until they paid up. I had only been there a couple of months when I pulled a delinquent file that I was meant to work on only to discover the name of one of my school friends. He and I weren't best friends, but I knew him well enough to know that he came from a poor family and had always struggled to pay for his education. I wrestled with the idea of calling him for around ten minutes before I put my coat on and left. I carried the delinquent file with me and dropped it into the first trash can I came to. It just didn't seem worth what they were paying me. I went home and took a long shower before doing anything else—like looking for another job. Of course, they undoubtedly had other files on my friend and most certainly went ahead with harassing him for payment. But at least I didn't have any part in it.

Next, I worked for the billing department in the Detroit Emergency Hospital downtown. I was the hospital's "qualification officer." It sounds fancy, but my role was just to find out if patients had insurance—and if so, which insurance—before we admitted them.

I was stationed at the hospital emergency entrance. Once a patient was brought in, the emergency room would triage them and I would go through the admitting paperwork with them. We never turned anyone away even if they didn't have insurance or the means to pay for care. If someone didn't have insurance, the hospital would still see them and try to find ways to collect later. My job also included looking at the obituaries every day to see if anyone who died owed the hospital money; if so, the hospital investigated whether they had assets or insurance so we could collect.

I worked the night shift and the hospital's trauma center was the best in the city, so I saw a lot of traumatic injuries. I primarily saw victims of gunshot wounds, stab wounds, and traffic accidents. I also saw the results of how the police treated my race, and much of it wasn't pretty. Late one night, for example, the ambulance brought in a young black man with a gunshot wound. He had been shot in an altercation with the policeman who accompanied the ambulance to the hospital. When I saw the giant hole where the bullet had exited, I said (as much in reflex as anything else), "My God. What caused *that*?!"

The policeman grinned and pulled a 357 magnum out of a big holster on his hip. He waved it about, then held it out in front of him, putting it on display. "I shot him with my .357! *This* is what caused it!" he said proudly.

I was exposed to a fair amount of violence in my early life, especially when members of the black community settled disputes on their own before the Bell County Sheriff began patrolling the black neighborhoods. I had concluded then that anyone who shot someone else should not be proud of it. In my world, it was a failure that meant they could not resolve the situation any other way. And white police officers certainly shouldn't be proud of shooting a black person. I thought they understood so little of each other that there was a high likelihood of misunderstandings leading to gunplay. And that is without even considering the effects of the rampant racism that the Detroit Police Department was known for. They seemed to harbor the deep level of racism that is always dangerous in those who have the authority to carry weapons and who are permitted to choose when to use them.

During the time I worked at the hospital, I saw the result that awaited many members of my race, and it was depressing. The injuries were often horrific, and I was reminded again how unsuited I was for the medical profession when I started losing weight. I was already thin when I began the job, and after four months at 6 feet, 1 and 1/4 inches, I had gone from 175 to 155 pounds. I wasn't sleeping and I was a nervous wreck.

My days at the hospital were dark, and I began to feel like I'd wasted all my educational efforts. I was especially bothered by the sacrifices my family had made for me—I wasn't in any way fulfilling their dreams for me, and it troubled me a great deal. I had spent four years at Wiley and another three at Wayne State Law, and it had led me to a job admitting gunshot victims to the hospital. I had a recurring nightmare that involved the many relatives and acquaintances who had told my parents they were wasting their money sending me to school. When I quit that "good job" at the foundry in Saginaw, my mother heard about it many times, mainly from relatives back in Texas who "only wished [they] could have a job as good as the one Lil' Brother had just given up." Thankfully, my mother and stepfather had their eyes on a higher prize for me from the beginning.

So, feeling like a failure after four months at the hospital, I began to broaden my horizons. I considered New York or even Canada, but, fortunately, something else presented itself before I could head north. Several of my friends saw me hanging my head and suggested I try the West Coast. One was a CPA who had an uncle in Los Angeles. The uncle had his own law practice, and my friend thought this uncle might be able to advise me on where to get a law job on the West Coast. The more I thought about it, the better it sounded. Back then, the West Coast held certain exotic notions about Hollywood, the Wild West, and beatniks. New ideas seemed to start and flourish there.

Some of my friends had even been to San Francisco, and several of them said, "Man, if you ever get a chance to go to North Beach in San Francisco, go! It's full of all kinds of hip people, and they all get along with blacks."

When I decided to try my luck on the West Coast, I took a leave of absence from the hospital and came out to San Francisco. At the time, I was sharing an office with one of my former law school classmates, still working at night and trying to start a practice. After three days in San Francisco, I called him to say I wasn't coming back and he could have the books and other items I had left there. I hadn't found a job yet, but after three days in San Francisco, I knew this was home and I wasn't going back.

Moving to San Francisco meant leaving my family behind, including my little brother. During my three years at Wayne Law, I'd mostly seen Robert when I returned to Saginaw to work summer jobs. Going to Law School in Detroit allowed me to spend more time with him than I had while I was at Wiley, but we were nineteen years apart. This engendered a relationship that was more like that of a distant father and son than an older and younger brother. He knew me more from the stories our mother told him than anything else. And, as I had survived into young adulthood reasonably intact with only a few derailments, I am led to believe she used me as a role model for him to follow. He was nine when I moved to California, and from what our mother told me, he always wanted to live near me.

Much later in life, Robert and I were reminiscing when he told me something that made me both proud and humble. I asked him what life was like as he grew up in Saginaw after I moved west.

"Well," he said, "I was always really proud of you. All the other kids had their stories, but I was the only one who could say my big brother was a lawyer in San Francisco."

After Ina and I married, we visited Saginaw when Robert was still "that little fat boy" in grade school, and again when he was "that active young man" in college. Though our mother wanted him to attend medical school (he certainly had the grades for it), he came out to San Francisco as soon as he graduated, and I helped to get him into University of California, Hastings College of the Law (now the University of California College of the Law, San Francisco).

Upon graduating from Hastings and successfully passing the bar exam, Robert joined my firm—Brown, Dearman, and Smith—and stayed with us until I left the practice when I was appointed judge in 1977. Shortly after that, Robert joined the San Francisco Public Defender's Office where he worked as a public defender and city attorney until he suffered a massive stroke. Although he recovered, he was unable to return to full-time work.

Robert raised three children as a single parent. His youngest was only one year old when he took on the role as sole parent, and the oldest was nine. His daughter, Jessica, was like a mother to her younger siblings, Matthew and Joshua.

All three have graduated from college and are thriving. Jessica now works for a large nonprofit in the Bay Area. Matthew works for a major bank in Seattle, and Joshua is a soon to be architect with a global architecture firm. Robert's success and the success of his children is further fulfillment of our mother's dream.

Robert and I are much closer now than we were during those early years, and Sundays often find him at our house joining ten or twelve other family members and friends to break bread, discuss (argue about) current events, and reminisce about the old days with stories that are mostly true. He is very curious and loves to travel. He has been around the world a few times over the years, seeing many other countries and cultures. I am proud of him and what he has accomplished in life.

Robert Jr. and Mr. Robert

We have gone back to Texas together for several family reunions, and I think, after all these years of other family members confirming my stories, he has finally come to accept my "tall tales" of life on the farm as also mostly true. It's no wonder he found them hard to believe. Thinking back, I sometimes do, too. Life in the South was always very different from life anywhere else. The evil relics of slavery lived there for many years after the institution itself died, and those relics seem so barbaric they're almost impossible to believe for those lucky enough to have avoided them.

Chapter 13
Moving West - 1959

In 1959, two years after graduating from Wayne Law, I was no closer to a life in the law than I had been before entering law school. I wanted to leave Detroit, but Saginaw seemed dead to a young man in his twenties who was ambitious and curious about the wider world. My mother wanted me to move back there and open a practice since there was only one black lawyer in town at the time. I thought there was a reason for that.

Back then, most blacks with a serious legal problem would go to a white lawyer thinking they would get better legal representation. Black lawyers really had to prove themselves, even to their own people. This was caused by a combination of factors. First, there were so few black lawyers that no one had much experience with them. Second, the legal system was run by the white establishment and blacks (often rightly) thought it would be biased against black lawyers. Finally, and most troubling, there was still a perception in much of the black community that their compatriots just couldn't perform as well as whites.

The white culture had promulgated this racist trope for so long that even some in our own race believed it.

Though the modern Civil Rights Movement had officially begun sometime between May 17, 1954, when *Brown v. Board of Education* invalidated "separate but equal" school facilities, and December 1, 1955, in Montgomery, Alabama, when Rosa Parks refused to give up her seat on a city bus, it was still a nascent movement in 1959. And, although I was acutely aware of it, the larger parts of the movement had not yet touched me.

As of 1959, the South had not yet started to change in meaningful or widespread ways. In fact, 1959 was the year that Prince Edward County, Virginia, was delivered a court order to begin desegregation based on the *Brown* decision from five years earlier. Rather than integrate, the county, following the state strategy of massive resistance, closed the entire public school system for five years. Instead of funding public schools, they provided vouchers for all students to attend private institutions, knowing full well that there were no black private schools there. Black kids either had to move or skip education altogether. The white kids used their vouchers to go to nearby private schools with other white kids.

For me, the Northeast had served up various levels of racism, auto plant hard labor, and menial jobs of various kinds. With a brand-new law degree, I felt I was on the cusp of opportunity, but it seemed like it just wasn't working there. And if it did, it would involve fitting into a very straitlaced and hidebound world where black opportunity was still quite limited compared to that of whites. It was primal. I could practically feel the opportunity I had been working towards for so long slipping between my fingertips.

By then, Mother had graduated from working as a domestic and had been employed by John Roxborough's insurance business in Detroit for about a year. She saw how frustrated I was and approached Mr. Roxborough about a job in the law. He was a mover and shaker in the Detroit Republican Party and was well-connected to the power structure there.

Detroit was a different place back then. The first part of the twentieth century saw it rise as Motor City to the fourth-largest US city and one of the most successful working-class cities in the world. By 1918, half the cars in America were Ford Model Ts made in Detroit. By 1932, the Ford River Rouge industrial complex was the largest integrated factory in the world with its own docks, railway lines, power plant, and over 100,000 workers. Detroit was the model of a successful industrial city in the most prosperous nation on earth. The city had low unemployment, relatively high wages, and a peaceful environment. Then, the Great Depression of the 1930s devastated demand for autos, along with everything else, and Detroit suffered mightily. Many of the black Southern workers who had come north in the Great Migration a few years earlier were the first to lose their jobs, and they spent years in the unemployment lines as racial animus increased. Making things much worse, there was no unemployment insurance until 1935 when FDR pushed the Social Security Act through Congress and Michigan followed with its own in 1936.

The Second World War revitalized industry across the US, but especially in the auto plants that were converted into assembly line production for planes, tanks, trucks, and autos. Following victory, the entire economy was booming, GIs were coming home by the millions (most with pockets full of dollars), and car ownership surged across the US. The factories of Detroit converted back to auto production, along with factories across America, and the boom continued.

The 1930s and early 1940s were tumultuous for all industrial cities, especially Detroit; 6,000 federal soldiers were called in to quell the rioting in 1943. Of the thirty-four people killed and 433 injured, most were black, and they were killed or injured by either the police or soldiers. All of the dead blacks were killed by police, but none of the whites who died were killed by police. Then, when black veterans returned from World War II a few years later, they could not find jobs as easily as their white counterparts, and the jobs they did find were of a lower quality. When other Northern cities were implementing civil rights initiatives, Detroit, controlled by pro-business Republican mayors, was searching the Deep South for white men to increase the notoriously brutal racist police force.

The Detroit Police Department's reputation was built up under a string of Republican mayors. From 1913 through 1962, fifteen Republican mayors served a total of forty-two years. During that time, there were only three Democratic mayors who held office for a total of seven years (1923–24, 1930–33, and 1948–50). Detroit was a Republican stronghold, and the Republican Party stayed in power largely by using race to drive a wedge into the city's large working class. (Remember when Clarence Darrow came to Detroit in 1925 to help Dr. Ossian Sweet with his problems?) I didn't know all the details at the time, but I had become intimate with the results when I worked for the hospital.

My last few months in Detroit were a very low time for me. When I walked into the meeting room for the Republican Party in Detroit, where John Roxborough had arranged for me to be "introduced around," I felt very much as I had when I realized I couldn't go on working at the hospital. In addition to owning an insurance business, John Roxborough had been Joe Louis's business manager and was well-known in both black and white circles around Detroit. The idea of an introduction from him was dripping with job prospects. Mother had introduced us and he had appeared optimistic—excited even—at the prospect of introducing a new young lawyer to the local party as his acolyte. But from the moment I walked into the room, I felt like a bantamweight tiger trying to break into a pride of heavyweight lions. I walked halfway down the aisle toward the empty seats at the front of the room before I turned on my heels and escaped as fast as I could without running.

The hospital job that caused me to lose so much weight had clearly shown me what Republican policies had done to Detroit over all those years, and especially what it had done to minorities. Besides that, I had been active in left-leaning activities in Detroit while I was in law school. Admittedly, that had initially been driven as much by the prospects of meeting pretty young ladies all afire for the cause as it was by a deep-rooted understanding of class and race politics. (Though I had lived it in Texas where it wasn't named.) I had neither the vision nor the self-confidence to lead my people to some promised land, but throughout college and law school, I paid keen attention to progressing civil rights—we all did.

At Wayne State, my friends and I boycotted a bar that wouldn't seat blacks until they did. When I worked a summer job at a resort, our little group of black and white seasonal workers had successfully boycotted a local restaurant where "no blacks allowed" signage was displayed and enforced. The success of those and other small demonstrations had convinced me of the power of direct action and the power of the purse— the black purse. I saw firsthand that change was coming. From the time I was in college and throughout law school, our late-night discussions almost always gravitated towards what was happening in civil rights and how we could help.

We had watched the progress driven by *Brown v. Board of*

Education in 1954, then Rosa Parks and the Montgomery bus boycott in 1956. The Southern Christian Leadership Conference (SCLC) was formed in Atlanta in early 1957 by Dr. Martin Luther King Jr. along with Charles K. Steele, Fred L. Shuttlesworth, and sixty other black ministers and civil rights leaders. SCLC was originally dedicated to abolishing legalized segregation through nonviolent action, and Dr. King was chosen as its first president. It struggled at first with only one full-time employee, a secretary, but it became a major force for civil rights after a few years.

Central High School in Little Rock had been forcefully integrated in late 1957 against the orders of Arkansas Governor Orval Faubus and the Arkansas National Guard. Nine heroic and resolute black teenagers endured routine harassment, violence, and local rioting throughout the process. The local NAACP had vetted them and trained them to endure the punishment they would experience while responding to it nonviolently. Ultimately, President Eisenhower sent National Guard troops to take control of the state's national guard and quell the violence. We all watched this with rapt attention, eyes glued to the violence and drama unfolding on television.

Many of us had studied the law with an eye to changing it. And beneath it all, my mother and grandmother had both been clear when they raised me. I could tell right from wrong and black from white, and rubbing elbows with the Young Democrats in Detroit, both black and white, had shown me the possibility of the races working together to make change. At least there was passion in the YD. There were clear and present ideals, and a fire was burning in the bellies of the change agents that I didn't see in other organizations.

When I walked into that Republican meeting sponsored by John Roxborough, I passed row after row of white men sitting straight-backed at attention towards the front of the room. I was overcome with the visceral smell of conformity laced with sycophancy, which advertised the status quo. In my mind, it smelled distinctly like a pool hall men's room gone way too long without cleaning.

In spite of how much I needed a job, even a patronage job, the whole thing seemed artificial to me. When I was halfway to my seat, I felt like I would disappear altogether. I made an about-face, escaped with my future unsullied, and never talked to my mother again about help from John Roxborough or the Republican Party.

I had been frugal while I worked all of those jobs after law school, and I had salted away a small nest egg to stake some future plans. When I counted it up, I had enough for the plane fare to California and a little walking around money, but not much else.

During that time, I wasn't a stranger to the racetrack—and I was lucky. One weekend, I studied the forms and made a plan. I took five dollars to the racetrack and played a few races until I found myself with fifty dollars in my pocket. I had always pulled for the underdog in sports, in life, and even at work, so I took a deep breath and bet it all on the nose of a longshot hunch, a horse from New Zealand named Bootbard. He came in first and I won $3,000! Now I had enough to get to Los Angeles, stay awhile to look around, and even get back home if I wanted to. My future was sealed by a lucky bet!

One of my friends helped me find the cheapest flight to LA possible. It was a charter flight and it was about two-thirds the cost of the other flights. They cleverly called it a "red-eye." This wasn't my first flight—that had been when I flew from Detroit to Washington, DC, to see my girlfriend a few weeks before. I have never been a big drinker, but on that short flight, this country boy had two old fashions to calm his worries and felt no pain during the entire flight. That flight wasn't a red-eye, either. When I saw that description of the flight I was considering taking to LA, I didn't know what it meant, but I thought it couldn't be good. Nevertheless, I went to the travel agency and bought my fifty-eight-dollar ticket, one way.

This flight was long, too. It was cross-country and was scheduled to take about six hours. I packed a small bag, shined my shoes, put on a tie and a sport coat, and lit out for the airport. I walked to a downtown hotel and took an airport bus to the Detroit airport. We arrived after dark, and I found the obscure gate assigned to my charter flight off by itself at a lonely end of the terminal with a small crowd of people huddled around the desk. When the boarding announcement came, we walked out onto the tarmac and over to the stairs they had rolled up to the door of the plane. We had no sooner boarded and begun to roll out toward the runway when the pilot came on the intercom.

"Well, folks, it looks like we have to return to the gate to have some parts replaced. Our last engine check showed the performance of a couple of parts just out of safe levels. We'll have those replaced and be in the air in no time."

My mind started to find excuses to get off this plane. *Engine parts!*, it screamed. *Out of safe levels?! In the air in no time?! Just take your time . . . no hurry here!*

It seemed like it took forever for those parts to be replaced while we sat in that hot, stuffy steel tube like a bunch of doomed sardines. The whole time, I kept thinking about recent airline crashes that had been in the news. In 1955, a prop plane carrying passengers on a commercial flight crashed after one of the engines caught fire. When the pilot tried to make an emergency landing, a wing fell off. I thought, *A wing fell off?! All thirty occupants were killed?! They were all killed?!*

And, in February 1959, just a few months before my flight, a much bigger propeller-driven airplane had crashed into the East River while flying into La Guardia. This had surprised me; for some reason, I thought, bigger planes should be safer. Sixty-five of the seventy-three people on board were killed in that crash. *Sixty-five of seventy-three were killed?!* I furiously began calculating the percentages in my mind. *Let's see. Sixty-five divided by seventy-three. That's . . . that's . . . that's . . . over 90 percent died!*

Most recently, just a month before my flight, a four-engine jet (*like this one*, I thought) did a barrel roll on a training flight when landing. It crashed and killed everyone on board. *Killed everyone onboard?!*

It seemed like we sat there forever while they worked on the plane and I stewed about it. It's a good thing they never opened the doors or I might still live in Detroit. Commercial jets were still new at the time, and I began thinking about how many things could go wrong with something that new.

When I tried to join the air force back in 1949, the British had just unveiled the world's first commercial jet; it wasn't until 1952 that they began carrying paying passengers. But the British Overseas Airways Corporation's de Havilland Comet, that first jet, had a series of fatal crashes in 1953 and '54 that led to grounding the entire fleet until 1958, the year before I took my flight to LA. When they analyzed the crashes, they discovered that flying at much higher altitudes (and at lower pressure) caused the pressurized fuselage to expand and then contract again upon landing. Enough of those cycles weakened the fuselage so much it eventually split—and that last time, the whole plane exploded.

My flight was on a Boeing 707, a jet that had only been in commercial service for a year. I would have been much happier on an old DC-3, a twin propeller-driven plane like the one I'd taken to Washington, even if it would have taken twice as long.

Finally, we took off and my thoughts wandered to what they might have left off or what corners they must have cut to offer such a cheap flight. I was exhausted, so I finally fell asleep, and when I woke up, it was daylight. The *thump, thump* of the wheels going down had woken me, and I looked out the window to realize we were landing. To my horror, the wings were flexing up and down much more than I thought they should and the ground was coming up at us much faster than I thought it should.

I was extremely glad to step out of that plane, get onto the asphalt, and begin walking to the terminal. It was all I could do not to get down on my hands and knees and kiss the ground. Of course, I didn't do that, but I did stand on the tarmac for a few minutes breathing in the California air. The bright, sparkling early-morning sunshine springing out of the blue California sky felt fresh, like a harbinger of good things to come.

The author at age 28, new to San Francisco

When I crossed the continent to get to California, I was participating in an updated version of the migrations that have happened throughout California's history.

For example, gold had precipitated dangerous expeditions and started wars for thousands of years, but the California Gold Rush in Coloma was the only place where an average person could venture alone into relatively unclaimed land and use simple tools to dig out enough gold in a few months to return home rich. Significantly, the wealth gained here did not go to monarchs or religions but to ordinary people.

During the first years of the Gold Rush, California had no established government or law enforcement controlling the gold fields. This led to a wild and single-minded free-for-all that forever changed hundreds of lives every single day. Because of this, it is understandable that the Gold Rush precipitated one of the largest mass migrations in US history. It was a once-in-a-life-time opportunity that drew people from across the globe. It was not until 2010 that the number of native-born California citizens surpassed the number of Californians who had migrated from somewhere else. During the Gold Rush era, not so long ago, almost everyone was from somewhere else. Because of this, it is understandable that San Francisco developed such tolerance for the unusual and different.

The earliest ethnic breakdown of the San Francisco population comes from 1847. That year, the total population was 459. The data shows that there were ten African Americans and 375 whites, with the remaining people having American Indian or Pacific Islander heritage.

When gold was found at Sutter's Mill on January 24, 1848, San Francisco was a small, sleepy port trading village with a population of 800 and just over 200 frame and old adobe buildings. Though Sutter's Mill tried to keep the discovery quiet, the news got out in March and was spread locally, both by a San Francisco newspaper and by Samuel Brannan, who owned the only store between San Francisco and the gold fields. Brannan had learned of the gold find some weeks earlier and bought up all the picks, shovels, and pans he could find. Then he ran through the streets of San Francisco shouting, "Gold! Gold on the American River!" He had paid twenty cents for the pans and sold them for fifteen dollars. By mid-June, three-quarters of San Francisco's male population had left for the gold fields, and men from around California soon followed. Thousands of people from Oregon, Mexico, Chile, Peru, China, and the Sandwich Islands (Hawaii) headed for California in the summer and fall of 1848, all before Americans on the East Coast had a clue of what was to come. Europeans—principally from, Spain, Portugal, France, Germany, Belgium, Ireland, and England—would soon follow. African Americans came too, most of whom were free when they arrived.

So many Chinese arrived in the 1850s that the government first passed laws limiting their numbers and finally passed the Chinese Exclusion Act in 1882, the first US law to place broad restrictions on immigration, including suspending Chinese immigration for ten years. This law was extended and expanded to include other countries as soon as its term expired, and it provided the foundation for the immigration laws that exist today.

When Eastern newspapers picked up the news of gold in the California hills, including papers in New York, practically every ambitious male on the East Coast began making plans to move west. President James K. Polk announced the extraordinary abundance of gold in December 1848, and the stampede was on, driving Americans to migrate to California en masse. Before the Gold Rush, California's approximate population was 12,000. One year after gold was discovered, it had surged to over 100,000. A few years later, over 300,000 people from every state in the nation had moved to California—about half by land and the other half by sea. Either way, it was a long and arduous journey made mostly by young males. Black, white, and every shade in between, the forty-niners, as they came to be called, were mostly Americans, though a substantial number were also from outside the country. By 1850, about a quarter of California's population had been born outside the US. In only a few years, the tiny port of San Francisco had grown into California's largest city. It was a raucous frontier metropolis with a thriving economy and a population that was nothing if not cosmopolitan.

Many African Americans had seen the Gold Rush as a terrific chance at economic fortune as well as a unique opportunity for greater racial equality in the soon-to-be free state of California. They perceived California as offering them better conditions than any other state in the Union. But an extensive body of discriminatory legislation was passed in 1851 to protect white interests. Among other things, it prohibited African Americans, Chinese, and Native Americans from testifying against whites in court, showing the depth of the state's brutal racism.

Despite this law, the African American community was making gains, and San Francisco's black population began to organize. In 1862, they sensed growing white support from exigent Civil War issues and formed the Franchise League to campaign for voting rights. They also campaigned to end the testimony restrictions that allowed white people to mistreat or steal from black people (along with Indians and Chinese) almost at will. This was because wronged blacks could not testify against whites; unless a white person supported the black person's side of the issue, the white would always prevail.

The Franchise League's efforts saw fruit in 1863 when the California legislature removed discrimination in education (but only on a separate-but-equal basis) and repealed the testimony restriction. By law, a black man now had an equal chance against a white man in court.

San Francisco established California's first public school in

1851. By the end of 1863, when separate-but-equal education was instituted, the city's black public school had seventy-six students in regular attendance. Throughout the Civil War, we campaigned for better schools everywhere, and in 1863, we legally got access to California public schools, but practically they remained separate but equal. However, because there were many small communities in California with too few blacks to support a separate school, a campaign to remove this restriction grew. Most of California had already admitted blacks into integrated schools by 1875 when San Francisco officially ended school segregation. And in 1893, the California State Assembly passed an anti-segregation statute that ended streetcar segregation. While slave codes, Black Codes, and Jim Crow laws were restricting blacks across the South, essentially extending slavery in another form, the West was making steady progress.

Because San Francisco's black population was small before World War II, blacks lived throughout the city, often next door to whites. De facto segregation did not begin in earnest until after World War II when the black population grew substantially. The new black residents were often from the South. They had noticeably different speech and customs that they brought with them.

Before this influx, both blacks and whites had dressed up to go downtown. Women often wore white gloves and men always wore hats. The established black San Francisco community had successfully adopted many white customs to better fit in, and both races were often aghast at the language and customs of the uncouth, uncultured, raucous bunch of Southern immigrants who spoke a language quite different from the King's English, with manners to match. Things changed dramatically between 1940 and 1950 for San Francisco's black population, which increased by 800 percent in one decade—the largest black population percentage increase of any major West Coast city. Among the changes was the compartmentalization of the black population. Black neighborhoods emerged—most notably, the Western Addition and then the Bayview-Hunters Point.

The year I moved to San Francisco, 1959, California again led the way in civil rights by passing and enforcing the Unruh Civil Rights Act, a landmark law that prohibited discrimination of any sort in almost every setting. It is amazing to me that this law was not passed until the year I moved here, but it would be decades before similar laws were passed and enforced in the Southern states I had recently left.

The Unruh Civil Rights Act states,

"All persons within the jurisdiction of this state are free and equal, and no matter what their sex, race, color, religion, ancestry, national origin, disability, medical condition, genetic information, marital status, or sexual orientation are entitled to the full and equal accommodations, advantages, facilities, privileges, or services in all business establishments of every kind whatsoever."

Beyond establishing equality, the Act provides both injunctive relief and damages, which means violations of the Act could result in losing certification or shutting your business down and/or having a monetary punishment, so it does have teeth—it took long enough.

In 1963, California passed the Rumford Fair Housing Act, which prohibited racial and other discrimination when selling or renting housing. In 1964, however, California voters overturned the bill. It wasn't until the federal Fair Housing Act passed in 1968 that housing discrimination became clearly illegal and we were able to actively fight it across the country.

Even so, many realtors and property owners continued to discriminate against African Americans so we had to build a solid case in each violation.

When I arrived in California amid all this change, the first place I went was to Hollywood and Vine in Los Angeles. It was famous at the time for 77 Sunset Strip, a 1959 TV series. A real hit at the time, several of my friends in Detroit who had been to LA insisted that I should see it. I don't know what I expected, but when I got there, it was like, "OK, seen it. Now what?" So, I rented a room in the local YMCA and started looking for work. Back then, the Y had hotels in cities around the country; these hotels were known to be spartan, clean, cheap, safe, and well-maintained. It was perfect for me.

My friend's uncle had a law practice in LA, but he wasn't hiring. He referred me to several other law practices around the city, but there were no openings for a young man who hadn't yet passed the California Bar. After a week of striking out, I applied to the Los Angeles Police Department. It wasn't lawyering, but at least it was applying the law. I figured my law degree would give me a leg up, but that wasn't the case. In fact, the officer who interviewed me told me they were reluctant to invest in a new law school graduate who would likely quit as soon as he passed the bar. Whether this was cover for their reluctance to hire blacks I'll never know, but it did make sense, and my long-term plans had never included the police force. In fact, LA reminded me of Detroit in many ways, and I wasn't particularly impressed. It just seemed to me like another big, impersonal city.

My friend's uncle suggested I try San Francisco. "If I was starting my law career," he said, "I would look in San Francisco." But, he also recommended Portland. Later that same day, I saw a notice on the YMCA bulletin board advertising a ride to Portland that only required splitting the cost of gas. So, I headed north.

One of my law school friends lived in Portland, so I called and he told me I could stay with him while I looked for work. My traveling companion and I left LA the next morning and managed the 1,000-mile trip in one very long day. My cost was $5.50. Late that night, the driver dropped me off at the Portland YMCA, where I stayed for the night. The next day, I found my friend from Detroit, dropped my small suitcase at his house, and started looking for work. Prospects there turned out to be no better, so after a fruitless three-week job search, I joined another friend on a road trip. He dropped me off in San Francisco on his way to LA. It was August of 1959.

I was beginning to run low on funds and was dipping into the money I thought I would need if I had to return home. It was a low time, and as I hadn't even gotten a whiff of a job, I thought of giving up and going back to Saginaw. At least I had family there. But that felt like surrender, something I had never accepted graciously. And since I had gone all that way, I felt like I owed it to myself to at least give San Francisco a try. After all, friends in Detroit had said it was a place that welcomed everyone, and they'd said opportunities for blacks weren't so restricted there. I had used up all my Northeast connections, so I had my friend drop me off at the Embarcadero YMCA.

After a couple of nights there, I was out late looking for work when I passed a small hotel in North Beach that was cheap and clean. My Detroit friends had sung North Beach's praises, so I decided to move. After I checked into the hotel, I found a little club down the street where I could nurse a beer while listening to a set or two of good jazz. The doldrums overtook me for the next few days as I first searched the yellow pages for black law firms, then the help wanted pages of the *Examiner* and *Chronicle* newspapers looking for any type of work, followed by phone calls and pounding the pavement to follow up on those leads. The next few days were a combination of looking for work during the day and going to North Beach jazz clubs and coffee houses at night. I was astonished at how friendly everyone was, especially the white folks I met. Maybe that was because I primarily met North Beach residents since that was where I was staying. Back then, North Beach was full of beats, poets, jazz musicians, and jazz lovers, and none of them seemed to be reluctant about establishing friendships with other races. There was a different vibe there from anywhere I had ever lived.

You have no doubt heard the phrase "Not sure, but I'll know it when I see it." Well, that's exactly how I felt a couple of days later when I suddenly realized I was home. The people in San Francisco were so friendly, the barriers between races seemingly so low, the food so good, the weather so agreeable, the jazz so available, and the women so fine. I just felt like I was home! Bizarrely, and without being able to define why, it felt like paradise. Talk about blind optimism!

I had found a home, but I still needed a job.

A couple of nights later, I was sitting in the Jazz Workshop, another North Beach jazz club, examining the very bottom of my wallet, counting my nickels, and bemoaning wasted shoe leather, when a friendly voice called out. "John? John Dearman? What are you doing here, dude?" It was Andy Peterson, a white friend with whom I had worked at the Detroit Department of Social Services.

After some backslapping, I confided my fear that I would starve at this rate, or at least move onto the streets if I didn't find something soon, very soon.

"Why don't you try the San Francisco Department of Social

Services, John? I work there, and I know they are hiring. I'll get you on," he said.

The next day, I went to the San Francisco Department of Social Services and applied for a job. They hired me on the spot, based, I am sure, on Andy's recommendation. A few minutes later, I met a lovely young woman named Ina Flemming.

Just like that, I'd found a job. As it turned out, I'd also found my wife, with whom I would spend a lifetime. With her help, I'd have a successful career in the law as well. Only I didn't know it yet.

Back in 1959, North Beach had a much more European atmosphere than the rest of San Francisco. The city's neighborhoods all had distinctive ethnic influences, and North Beach was an Italian neighborhood with a cosmopolitan flavor. Most of the real estate was owned or managed by Italians, often first-generation Italians. My ten-minute strolls through the neighborhood always produced several encounters with unfamiliar European languages, one of which was always Italian. In addition, the mores the Italians brought with them from the old country had great regard for artists and poets—they thought the job of an artist was as legitimate as any other, and not something just anyone could do. As a result, artists and poets gravitated to North Beach. Rents were low and the weather was generally balmy. All of this led the beat and artist communities to flourish. The resulting culture was very liberal. It was quite different from the racism I had known in the Northeast. I felt like San Francisco was entirely devoid of racism, and by comparison, I suppose it was. It would take me a few months to see the different and often subtler—but no less restrictive—racism that existed here.

After I got the job with the Social Services Department, I

moved into a small place in North Beach where I stayed for the next three weeks. The weather was great and everyone seemed quite friendly back then. At that time, the neighborhood was full of "characters" and very laid back. I guess that was a part of the beat culture. I was out almost every night, soaking it up.

One of the poets I met was quite friendly and we hit it off right away, but he disappeared. a few months later. The next I heard of him was a couple of years later when a mutual friend told me he had become famous in Europe. Years later, I bumped into him on a sidewalk in North Beach and he remembered me. Out of the blue, a familiar voice hailed me. "Hey, John. What are you doin', dude?" he asked.

"I'm finally lawyerin'," I told him. "I heard you hit it big and are a famous poet now."

"Well, a little," he said. "Why don't you give me your card, man? I never know when I might need a lawyer."

I did, and we went to a jazz club on Broadway to catch up. I never heard from him regarding legal work, but it was thrilling to know a famous poet!

After I had been in North Beach for a few weeks, I met a black man who was quite friendly. His name was Carlos something. One reason I can't remember his last name is that back then, we seldom used our given names when talking to each other. It was "dude" or "man" or some other hip street lingo. But we were good friends nevertheless. I was about seven years older than he was. He was tall and muscular, and from the way he acted, I first took him for a gigolo. He could have just been a rich man, but all I knew was that he never seemed to work, always had money, and seemed to know every pretty woman in San Francisco. Years later, I saw him again. He told me he was married and had been driving a streetcar for a living until he hit a man who died and he quit over it. I never saw him again after that.

I had been hanging out in North Beach cafes where people played a lot of chess, and I was watching Carlos play one day. He asked me if I knew how to play, and when I told him I didn't, he offered to teach me. We became chess bums, playing almost every day. We laughed a lot and had a great time for about three months before I managed to beat him for the first time. I had been paying attention and studying books on the subject, and after that first win, I beat him three more times the next week. Suddenly, he was "busy" and we seldom played again. But we stayed friends for years, and I would see him almost every time I went back to North Beach. Some people are like that. They hate to lose so much they aren't willing to play! Not just chess, but in other walks of life, too. That never seemed very sensible to me. If you aren't willing to lose, you'll never try anything new.

My haunts included a number of places that had several things in common: they were cheap, they had live jazz, and they didn't mind if I nursed a coffee or a beer for hours while I studied for the bar exam. I had a job then so I had money, but I was still establishing myself. Being frugal had also been ingrained in me for decades.

The Coffee Gallery was one of my favorite spots. They had local jazz musicians playing during the afternoons, evenings, and weekends. The Cellar was another hip spot where I spent a lot of time, as was the Jazz Workshop. I continued frequenting them for the jazz even after I was married and my first child, Tracy Ina Dearman, was born. I would often take my wife, Ina. She also had a sincere attraction to jazz music.

There was a tiny cafe on the corner of Green and Columbus where Carlos and I spent hours playing chess at a window table and drinking coffee while he hailed everybody who walked by. He seemed to know everyone in North Beach. Of course, the fact that he was a tall good-looking dude didn't hurt, but he did talk a lot of trash, especially to beautiful women walking by.

Patty O'Sullivan was another "character" in North Beach. I believe he was a poet, but what I remember most vividly about him was his dress. He dressed very stylishly and eccentrically, usually wearing a cape to top it all off. After a rain, he was always throwing his cape over puddles of water with a flourish in front of pretty women. He was also quite flirtatious and a good talker. I think that was his undoing one day when he floated his cape over a puddle in front of a particularly beautiful young woman and made a few risqué remarks. Turned out the man with her was her husband, and he had no sense of humor at all. The husband took offense and stabbed Patty. I think Patty left San Francisco after he got out of the hospital. I never saw him again.

Vesuvio Cafe on Columbus was another spot I went to regularly. There, we could sit for hours and talk to Whitey, the young bartender with a thick head of white hair, while drinking thirty-cent beer. I was walking near the cafe one day when I bumped into Dante, a friend from college and we rekindled our friendship. Dante had moved to San Francisco just a few months earlier and was, like me, still getting used to this new and very different environment. He was working at the Discovery Bookshop up the street from Vesuvio. It was owned by Frederick Roscoe and, through Dante, I got to know Frederick very well.

He and his family became good friends with me and my family. Some years later, Frederick's wife, Nancy, became a lawyer. For years, she did mainly criminal law with the

Hallinan Group, and we would often see each other around the courtrooms or at legal functions. Sometime later, they moved to Marin, where they threw huge parties for the left-wing literati. Ina and I enjoyed attending those functions. Frederick's eightieth birthday party was a big affair on a yacht in Sausalito. Ina and I went and had a terrific time, except for the long gangway we had to walk over to get on the boat. I wasn't at all happy about that. The wind was up and the bay was rough as we walked up the gangplank, which bounced up and down in the howling wind. I still couldn't swim, and the image of James, my childhood friend, floating face down in a Texas swimming pool, kept flashing in front of me.

Chapter 14
Early Days in San Francisco

I was standing at the front of a cavernous office filled with rows of desks that were interrupted by the occasional low partition. The manager who had just hired me on Andy's recommendation pointed out the different sections of workers, told me where the facilities were located, and showed me where my desk would be. I was trying to stay cool after suddenly realizing I was going to be able to support myself in the city where I had chosen to live. I had only been in San Francisco for two weeks.

Unknown to me, a beautiful young social worker sitting at the back of the room turned to her friend when I walked in and said, "My, my, June. See that tall, handsome man talking to Andy up front? That's my future husband. Yes, I'm going to marry that man!"

That was Ina Flemming, and though it would take almost a year for me to find out, my fate was sealed. I guess I am a little slower than she is.

Just then, June got a call saying a client was waiting for her in the interview room, so she went to her appointment. When she returned fifteen minutes later, she saw Ina up front talking to the new hire—me. We were standing close, touching each other's arms as we talked. We looked like we had known each other for a long time.

"Hmmm, that was fast, even for Ina!" she said. "They do make a good-looking couple, though!"

I hadn't yet discovered we were a couple. But I was certainly open to the idea. This new acquaintance was a beautiful, smart native San Franciscan. Trifecta! I had hit the jackpot! Once again, I felt like I was living under a lucky star.

Ina and I started dating right away, and my opinion of her didn't diminish. Her family had been in San Francisco for three generations. They were well-respected, friendly, and accom-

Ina Flemming

plished. Her grandmother, Georgia Edwards, was a founder of Jones United Methodist Church, one of the largest black churches in San Francisco. I still thought of myself as a bachelor, but, oddly, I had little desire to see anyone else.

Ina is the opposite of me. I don't talk much around strangers and I'm kind of withdrawn. But she talks to anybody, anywhere, anytime, about anything. She used to embarrass me to no end because, as she says, "What comes up comes out." She says, "John, I don't have any brakes on what comes up. Hey, this is what I'm thinking, this is what I'm going to say." I've gotten used to it. I have been lucky over the years. My best friends and my girlfriends (before I got married) were always the talkers. When we were out meeting people, I never had to worry because they would carry the conversation. Ina definitely does that. She loves attention. She wants to be the center of whatever is going on, and that's all right with me because I don't. I like to sit back and watch and learn.

A while after she and I met, she wanted to introduce me to her mother, and I agreed. As we drove to the real estate office where her mom worked, I had a toothpick in the corner of my mouth, as I usually did; for most of my life, that had been my habit. (These days, I don't use a toothpick; I use plastic now.)

Ina said to me, "You have to take that toothpick out of your mouth."

"Nah," I said. "That's me. Take it or leave it." I kept my toothpick in my mouth, and I met Bertha. I'm sure she was annoyed, but she never said anything—she got used to her son-in-law and his toothpick. She accepted it, and so did Ina. My wife likes to tell the story of how I was fifty-odd years old before I saw a dentist because I have such great teeth. It's the truth—I do, and it's because of the toothpick.

My experience with dentistry is one of the many ways I've been lucky in my life. What happened when I moved to San Francisco is another. Within two weeks of arriving, I had found a job I liked and was qualified for, and I'd found my mate for a lifetime. Not too much later, I met Willie Brown, who became my best friend and one of my lucky stars—and still is.

A few weeks after reconnecting with Dante, we corralled another friend from school, Sandy Joseph, and we all moved into a small second-floor apartment at 28 Clement Street. That address soon became known as party central. In fact, we held so many parties with loud music and louder laughter that the landlady asked us to move several times over the two months we lived there.

Sandy worked out of San Francisco as a merchant seaman. He was originally from Detroit and had been at Wayne State when Dante and I were. He was good friends with Dante and had been a part of the little group that would study and socialize together.

As long as I have known him, Dante has been one of those people who draws others to him. When we were in college, before I got to know him, I would see him nearly every day in the Student Center lounge with a little interracial group (very unlike Detroit then). They sat together around a couple of tables, always talking quite animatedly. After a few weeks, he came over to me and asked me to sit with them. So I did, and for the next three years, we had some far-ranging and interesting conversations about everything under the sun. He has always had eclectic interests, and he digs deep into any subject that interests him. I suppose that's why he majored in philosophy in college and later earned several master's degrees.

I once asked him why he had invited me to join them. He told me he'd noticed the giant stack of books I always carried and figured I must have something interesting to say. Whatever the reason, it was my good fortune.

I once suggested he go to law school and become my partner. I thought that with his endless curiosity, his knowledge of people, his ability to talk to anyone, and his sharp, quick mind, he would make a great lawyer. Not too long after we lived together, Dante went to Europe and met a lovely young woman in Germany whom he married. He came back to San Francisco and introduced us to his new wife, whom he had brought back from Europe. Antonia and Dante also lived in Europe for years. We joined them there for several vacations during which they graciously acted as wonderful tour guides. We have stayed in touch all these years, and our families have grown quite close. I performed the wedding ceremony for both his son's and daughter's weddings; ten years later, when his daughter and her husband wanted to renew their vows, I did that ceremony too.

Even now, after sixty-plus years, we remain good friends. Dante and Antonia now live in Ramona, California, a suburb of San Diego, where Dante taught high school for about twenty years. We see them every few months when they come to San Francisco to visit and join us for a family dinner.

The author and Dante Cosentino

By 1960, I had found my new home city, moved into an apartment, started building a real network of friends, and secured a job to pay my way. It was time to go back to pursuing my real work. So, I signed up to take the California Bar Exam. But I was still bathing in the newness of the city, going to jazz clubs regularly, and seeing Ina almost every night. As the exam date loomed closer, I met Willie Brown. I knew of Terry Francois, who was both a lawyer and the president of the local NAACP. I went to his office to ask if he could suggest places where I could apply for work as an attorney, and he introduced me to Willie.

Terry was born in New Orleans in 1921. He graduated from Xavier University in 1940, after which he earned a master's degree in business from Atlanta University. He served as a marine platoon sergeant in World War II and came to San Francisco when he was discharged to attend the University of California's Hastings Law School, where he earned a law degree in 1949. He was a lawyer for the NAACP early in his career, and in 1952, after only two years in practice, he sued the San Francisco Housing Authority, charging that it admitted only white and Asian families to its new city housing project. He won that case based on the Fourteenth Amendment, which requires each individual to be considered for a public benefit in a race-neutral fashion. (In other words, San Franciscans had a constitutional right to integrated public housing.) After that ruling, the San Francisco Housing Authority opened its public housing to everyone regardless of race. *The Sun Reporter*, San Francisco's black newspaper, said the ruling killed the "Dixie Housing Pattern." Mr. Francois was well-known and well-respected in the black community.

Conditions for blacks in San Francisco in the '50s were very different from those in the Deep South in many ways. In most ways, we were much better off in San Francisco, and the problems we had there were not nearly as brutal. But there was still a long way to go in some significant areas. True equality was still a way off. At the time, Terry was the president of the local NAACP. He succinctly summarized the situation in an interview he gave to one of the local papers: "In San Francisco, a Negro can eat almost anywhere," he said. "But [he] will have trouble finding a job that will enable him to pay for his meal."

Even after the public housing case, housing was still a problem for San Francisco blacks. Under Terry Francois's leadership, the NAACP focused on using the courts to open up employment and housing opportunities for blacks. I agreed that those were the two most important areas to focus on, so I was anxious to meet Mr. Francois and see what I could do for the NAACP. Because I was still determined to find a job in the law, I sought him out at the law office he shared with another lawyer in an old building in the Fillmore District at 2085 Sutter Street. I had been told that, as the best-known black lawyer in town, he might be able to point me towards relevant work. He explained that the NAACP was trying to get blacks into a number of industries that had not hired many (or any) in the past. He said there were no black insurance adjusters in San Francisco and suggested I apply at some agencies to support the NAACP's effort to integrate that industry. For me, it was two birds with one stone.

I took the list of insurance companies he gave me and started applying. Over the next week, during my lunch hour, I went in person to all the companies he referred me to, but no one hired me. It was always "Sorry, we don't have any vacancies at this time." Only one called me back. When I applied there, the man talking to me said, "I'm sorry. We don't have any vacancies at this time." But then he looked through some papers and said, "But it looks like we are going to have one soon. Why don't you call back in a few days?" When I left, I thought I had a job, but when I called a few days later, he told me, "Sorry. I thought we were going to have a vacancy, but now it looks like we aren't."

The day after Mr. Francois gave me the list of companies, he said, "There is someone here you might want to meet. You are both from Texas and seem to have a lot in common. He's already been out here a few years, so he may have some insight on where you should focus your energies."

I walked into the adjacent office. A smallish black man was

sitting at a desk engaged in an animated conversation with someone on the phone. He waved at me to wait until he had finished.

"No, I don't think that would work," he said into the receiver. "Well, OK, I'll meet you. Let's see. Let me check my calendar. Not Monday, but Tuesday afternoon after the organizing meeting should be all right. The Top of the Mark? Why don't we make it Cafe Society or Virginia's Hickory Pit out in the Fillmore? OK. Cafe Society it is then."

He hung up and turned to me. "What's up, dude?"

That's when I introduced myself to Willie Brown, who would become my lifelong best friend. Later, he told me there was no one on the other end of the line that day, but he never wanted anyone to think he wasn't busy with important work, especially the all-important first time he met them.

I ran into Willie at a clothing store on Union Square the next week and again a few weeks later in the automobile dealership on Van Ness Avenue. We were laughing at how neither of us could afford to buy a new car, or a used one for that matter. As Willie has expressed it, "Neither of us had two nickels to rub together." But we both wanted to be prepared when we did.

That was when it really came to me how much Willie and I had in common. Aside from our obvious sartorial and automotive interests, we were both from Texas, we had both grown up poor, we were both new lawyers, and we both shared an interest in civil rights and politics—although saying Willie was interested in politics is like saying a fish is interested in water. We have been friends, business partners, and political partners in our efforts for blacks, minorities, and politics in general for over sixty years. Without his friendship, advice, and help, I would not have been able to accomplish nearly as much as I have.

The Journey

Soon Willie and I were palling around together on any night I wasn't with Ina. We went to political events, meetings, or clubs together all over San Francisco. The Civil Rights Movement was beginning to gain traction and members of the black race were demanding their rights and getting more attention around the entire country. Willie was very outspoken in his effort to improve things for blacks. Willie and I even attended a Cesar Chavez worker's rights march in Fresno California.

When I told Willie about the lovely young woman I was seeing, it turned out that he knew Ina. In fact, she attended Jones United Methodist Church, the same one he did. The black culture in San Francisco was pretty small and knowing the people within it wasn't that unusual, especially for Willie, who has always wanted to know people's connections. He laughingly called Ina "that little rich girl," and I asked why. He told me Ina's mother and adopted father had owned a nightclub, the California Jazz Club in the Fillmore, when it was in its heyday. He said both Frank Sinatra and Billie Holliday had played there. He also told me that Ina's family had been among San Francisco's early settlers. Willie said her mother was a real estate broker and her grandmother owned a large apartment building on California Street in addition to various other properties around town. Ina's parents used to feed him and some of his friends when he was in college—they could afford it.

Willie told me he had grown up in Mineola, Texas, a small town of about 3,500 located eighty miles east of Dallas and two hundred miles northeast of Falls County, where I grew up. Even though Willie grew up in a small town and I grew up on a farm, we had both experienced Deep South racism and poverty and were both glad to be in San Francisco. He had moved to the city in 1951, immediately after high school, to live with his

223

uncle Itsy. He had originally wanted to attend Stanford since it was one of the best schools in the country, but when he went down for his interview, he discovered he lacked the qualifications to be considered for Stanford or any of the top-tier schools in the Bay Area. Luckily, his interviewer also taught at San Francisco State and was impressed with Willie's ambition. The interviewer got him a probationary admission, and Willie got himself off probation during his first semester. He worked his way through college as a janitor, a doorman, and a shoe salesman. He also told me his uncle Itsy ran a gambling establishment in the Fillmore where Willie had acted as lookout/doorman for a few months just after he moved to the city.

When Willie was at San Francisco State, he joined the Young Democrats and got to know John Burton, who was very active in YD issues and causes. Willie suggested that I also join the Young Democrats and meet John Burton, a young mover and shaker in local politics. John and I immediately hit it off, and he soon became one of my best friends, too. He ran for president of the YD in the next election, at the end of Joe Beeman's term. John Burton asked me to run with him as vice president and we won.

John's older brother, Philip, was one of the founders of the San Francisco Young Democrats (YD). He, Carlton Goodlett, and others founded the organization in 1950 to be an active political group for young Democrats who work or live in San Francisco. Philip was elected to the California Assembly in 1956, at the age of thirty, to represent San Francisco. Beginning in 1964, he served in the US House of Representatives for twenty years. Among his many accomplishments, he was instrumental in establishing the Golden Gate National Recreation

Area. The Burton family has been a powerful political force in San Francisco for over fifty years, only losing two elections among the entire family in all that time.

Willie had gone directly from San Francisco State to Hastings College of the Law. He had passed the California Bar in 1958, a year before we met, and he asked if I had it on my to-do list.

"So, Dearman, you going to take the bar?" he said.

"Naw," I said. I'd signed up but didn't intend to take the exam. "I haven't studied much and I don't think I can pass it. Besides, I've been having too much fun to study." During my first few months in San Francisco, I went out in North Beach almost every night, taking full advantage of the San Francisco singles scene.

"What the hell, man? You paid for it, didn't you?" Willie said. He has always had a way of cutting right to the heart of a matter. And his logic is usually pretty good, too.

"Well, yeah, Willie. I guess it wouldn't hurt, would it?"

"You can retake it if you fail," Willie said flatly.

So, I began cramming for the bar exam even though I only had a few weeks to study. Predictably, I failed—but barely.

"No problem," I told myself, "I'll get it next time."

The sting of failure was sharp, and I even considered going back to Saginaw, where I could use my Michigan license. Bertha, Ina's mother, was instrumental in talking me out of that.

"You'll always regret not giving San Francisco enough effort," she said. "If you give up so soon, you'll always wonder what might have been."

She had a point. Besides, I was growing more attached to Ina by the day.

It didn't help that I knew exactly why I had failed. I hadn't prepared for the exam. I had been lazy and hadn't taken it seriously, and that was particularly hard to accept. So, I decided to stay in San Francisco and give it another try. I was determined to pass the next time. This failure thing wasn't going to become a habit. Besides, it was embarrassing!

Ina didn't like it either. She had her Masters in Social Work from the University of California, Berkeley. She knew how to study

Ms. Bertha Flemming, Ina Flemming's mother

and she was focused. She wouldn't let me fail, especially at something so important to both of us. Ina has an unwavering positive attitude about everything in her life. As far as I can tell, she has always had it. Her attitude is that there isn't anything she can't do if she applies herself. Ina has tested as a genius, so there is some reason for her thinking that. She was kicked out of two schools when she was younger, but that was because she disagreed with how they did things and she let them know. Just being around her makes you think you can do anything, too.

"Let's make a plan, sign up again, and get that little exam out of the way," she said. So, I signed up to take it again.

Ina and I were going strong by that time. One night, she announced, "I'm going to be married by Christmas."

"Good luck," I said.

I still didn't know my bachelor days were over . . . and had been for some time. Like I said, I guess I am just slower than Ina is.

In his book *Pride and Memory*, my friend Dante succinctly

recalls that time: "While John was working as a social worker, there was a young woman (also a social worker) who came to visit him quite often. Her name was Ina and she pursued John until he turned around and caught her. They were married shortly before I left San Francisco."

Ina suggested we get a marriage license. I agreed, but frankly, I wasn't too enthusiastic about it. I was aware of the expiration date, but I feigned surprise when the license expired. Ina was not happy. So, we got another license.

As Thanksgiving approached, Ina said, out of the blue, "I have a child placement client in Santa Rosa who I need to go see today. Why don't you come, too, and we can get married in the Santa Rosa courthouse?"

I knew the courts would close at noon that day and we would be just a little too late to make it happen. So that part of my plan worked. I had gotten a ring earlier but hocked it when money was tight. I foolishly thought I could skate on this by not having to produce it at a service. But on the way back from Santa Rosa, Ina got it out of me.

"You what?!" she said.

"I hocked it."

"It was cheap anyway," she said.

"It was worth enough for the pawn shop to take it," I responded defensively.

A few weeks later, after I had retrieved the ring, Ina said, "Let's get married today. A friend's husband is a minister and he can do it." Ina was determined not to be a "twenty-five-year-old old maid."

"Now?" I said. "Right now?"

"We can go after work," Ina responded.

It was settled. The goose was cooked.

I still didn't have a car, so Ina borrowed her mother's car. On the way to the church with Beverly and Harold Dent (who would be our witnesses), the car caught fire.

Harold and I were checking the engine and extinguishing the fire. Ina and Beverly were in the car when Beverly said, "Ina, don't you think that's an omen?" Ina said, "No, I'm getting married today."

She was undeterred. After we put out the fire, we caught a cab to Ina's friend's church. We were married that Thursday night.

In spite of everything, I still felt reluctant, because I didn't want people thinking we got married on a Thursday and went right back to work. I told Ina I didn't want her to wear her ring until the following Monday. She agreed not to wear the ring until later.

She really did promise.

The next day, Ina wore her ring to work and showed it to everyone in sight.

The department head and many others spent the day congratulating me, and it was public. So much for the bachelor-for-life plan. It wasn't that I had anything against marriage so much as I wasn't sure I could provide for a family. I had watched Uncle Jace's efforts for

The author and his wife, Ina.

years as he struggled to raise his children back in Texas, and I really didn't think it was fair to bring children into a world of poverty and want. But Ina had a different viewpoint. Like everything else, she was optimistic about this, too. And, as I have learned, her dogged optimism always removes barriers to the things she wants in ways that are truly astounding.

After Ina and I married, I got serious about the bar exam. I had already worked with John Bussey, San Francisco's first black judge—at the time, its only black judge—in a study group he ran, so I had a pretty good start on studying. But at Ina's urging, I took leave from the Social Services Department and made studying my regular job. I got up early and saw Ina off to work each day. Then I would study for two hours at a time, taking regular breaks and taking lunch from noon to one. By the time the exam rolled around, I felt bad watching Ina leave for work every morning. Growing up in Texas, we had been taught it wasn't manly to let your woman earn your living for you. If anyone was going to be without a job, it should be her. Not working rubbed me the wrong way, and as exam day approached, I began to study even harder. Two failures were enough, thank you.

Then, two days before the bar, Ina was admitted to the hospital.

She had been having symptoms since she was at UC Berkeley that the doctors had yet to diagnose. There were times when I'd noticed things weren't right—like her dropping things or missing the cup when she tried to pour coffee. Ina would make light of them, but I had my suspicions—I'd had a friend in law school who had been diagnosed with multiple sclerosis (MS) and had similar symptoms. I never made anything of those incidents. I just ignored them. I didn't want to burden Ina with the severity of what I thought she might have. After all, she had seen her doctor about it and he had found nothing.

This time, Ina's mother took her to a different doctor.

The night before the last day of the multi-day bar exam, a friend called. "Isn't it horrible that Ina has MS?" she said.

I didn't know because Ina and her mother had decided not to tell me—they didn't want to influence my test results. I guess that was smart since I could only answer two of the four essay questions on the exam the next day. Every time I looked at the page, I thought of Ina.

I was sure I had failed again. And my new wife, whom I had finally realized was the love of my life, had multiple sclerosis. The exam outcome suddenly seemed minor compared to what Ina was facing—what we were both facing. But now I needed to pass more than ever. I needed to be able to take care of Ina in a very uncertain future.

After the exam, I went to pick Ina up from the hospital. She was packed and ready to go. As I walked into the room, she was sitting on the hospital bed looking very small as she stared out the window with an uncharacteristically frightened look on her face.

"Hey you," I said. "You ready to go?"

Ina didn't look at me but went to the closet to get her coat. She put it on slowly, still not looking at me.

"This bag all you have?" I asked as I picked up the small suitcase.

"John?" she said looking at me with sad but steady eyes.

"Yes?"

She told me the doctor had diagnosed her problems as the symptoms of multiple sclerosis and tests had confirmed it.

"John, you can have an annulment if you want," she said. I thought I could see tears in the corners of her eyes.

"You know, Ina, we said in sickness and in health, didn't we? Well, I meant it."

She said nothing.

"Now, tell me if you have anything else to take home," I said.

"Nothing else. Let's go home."

Some weeks later, the letter from the State Bar of California arrived. As I held it, I took a deep breath. Here was my future. Here was *our* future. I tore it open.

I passed!

Now, even with all the uncertainty facing us, I at least stood a good chance of being able to support Ina and provide for her through whatever her disease held. I called Ina and she was ecstatic. I jumped into the car her uncle, a merchant seaman, had left for us to use while he was at sea and raced downtown to share the good news with friends only to be pulled over on Van Ness for speeding. The police officer must have thought I was out of my mind when he handed me the ticket and I happily tried to explain how it was really a ticket of good luck. It was June 1961.

Ina has always been optimistic, even when it seemed to the rest of us that there was no reason to be. For example, when the Kaiser doctor diagnosed her with MS, he told her it would get progressively worse until there would likely come a time after which she would not be able to walk.

Ina replied, "Doctor, I'll walk until I die." This did not surprise me. She is very independent. She likes to do things her way, and she likes to do things herself. She has faced and overcome many obstacles in the years since.

After Ina's diagnosis, we moved from our second-story apartment to a big house out on Eleventh Avenue. The house was owned by Ina's aunt, Fanny. Fanny was one of the most generous people I have ever known. She was the first black woman accepted to the Merchant Marines, and she was at sea most of the time, so she was glad to have her sister Bertha, Ina's two brothers, and the two of us living there. She could trust us to take care of the place while she was gone.

We needed income until I received the bar exam results, so I took a job with a local private detective who was investigating theft at the Hills Brothers Coffee warehouse. Bags of coffee had been going missing for some time, and it was beginning to add up. After a few months there, I discovered that the women would put small bags in their bras, taking them home every night. Large sacks of unroasted beans were also thrown out of a second-story window to a waiting truck during the night shift. Then they were driven off and disappeared. I gave the information to my supervisor and they took it from there.

My work at Hills Brothers led to a job at Burns Detective Agency doing security at Candlestick Park during the 1961 baseball season. One particular incident led to my initial meeting with Willie Mays.

A few months after I started, I showed up before the game to get my assignment. I was once again assigned to the outfield bleachers. My job involved standing around, mostly waiting for something to happen. All of us security guards had a short nightstick to protect ourselves and a holster to carry it in, which hung off our belts. I kept my nightstick holstered, but some of the younger guards liked to walk around with the stick out, slapping it into the other hand like a beat cop out of a 1920s silent film. Management must have known about this because no one hid it. But I always thought that was a short-sighted thing to do. It seemed like folks were there to enjoy the game and have a little fun, not be harassed by a hyped-up cop wannabe.

Just after the game started, I was standing at the bottom of the bleachers and had a good view of the section. I looked up to see three large toughs sitting together on the top row of the bleachers. They hadn't been there when I looked a minute earlier. About that time, another one climbed over the back of the bleachers and joined them.

I walked up the stairs to the top row and stood next to them. "What's goin' on fellows?" I said.

They were passing a pint of whiskey in a brown paper bag back and forth as they sat in the sun. They mumbled something that sounded like, "Nothin' . . . not much . . . jus' watchin' tha' game . . . what's it to ya?"

"Well, I just saw you climb over the back and sit down. You sneak in through a hole in the fence?"

"Huh?"

"It just happens I am supposed to stop folks like you from sneakin' in."

They all seemed to take umbrage at once.

"Aw, man, jus' leave us alone! Ain't hurtin' nobody. You old fool, what's it to you? You got a problem with that?!"

I thought a few seconds.

I'm not gonna face three people with this lil' ass stick ran through my mind.

"Nope. No problem at all," I said. "You boys enjoy the game."

I walked over to the next section, where I could stand in the sun and watch the game in safety while they slapped each other on the back, laughed, and continued passing the bottle. Before the game was over, I heard the bottle break against the concrete stairs where they had thrown it.

It didn't seem like complaining about it would do any good, but I thought about it all evening. The toughs obviously had no problem breaking the law, and they were big and muscular. And the more I thought about it . . . mean and dangerous. They could have been carrying knives or guns, and all I had was the short mini nightstick they gave us to enforce things and keep order. I have never liked the idea of taking a knife to a gunfight, and that is what it felt like to me.

233

I had noticed several of the boss's friends "guarding" the seats behind home plate. Not only did they have a much better view of the game, but the worst the fans in that section would likely do was complain there wasn't enough mustard on their kid's hot dog. Those guards seemed to be watching the game and enjoying themselves immensely. Then there were the rest of us riding herd on the outfield and bleacher seats, expected to risk our lives trying to keep order in that sunny cauldron of mean drunks and ne'er-do-wells.

It seemed to me that Burns was giving all the sweetest spots to the white employees. The rest of us—the blacks—were always stationed in the outfield or the bleachers. The more I thought about it, the madder I got thinking about how little they were paying us while screwing us with the worst spots and expecting us to risk our lives over a few dollars. So, the next day, when the entire security department had a regular meeting, I spoke up.

"It seems to me that all the good spots are being given to the white folk," I said.

The meeting included the entire security crew, and out of thirty or so, twenty-five of us were black. Of the five others, three were supervisors and the other two were their relatives. I had primed the pump in the employee locker room before the meeting by carping about the plum assignments always going to the white employees, and I had done a pretty good job of getting everyone riled up. As I spoke up, it began to sound like a church meeting with call and response.

"That's right!"

"Ain't right!"

"Discrimination!"

A few other supporting phrases came out of the crowd.

"All assignments are given based solely on seniority," said one supervisor haughtily.

"Everything's completely fair," said another.

"Yeah? Well, I was here at least a month before him," I said pointing to a young white man, the main supervisor's wife's little brother.

"Ah' wonder what the NAACP would have to say about it," I said. "Maybe I should ask them."

"No need to do that," the main supervisor said. "Give us a day to review the assignments."

"Dearman, you are assigned to the third base side of the home plate section," was the first assignment the next day. I tried not to smile too much as the older guys got better assignments too.

As I enjoyed watching the game in the warm sun behind home plate, I looked out toward the bleachers, squinting to make out the details from that far away. Sure enough, the four toughs were sitting in the top row cavorting with each other while passing around a brown paper bag. Standing at the bottom of the bleachers was the young white man, doing his best to ignore them. I thought I could see him trembling from across the field.

Of course, here in the not-so-cheap seats, my responsibility was mainly to make sure no one got drunk enough to disrupt the game or annoy the swells. Everything was going well until late in the sixth inning. The Giants were on defense when a highly intoxicated and overexuberant young fan leapt the fence on the first base side of home plate and immediately began running the bases and waving to the fans. I started to go after him but quickly realized that if I just stayed put, he would soon meet me as he rounded third and headed for home, so I waited. He was exceptionally fast for a drunk and was nearing home plate when I tackled him. For some arbitrary reason, I was determined not to let him reach home. After I pulled him up with his arm locked behind him, I realized the only way out was through a door in center field, so I marched the stumbling drunk past second base toward the outfield fence. As we neared the wall, we approached Willie Mays.

"Hi, Willie," I said. He looked just like his photos in the newspaper, like he was really enjoying his job.

"Say haylew kisgdos," said the drunk.

Willie flashed that famous smile at us and nodded.

"Hey," he said. He was having a good laugh at the boos I was getting for stopping the drunk from weaving around the bases.

As I pushed the drunk through the door and off the field, I realized the fans had been booing me all the way, chanting "Let him go! Let him go!" as we walked. But that didn't matter to me because I had just met one of my heroes. I had met the great Willie Mays! Later, after I became a judge and Ina and I began going to fundraising events around town, I saw him and his wife, Mae, on many occasions. They were truly two of the most gracious people in San Francisco.

Up until World War II, there had been so few blacks in San Francisco that there was a running joke that if you were black, you probably knew them all. The city had developed a very liberal reputation even though the majority of the white population was less than enthusiastic about it.

Only low-level jobs were open to us then. For the most part, women worked in the domestic trades as maids and servants of a sort. The few black males worked as laborers in the city's scarce non-union industries. Aside from the International Longshore and Warehouse Union (ILWU) and the Marine Cooks and Stewards Union (MCS), unions in the city were quite racist, and most did not accept black members. While the number of black residents increased during World War I and shortly after, so did the white population. Blacks were still a small minority in 1940, accounting for less than 1 percent of the population. That all changed during and immediately after World War II when blacks flooded the Bay Area to work for the large shipbuilding and supporting industries that developed. By 1950, we accounted for nearly 6 percent of the population, an increase of about 800 percent. Because of the labor shortage, blacks in the shipyards learned skilled trades and professions, allowing them to be promoted into much higher positions than they had previously been able to obtain. A big percentage of these new San Franciscans were from the South and the Deep South.

According to the 1940 and 1950 censuses, San Francisco's population was 634,536 in 1940, out of which only 4,846 people were black (0.8 percent). By 1950, the white population had increased to 775,075 (a 22 percent increase). However, during the same time period, the black population grew to 43,460—an increase of almost 800 percent. The black population of the entire Bay Area rose at similar rates, with Richmond and its nearby shipyards seeing the largest relative increase of blacks from 270 to 13,374. That is a 4,853 percent increase! By 1960, there were 83,104 blacks living in Oakland out of a total population of 367,548. Almost a quarter of the population was black.

While the severe World War II labor shortage forced industries to accept and even promote blacks, we were, for the most part, still relegated to low-skill, low-wage jobs unless there was no alternative. Most white unions, if they accepted us at all, segregated blacks into "dependent auxiliaries" where we paid the same dues but did not have the same representation. The ILWU was the only union that had always given black workers a fair shake.

During World War II, San Francisco's Western Addition

neighborhood grew into its heyday as the Harlem of the West. Known for having the most vibrant jazz scene on the West Coast, it retained a wide ethnic mix and gained a reputation as one of the most diverse neighborhoods in San Francisco. Back then, employment in the neighborhood was high, the crime rate was low, and it became the place to be for the city's blacks and jazz lovers.

With the shameful World War II internment of California's Japanese American population, African Americans became the most visible and dominant minority. The relatively benign prewar racist attitudes towards a tiny minority were replaced by a harder view of the larger black population, which was nearly 60 percent in the Western Addition. This new attitude was actively influenced by virulent racists from the Deep South who had also migrated to work at the shipyards. Houses and apartments in the Western Addition filled with newly arrived blacks as WWII developed, and in the early to mid-'40s, the neighborhood was a vibrant boomtown of theaters, hotels, bars, restaurants, billiard parlors, jazz halls, and, of course, casinos. After the war, however, things sharply resembled Detroit in that blacks, last hired, were then first fired. The safe, prosperous black wartime neighborhood became filled with out-of-work folks, crime, and blight.

The shipyard employment during World War II had brought enough money into the black community that it created heretofore unseen problems, challenging San Francisco's image as a liberal bastion. In 1951, for instance, Mrs. Orelia Duncan and her adult son moved into their newly purchased home on Rhode Island Street in the Potrero Hill neighborhood. Three weeks later, Mrs. Duncan found a one-foot-tall, kerosene-soaked cross burning on her front porch. A local newspaper reported that it took police two and a half hours to arrive, and when they finally did, they advised Mrs. Duncan to forget about the "kiddish prank."

But the neighbors' response was encouraging. The same article reported that five of Mrs. Duncan's white neighbors visited about a dozen homes in the immediate area and polled more than twenty-five residents. All but one agreed that Mrs. Duncan and her son had a right to live there. She later said the neighbors' goodwill mission had calmed her immediate concerns.

At that time, attitudes were at best marginally ambivalent, but a violent undercurrent showed itself more often than one would like. A little over a year after Mrs. Duncan discovered the cross on her porch, a burning cross scored with "KKK" was planted near the intersection of Geary and Steiner in the heart of the Western Addition. Many people witnessed the blazing cross, but no one could explain how it got there. It was clearly a response to the Harlem of the West turning into a neighborhood of out-of-work blacks when their shipyard income had dried up.

The Western Addition was declared a center of urban blight in 1948. Soon thereafter, it became a target of urban renewal, a concept that started at the national level with generally good intentions of cleaning up neighborhoods for the residents. When implemented at the local level, however, it proved to be a brutal way of emptying poor blacks from their neighborhoods without returning them to improved areas.

Declaring an area officially blighted allowed the local government to take over private property through eminent domain and then rebuild it. It was a nationwide experiment in which well-meaning civic planners and proponents razed and replaced large swaths of older, economically depressed neighborhoods with bigger buildings, theoretically resulting in lower crime, economic growth, and a higher standard of living.

Predictability, the commitment to bring residents back into the neighborhood to live in the more modern buildings was largely a hollow promise; instead, profit was maximized. The Harlem of the West disappeared under redevelopment bulldozers soon after the first demolitions began in 1956 and the Redevelopment Agency destroyed the Western Addition.

This was roughly the situation when I arrived in San Francisco in 1959.

The Civil Rights Movement was quickly gaining steam on the East Coast and would soon reach the critical mass necessary for dramatic change. There were new calls for a fundamental strategic shift from litigation to direct action, many from well-respected movement leaders. Since 1960 was an election year, that gave us an opportunity to use the time and our votes to make an impact. Just before I moved, A. Philip Randolph, a longtime leader of the movement, spoke to an audience of 3,000 in New York's Carnegie Hall. Thousands more were turned away once the auditorium reached capacity. During that speech, he indicated that Negroes need to demand something more than we have been given for our votes:

> They have demonstrated that when a conservative body of bipartisan members produces a practical proposal such as federal registrars in the South to guarantee registration and voting they will ignore and even seek to discredit the proposal; and yet they expect us to regard the maintenance of the Commission as a concession. To illustrate the absurdity another way—when we are hungry, they keep the bread and offer us the wrapper.

While A. Philip Randolph was calling for disrupting the upcoming pre-election party conventions with marches, the deceitful practice of Democrats supporting black civil rights before Northern audiences and assiduously avoiding the issue before Southerners rankled all of us. Mr. Randolph's ideas sparked others to question what they could do in their own neighborhoods. In contrast to the notion that the explosion of civil rights actions in the '60s was a spontaneous reaction to years of oppression, much like a pressure cooker will explode after heating for too long, the movement and its actions resulted from years of discussions and planning, much of it surreptitious on a local level. Seething and planning sometimes found a nexus when it was just time.

Like the small group I belonged to at Willey College, four exceptional young men enrolled at North Carolina Agricultural and Technical University met for bull sessions that soon turned into discussions of what they could do to help the movement. About the same time that I was getting on the plane for San Francisco, these men were boarding, too—in their case, buses. That Christmas, as one of them returned to college from his home in New York, he was refused service at the Greensboro Greyhound bus station. He was told to take a seat in the back of the kitchen with others "of his kind." This was the straw that broke the camel's back of a hundred years of Jim Crow segregation on top of 250 years of slavery in the US. All four of these men (Ezell Blair Jr., Franklin McCain, Joseph McNeil, and David Richmond) had similar experiences, and together they decided they'd had enough. As they banded together and committed to act, they didn't realize their actions would ignite a movement, change a nation, and inspire a world. They also inspired us in San Francisco and changed my life.

On Monday, February 1, 1960, they became known as the Greensboro Four when they began a nonviolent protest at four thirty p.m. at Woolworth's "whites only" lunch counter where they ordered coffee, were refused service, and then were asked to leave. They stayed at the counter, expecting to be arrested, until the store closed at 5:00 p.m. Surprised at still being free, they returned to campus, where they recruited other students to join them.

The next day, the four young men returned with twenty-five other male students and four women. They all sat at the lunch counter from eleven o'clock a.m. until three o'clock p.m. while they read and did homework. Meanwhile, whites gathered behind them to heckle and threaten them as they were refused service. A television crew, reporters from both local Greensboro newspapers, and a contingent of police officers monitored them.

The sit-ins filled the local news, energizing students across the community. That night, they met with college officials and concerned citizens to organize the Student Executive Committee for Justice and committed to continue the demonstrations. The committee sent a letter to the president of F.W. Woolworth in New York requesting that his company "take a firm stand to eliminate discrimination." The same day, the NAACP voted unanimously to support the sit-in at their regular monthly meeting.

The next day, over sixty students, more than twenty of them women, returned and occupied every lunch counter seat while they again studied and ignored the angry crowd, which now included KKK members. This time, they were joined by students from Bennett College and Dudley High School, both local schools, many carpooling from school to downtown. They sat all day and replaced each other at the counter in shifts.

On Thursday, more than 300 students from the three local schools again occupied every seat at the lunch counter. That day, three white female supporters from the Women's College of the University of North Carolina joined this now interracial group. Each day, the crowd of whites had grown nastier, and the KKK was agitating everyone to "protect their city." The Executive Committee for Justice responded by sending another group of students down the street to S.S. Kresge & Co., where they occupied its basement lunch counter, too. That evening, student leaders, college administrators, F.W. Woolworth, and Kresge officials held talks. The stores' representatives said that as long as other downtown stores remained segregated, their stores would refuse to integrate. Their argument was that it would create a competitive advantage for the other stores as it would drive white customers away from the integrated stores. The students vowed to continue the sit-ins, and the meeting ended without progress.

By then, the national press had picked up the story. Willie and I attended a house meeting in San Francisco with twenty or so other left-wing "liberals" (mostly white) where we exchanged ideas about what we could do in California to support the sit-ins. It wasn't lost on us that our interracial group could meet together without incident while interracial groups in North Carolina, Alabama, South Carolina, Mississippi, and the other Deep South states risked their lives every time they met or otherwise socialized together.

The next day was Friday, February 5. When the demonstrators arrived at Woolworth's, they found a group of fifty racist whites occupying most of the seats at the lunch counter. Some additional white students from area colleges joined those white protesters. The demonstrators took the remaining seats and tried to study as they had before. These new white protestors were more incensed than the others had been, and they began yelling and threatening the protesters. Police removed two of them for disruption and swearing, and by three o'clock p.m., the crowd had grown to more than 300 people. Three more whites were arrested, and the store closed for the day at five thirty p.m.

Woolworth's store representatives met with the students again that night and objected vociferously to the group targeting only two stores—theirs and Kresge. They asked school administrators to stop the student protests, but administrators responded by saying they had no power to tell students what to do off campus and out of class. The administrators did, however, recommend that the stores temporarily close the counters. They contentiously debated these issues for two hours before ending the meeting.

Early Saturday morning, a group of 1,400 students met in an auditorium on the NC A&T campus and voted to continue the protest before many of them headed downtown to Woolworth's, where they filled every seat as soon as they opened, preventing any of the whites from sitting when they showed up. By noon, the store was packed with more than 1,000 people on both sides, and at 1:00 p.m., a caller said a bomb was set to explode at 1:30. The store closed and the demonstrators quickly left, going down the street to occupy the Kresge counter again. People were arrested outside both stores. That night, a group of 1,600 students met at NC A&T and voted to stop the demonstrations for two weeks to let Woolworth's decide if it would change its policy towards Negro customers. Predictably, local leaders established committees to study the issue.

On February 22, the stores opened again with segregated lunch counters. By then, the demonstrations had spread to thirty cities in eight states. By the end of March, the demonstrations had spread even further, to fifty-five stores in thirteen states. People from all walks of life in and around Greensboro had written over 2,000 letters to the management of both

Woolworth's and Kresge. Three-quarters of them supported integrating the lunch counters.

In San Francisco, the local movement kicked off on March 31 when Terry Francois, president of the local NAACP chapter, spoke at a local NAACP meeting in Longshoremen's Hall to start a boycott of local Kresge and Woolworth's stores in support of the Greensboro Four. By then, pickets and sit-ins were being held across the country in support of the Greensboro action, and similar actions spread across the South like wildfire. For example, in sympathy with civil rights protests in the South, 100 Vassar students picketed Woolworth's in Poughkeepsie. There were protests by college students almost everywhere outside the Southern states, and even a few south of the Mason-Dixon line.

In the late '50s, Terry Francois had said, "Blacks in San Francisco can eat almost anywhere they want, but they can't work in those same establishments." His famous summation was still accurate. Redlining in housing and real estate was also prevalent so that blacks could not rent or buy in many neighborhoods. And on top of this, the Redevelopment Agency was destroying San Francisco's most densely populated black neighborhood, the Western Addition.

On Friday, April 1, the Greensboro students renewed their demonstrations, and over 1,200 pledged to continue. By the next day, both Woolworth's and Kresge had officially closed their lunch counters. On Sunday, April 3, Thurgood Marshall, the NAACP's legal counsel, urged the students to keep the pressure up, starting an economic boycott of both stores.

Two weeks later, over Easter weekend, the SCLC organized a meeting of sit-in students from all over the nation at Shaw University in Raleigh, North Carolina. Ella Baker, one of the organizers, encouraged the students to form the Student

Nonviolent Coordinating Committee (SNCC, pronounced "snick") to make use of the synergy and momentum the burgeoning movement had gained. The next Thursday, forty-five students were arrested for trespassing at the Kresge lunch counter in Greensboro and were released without bond.

During this period, the San Francisco liberal movement, growing rapidly through its support of the Greensboro Four, was shocked by a wholly different though no less dramatic local event.

Shortly before I arrived in San Francisco, the House Un American Activities Committee (HUAC) came to San Francisco to hold public hearings. The HUAC was a conservative but powerful Senate committee headed by Joe McArthy. On the first day of the San Francisco HUAC hearings, May 12, 1960, many waited in line outside the hearing room in San Francisco's city hall hoping to gain admission, only to discover most seats had been given to known HUAC supporters. There were hundreds of protesters, most neatly dressed in a jacket and tie. Many were from area colleges, including San Francisco State and the University of California, Berkeley. The demonstration was a strange combination of raucous and polite as well-dressed protesters inside the city hall rotunda chanted "Let us in! Let us in!" while those few in the hearing room sang the national anthem. The next day, the protest grew, but even more HUAC supporters showed up with official "white cards" for admission. Almost no protesters got into the hearing room.

This time, a police riot squad turned fire hoses on protesters in the rotunda without warning, and many were washed down the marble staircase while police dragged others down the stairs by their feet, banging their heads on every step. Local and national news media called it a "riot" and blamed it on the protesters. In response, 5,000 people turned out on the final day, and the hearings were called off.

Part of the Southern strategy for segregation was to red-bait any advances. Integrating schools there and registering black voters was labeled a "communist plot," as was any other effort towards advancement. We saw it quite differently and, for the most part, we were accepting of anyone who wanted to help, regardless of their politics. Besides, most US communists and "fellow travelers" were more interested in improving life in the US than in subverting the government. They were especially interested in improving life for blacks and the working class.

This was one of the country's last HUAC hearings, and soon the local progressive movement claimed, "Not in San Francisco!" The HUAC demonstration is generally recognized as the birth of the local student protest movement. The newspapers noted that Vincent Hallinan—the presidential candidate who ran while imprisoned—was at the demonstrations, and one of his sons was among those washed down the rotunda steps. I would shortly find myself in a courtroom gallery watching Hallinan, one of my legal heroes, fight a case. He was soon to become a good friend of mine.

The HUAC demonstrations galvanized local liberals in ways the Greensboro Four could not. The demonstration had happened right before our eyes to people we knew—to our friends and neighbors. It helped to coalesce everyone in San Francisco and strengthen our support of the Greensboro Four. The local liberal movement began to refine its phone trees and expand its mailing lists. We could easily see the connection between local events and the events (though very different) in the Deep South. After the HUAC demonstrations, it was easier to mobilize a broader coalition for demonstrations and marches in support of the North Carolina lunch counter sit-ins.

In June, when college students left Greensboro for the summer, students from a local black high school, Dudley High School, pledged to replace them. Furthermore, the protests expanded to Walgreens and Meyers stores and continued through the summer.

On Monday, July 25, Woolworth's opened its lunch counters to blacks and Kresge followed the same day. The first blacks to sit down and eat next to whites at a Woolworth's lunch counter were four Woolworth's employees. More than 70,000 people had participated in sit-ins across the country in support and more than 3,000 had been arrested, all because four young black college students in the Deep South had had enough of being treated like second-class citizens, sat down at a lunch counter, and refused to move.

Soon, Kresge and F.W. Woolworth stores were desegregated across the nation, and the end of 100 years of segregation in the US had begun in earnest. However, segregation would not go quietly, and America would never be the same again. Blacks and supporters were galvanized across the country and unrest was spreading. But things would get worse before they got better. Confronting the deep evil of racism (which Willie and I had grown up with) would unleash violence of a kind most Americans could never have imagined. It would be confronted by a nonviolent movement led by Dr. Martin Luther King Jr. (MLK) and patterned after strategies Gandhi used until his death in 1948. He used his tactics first in South Africa in the early 1900s in the struggle for Indian rights, then in India to gain home rule from British occupation.

After protesters won the Woolworth's boycott, other local demonstrations integrated lunch counters in several places across the south. On October 19, 1960, MLK joined a student sit-in inside Rich's Department Store in Atlanta, Georgia, at the "whites only" dining room. He was one of fifty-two protesters arrested for trespassing. In the trespassing trial, sixteen of the fifty-two had their charges dismissed and thirty-five were released on bond, but the judge sentenced MLK to four months of hard labor in a Georgia public works camp. Presidential candidate John F. Kennedy called Coretta Scott King, MLK's wife, to offer encouragement while his brother, Robert Kennedy, called the judge and convinced him to release MLK on bond. MLK spent just one day in the camp, and many Americans, especially blacks, were convinced to support John Kennedy in the upcoming election.

Willie had met MLK in 1956 when he came to San Francisco for the forty-seventh NAACP National Convention to generate support for the Montgomery bus boycott in Alabama. I would meet him in May of 1964 when he spoke out against discrimination before 8,000 admirers during the Human Dignity rally at the Cow Palace.

MLK returned to San Francisco in July of that year to address the Platform Committee at the Republican National Convention. His goal was to persuade the GOP brass to include civil rights language in the party platform. "There will be no tranquility or cessation of demonstrations until every vestige of racial injustice is eliminated from American society," he said. The Republicans shunned King's ideas for their platform as they swung far to the right and nominated Barry Goldwater.

We were all impressed with Dr. King's backbone and commitment. However, Willie and I, recalling our experiences in the South, were concerned that he was becoming too visible and was putting a target on his back in that most violent region where many whites were determined to resist progress and integration. We shook our heads and said a prayer for him.

After World War II, Blacks across the country had sporadically mobilized against discrimination. By the 1960s, they reached critical mass and the modern Civil Rights Movement was born. It fought for an end to segregation with equality and fairness in education, housing, and employment opportunities. By the 1960s, almost exactly when I moved to San Francisco, the Civil Rights Movement reached California after beginning in the South. Once it took hold in the Bay Area, it brought together people from all races and backgrounds to fight against the social injustice that had become so ingrained even here. It was often brutal, and victories were hard-won. Some of the weapons that activists used in the fight were sit-ins, marches, pickets, and parades.

Meanwhile, in the South, riding the momentum of the student-led lunch counter sit-ins, students from CORE and SNCC organized the Freedom Riders in 1961 to challenge state segregation of interstate buses and the lunch counters and terminals that served them. The Freedom Rides were patterned after the 1947 Journey of Reconciliation bus rides led by Bayard Rustin, but this time they included women and would travel through the Deep South—Virginia, North Carolina, South Carolina, Georgia, Alabama, and Mississippi—to their destination in New Orleans. This was a *much* more dangerous route. After extensive training in nonviolent resistance, the group of thirteen Freedom Riders (seven blacks and six whites, some in their forties and fifties), led by CORE Director James Farmer, left Washington, DC, on May 4 on two interracial buses, a Greyhound and a Trailways. As they headed south, they would ride in the "wrong" sections of the buses, sit at "whites only" lunch counters, use the "wrong" facilities, and sit and mingle in all the places where they were forbidden in those states. Their purpose was to force the federal government to enforce the law.

The Journey

In 1960, through *Boynton v. Virginia*, the US Supreme Court had upheld the federal law that found segregation involving interstate travel and its associated facilities to be illegal. This ruling supposedly protected all interstate riders. Predictably, Southern states ignored the federal law and passed their own racist ones demanding segregation. At the time of the Freedom Rides, the federal government refused to enforce the national law.

Aside from a few trespassing arrests, the Freedom Riders encountered little trouble while passing through Virginia and North Carolina. But when they got to Rock Hill, South Carolina, John Lewis, a black man, and Albert Bigelow, a white man, were beaten as they entered a white waiting room together. Genevieve Hughes, a white woman, one of three women in the group, was also injured.

The buses continued across Georgia without incident, but on May 14, the lead Greyhound bus was met at the terminal in Anniston, Alabama, by a mob of 200 angry whites (including many KKK members) who threw rocks through the windows and slashed the bus tires. The driver managed to get the bus out of the terminal, but when he stopped a few miles outside of town to change the tires, white racists following in cars fire-bombed the bus. The Freedom Riders escaped the burning bus into the arms of the howling mob, who beat them unmercifully.

The Trailways bus was also attacked in Anniston, but they escaped and drove on to Birmingham, where they arrived on May 17 and were assaulted by a larger, more vicious white mob, some members of which used metal pipes and bats. Birmingham Commissioner of Public Safety Bull Connor later said he knew the Freedom Riders were coming and that there would be trouble, but he hadn't sent any police to protect them because . . . it was Mother's Day. The next day, newspapers in San Francisco and around the world printed photographs of the bombed and burning buses with bloodied riders tumbling out into the hands of mob members, who beat them to their hands and knees.

CORE could not find a replacement bus driver to finish the trip, so they called off the original Freedom Rides. But a SNCC activist organized an interracial group of ten students to replace them, leaving from Nashville, Tennessee. Attorney General Robert Kennedy negotiated with the bus companies and the governor of Alabama to continue the rides with limited police protection. On May 20, they departed Birmingham with a state police escort. However, the police abandoned them just before Montgomery, where a mob of racist white men, women, and children attacked the riders with bats, bricks, and tire irons when they attempted to depart the bus. Both John Lewis (who was on the original Freedom Ride) and Jim Zwerg sustained major injuries, and when a White House observer attempted to protect two of the women, the crowd knocked him unconscious with a brick. All of this was televised and broadcast around the world.

The next night, Martin Luther King Jr. led a service of 1,000 worshippers in support of the Freedom Riders at the First Baptist Church in Montgomery. A riot of racist whites erupted outside the church and MLK called Robert Kennedy to ask for protection. Kennedy sent 600 federal marshals, who used tear gas to disperse the white mob. Then Governor Patterson declared martial law in the city and sent the National Guard to restore order.

On May 24, James Farmer arrived to accompany the group across Mississippi, where they would have the protection of state troopers. They were met by several hundred supporters in Jackson, Mississippi, but when they attempted to enter the whites-only facilities there, the riders were arrested by the

Jackson city police. They were each convicted and fined $200 under a newly passed breach-of-the-peace statute. When they refused to pay, the judge sentenced each rider to ninety days in jail. Their mantra became "refuse bail, fill the jails!" They were then transferred to the state's infamous Parchman Farm, in the heart of the Mississippi Delta, where their mattresses and blankets were confiscated and they were given regular beatings, foul food, and repeated strip searches. As the summer progressed, newly recruited Freedom Riders arrived in Jackson to suffer the same fate so that, by the end of summer, over 300 Freedom Riders were guests of the State of Mississippi at Parchman Farm, all treated to the same conditions.

The Freedom Riders had failed to reach New Orleans, but the international attention, continuous news broadcasts, and reports forced US Attorney General Robert Kennedy to petition the Interstate Commerce Commission to enforce the law eliminating segregation in interstate transportation and enforce it. On November 1, 1961, the new order was put into effect across the nation with sanctions and penalties applied.

More than 400 Freedom Riders participated in the 1961 bus rides, including a contingent from the Bay Area. The Freedom Riders inspired all of us to embrace peaceful civil disobedience in our struggles across the nation, and our local brethren returned with experience in tactics and strategy on another level.

Willie Brown and I joined many others when we decided that the biggest problems for our race were housing and jobs. Accordingly, the first mass civil rights actions in San Francisco involved picketing businesses to hire more blacks in jobs of all sorts. Under the status quo, it was OK for blacks to wash dishes, but allowing them to progress into other jobs, like server, was not. Hiring blacks to wash and detail cars at the dealerships was OK, but allowing them to work out front was not.

Although the job situation was certainly problematic, the housing situation was more immediate for Willie and me. On May 29, 1961, Willie and some friends had gone to one of their houses after a Giants game when his wife, Blanche, called. She said she and a friend, Dorothy Lincoln, had been driving by some model houses in Forest Knolls, a new development on the western side of Mount Sutro overlooking the Pacific Ocean. She and Willie were looking for a new place to live, one that was closer to Willie's office and was more fitting for a lawyer's wife to entertain in. Forrest Knolls was in the geographic center of San Francisco and filled the bill in the other ways, too.

"Willie, we were just driving by and saw this house that was open. It looked nice on the outside, so on a lark, we decided to stop and take a look. We parked, and as we walked in, they all ran out. I'm not kidding. Buyers and agents all literally ran out of the house like it was on fire! They all ran into the garage and closed the door. I don't quite know what to do."

There had been problems like this before. Several famous instances had occurred just before I moved to San Francisco. When Willie Mays joined the Giants and moved to the city in 1957, before the team's first season here, he ran into a problem trying to buy a house on Miraloma Drive, next to St. Francis Wood, an exclusive community in the city's western hills with views of the Pacific Ocean. Willie offered to pay the owner the asking price and the owner accepted. The next day, the builder, who also owned property there, complained to the owner that property values would go down if a "colored family" moved in, so the owner backed out.

The whole thing hit the newspapers, first on the front pages in San Francisco, which was known as a liberal place, and then across the nation. It threatened to give the entire city a black eye. Mayor Christopher was publicly embarrassed, as were other residents, including the owner of the team who had just moved his franchise across the country. Willie's attorney was Terry Francois, and he got the NAACP involved. They all put pressure on the owner, who finally changed his mind and sold the house to Willie Mays. Willie did, however, pay $37,500, nearly 15 percent more than the originally agreed-upon price.

A year and a half later, some racist, clearly not a sports fan, threw a bottle with a hate note attached through the front window. This spooked Willie's wife, Marghuerite, who had grown up in the violent racism of Alabama, and she made Willie move back to New York. Their marriage began to fall apart after that. But Willie was having good seasons with the Giants and the fans in San Francisco loved him. His spectacular play made the team into a perennial contender to win their division and even the World Series. When he returned to San Francisco a few years later, he was alone. But he had liked the original house with the great views of the Pacific, so he bought another home in the same neighborhood. This time, his neighbors held a block party.

There were also plenty of neighborhoods where blacks couldn't live because of realtor redlining. That was the practice of designating particular areas as white-only and drawing a red line around them so everyone in the real estate office would know not to sell to blacks (or anyone not white). Ingleside Terraces was one of these areas. An issue arose there in 1958 when Cecil F. Poole, who had recently been hired to head the District Attorney's Superior Court Trial Division, attempted to purchase a home there. Local real estate agents refused to show him a house, so he and his wife worked directly with a property owner in that subdivision to arrange the purchase. They were the first blacks to move into the private residence park, paving the way for its eventual integration. But shortly after the family moved in, a cross was burned in their front yard. Robert Bilafer and Edmund Hass, both teenagers from prominent San Francisco families, were arrested and admitted they burned the cross there because they knew a black family had moved in. They denied knowing that Assistant District Attorney Poole in particular lived there, and he was satisfied to let the juvenile court handle the incident. Fortunately, there were no other significant incidents at the Poole house.

"Blanche," Willie said when his wife called from the house showing. "Why don't you just stay there and see what happens?"

So, Blanche and her friend stayed . . . and stayed . . . and stayed. More than three hours later, a black caretaker showed up. He told Blanche they were closing the house and wouldn't be showing it again that day.

The following Sunday, Willie and his family went to the housing development after church. He was joined by Terry Francois of the NAACP and a contingent of friends from Jones United Methodist Church. Willie had been a member there for many years by then and had worked in various positions. He knew almost every church member and had earned their trust. When they got to the model home in Forest Knolls, there were photographers and reporters from local newspapers waiting for them. As Willie thought, the sales representative had disappeared, so Willie, his family, and a gaggle of his closest friends sat down in the garage and waited. Soon they were told the office was closed for the day. On Monday, several local newspapers ran stories and photos of the well-dressed and polite Brown family—the perfect image of a well-dressed professional family . . . a black family. Willie and Blanche were hand-in-hand with their young children in front of the Forest Knolls sign trying to get in to see a model house. The photos were a developer's nightmare but a politician's dream. This turned out to be the start of his political career.

Willie told me later that he had no intention of buying the house because, at a little over $24,000, he couldn't afford it. In fact, he probably couldn't even afford the down payment. But because they wouldn't show it to him on account of his race, that made him both mad and determined to change things.

Blanche's trip to the model home that day was unplanned serendipity. But choosing how to follow up was not. The Standard Building Company, the model home's owner, was the largest housing developer in San Francisco. The company had built 14,000 houses in 1957 and was notorious for skirting construction, health, and fire codes through its influence with city hall. They were also notorious for not selling to blacks. Forest Knolls wasn't exactly chosen at random for the actions that followed. In the following weeks, Willie proved his organizing skills as protests became the cause célèbre among San Francisco liberals. Each day, blacks took turns being refused the opportunity to buy a house there. Oscar Peterson, the famous jazz pianist, walked the picket line with a growing number of future movers and shakers, many of whom pinpoint Forest Knolls as the place where they met each other. Willie had future judges, mayors, and senators picketing. They got to know each other there and learned to work together in ways that would pay large dividends later.

San Francisco mayor George Christopher expressed friendship to Negroes and paid ten dollars to join the NAACP. There was an election coming up. This wasn't Birmingham—there was no Bull Connor, and there were no fire hoses or dogs set on protesters. For the most part, we could sit or eat where we wanted, but there was still a serious problem with blacks living where they wanted to (and landing the jobs that would allow them to pay for it). A Berkeley sociologist wrote, "In San Francisco, it's James Crow not Jim Crow."

Willie brought the housing issue to the front pages of the newspapers and threw a little mud in the faces of those who claimed there was no discrimination in San Francisco, but he never bought a house in Forest Knolls and the housing discrimination issue was not settled. Mayor Christopher finally convinced the builder to show Willie a house, but Willie refused, saying, "I do not want to be an exception. I would not accept a private showing." He did, however, show his aptitude for generating support and publicity for an issue, and he became better known in the liberal and black communities because of it.

In late 1961, Ina was six months pregnant and we were looking for a new apartment. She scanned the newspapers and found an ad for a two-bedroom in the Marina District that sounded good, so she called to inquire. The woman who answered was quite pleasant and told Ina that, yes, the apartment was still vacant and she could see it the next day.

The next day, Ina and I went to the Marina. When we entered the apartment, the agent took one look at us and told Ina that she was very sorry but they didn't rent to tenants with young children, and it was clear we would soon have one. The day after that, I went to see the NAACP. A few days later, they sent a pregnant white woman to see the apartment. She met the same agent and immediately rented the apartment without issue. I never found out what happened in the end, but I suspect the owner was fined and, hopefully, forced to change her ways.

Willie ran for office in the California State Assembly in 1962, first running in the Democratic primary. Negro churches were the core of his campaign; his minister, Reverend Boswell, was his campaign chair. Willie ran against seventy-five-year-old Democrat Ed Gaffney, who had held the office off and on since 1940. In Sacramento, Gaffney boasted to a staff member, "I have a little nigger running against me. I'm going to teach him a lesson." To say he was out of touch is an understatement. He was also an old, racist man with antiquated ideas. But he was backed by most of the state Democratic Party bigwigs and the unions amid the not-inconsiderable Irish Catholic cabal in San Francisco. No one gave Willie much credence. No one in Sacramento expected an upset.

Willie raised money at first by asking local black ministers to pass the hat, collecting $700. In the end, his campaign spent $4,532.83 to Gaffney's $6,915.66, but his lack of political experience cost him the most. He did not focus on campaigning to specific neighborhoods or groups of voters. He didn't know California politics hinged on expedience at that level and had very little to do with issues, so he didn't make alliances with key players. Willie's attacks on Gaffney were positively mild by political standards. He outworked his opponent and was described as working at a "frenzied pace," but that only took him so far. There were 31,000 votes cast in the June 1962 Democratic primary, and Willie came within 916 votes of winning. He did extraordinarily well in the poorer districts.

For his entire life, Willie has stuck to the gist of his platform:

If I am elected, I will seek to end racial and religious segregation in schools, housing and employment. I am dedicated to the principles set forth in the Constitution of the United States of America and the state of California. I believe that every citizen should be judged not on his color or the texture of his hair, not on the manner in which he worships, nor on the basis of his place of birth. I believe that the answer to the problem of rising social welfare costs can be found without a reduction in benefits to the needy recipients. I believe it is wrong to take a person's life, whether it be taken by a private individual or by the state.

When his campaign chair sought to console him after the vote, Willie was nothing if not practical. He seemed not to be discouraged, saying it was just the first step and he had anticipated the loss. Knowing Willie, I thought he likely felt somewhat differently—the loss must have significantly stiffened his spine for the contests to come. Willie really doesn't like to lose.

In the early 1960s, grassroots black organizations and students from CORE, including students from Bay Area universities, primarily UC Berkeley and San Francisco State University, created the Ad Hoc Committee to End Racial Discrimination. Tracy Sims, an eighteen-year-old firecracker from Berkeley with exceptional energy and intelligence, was their very vocal spokesperson for many of the demonstrations. Their first order of business was to pressure local Bay Area companies to hire more minority employees in better positions. At the time, few Bay Area businesses offered job opportunities to blacks. Merchants said they were afraid black employees would attract black customers, scaring off whites. The committee's plan was to picket these businesses until they agreed to end their discriminatory practices or at least agreed to negotiate the issue in good faith.

Similar to the rest of the country, these grassroots organizations based their tactics on those of the Southern Civil Rights Movement. They planned nonviolent protests that would create confrontations and bad publicity for businesses. At the same time, they offered to end their actions in return for more and better jobs.

1963 was an eventful year for civil rights in San Francisco.

The Southern and national movements had begun some years earlier, but it began in earnest for San Francisco when the KKK planted fourteen sticks of dynamite in the church basement of the Sixteenth Street Baptist Church in Birmingham, Alabama on Sunday, September 15, 1963. When the dynamite exploded, four young African American girls were killed and fourteen others were injured. It was the third bombing in eleven days after a federal order had come down to integrate Alabama's school system. When thousands of angry black protesters assembled at the crime scene, George Wallace sent hundreds of police officers and state troopers to the area to break up the crowd. Two young black men were killed that night, one by police and another by racist thugs. These thoroughly evil actions once again ignited support across the country for the Southern Civil Rights Movement. Most people, having never lived in the South, had no idea such loathsome and maleficent people existed.

Three days later, in San Francisco, 2,500 people solemnly marched along Post Street to protest the tragedy and a crowd filled the street in front of the Federal Building to listen to speeches denouncing that horrendous event. It was but the city's first large demonstration attended by both black and white residents in support of the Southern Civil Rights Movement. There would be many more. The bombings had lit a fire under everyone here, and the demonstration was led by left and liberal activists who began sending supporters to the South to help.

Back in San Francisco, beginning in late 1963, the Ad Hoc Committee and others conducted marches in Oakland, San Francisco, Berkeley, and Richmond to protest for more and better jobs for blacks. There was a good reason for this. Things had changed radically for us. In 1940, black unemployment in San Francisco was 20 percent higher than white unemployment, but it was 71 percent higher by 1953 and 112 percent higher by 1963. We were losing ground. At the same time, the city's black population had increased from less than 6 percent in 1950 to more than 10 percent in 1960. And we were, for the most part, now living in three distinctly segregated neighborhoods: Bayview–Hunters Point, Fillmore Street, and what was left of the Western Addition.

Organizers picketed Mel's Drive-In diners in Berkeley and San Francisco, San Francisco's Sheraton Palace Hotel, and the automobile dealers on Van Ness Avenue's Auto Row. They also picketed Berkeley's Lucky grocery stores. Their efforts resulted in agreements to hire more blacks in better positions at all of these locations.

Willie and I were involved in all of this. We walked picket lines and sat in with everyone else. But we never went to jail. There were two good reasons for that. First, we had both grown up in the Deep South where once you were in jail, you could be —and often were—extremely mistreated. It was a very dangerous place to be. We wanted nothing to do with the inside of any jail, no matter where it was. We also thought we could better put our skills to work in service of the movement by defending people in court, and we could not do that from inside a jail cell. When arrests started, Willie was at the forefront of organizing a large bench of attorneys and planning strategic use of that resource. I happily served as part of that bench and was involved in almost every defensive effort.

After that, a string of sit-ins, dine-ins, pickets, and other creative nonviolent actions started in the Bay Area, beginning with Select Realty in San Francisco's Mission District in August 1963.

Members of CORE, the W.E.B. Du Bois Club, and other activist organizations settled on Select Realty as their first picketing action because of its discriminatory rental practices. Samuel Peitchel, the owner, was quite brazen about his racist practices. His agency only served whites, and he was open about refusing to represent black clients and trying to find them housing. But he made it seem that he was just as much a victim as anyone. He said he felt it was dishonest to take the ten-dollar rental service fee from a Negro when he knew the landlords on his list would not rent to them. "I don't make the landlords' policies," he said. "But if a Negro comes in, I'm going to be honest—I'm going to say I can't help him because I don't know of an apartment he can rent."

In the beginning, he said he couldn't stop "discriminating" against Negros and still make money, so he was going to get out of the business for good. But, of course, he didn't. He just kept up his discriminatory practices. Activists picketed for a month before he called the police and had them arrested for sitting down in front of the entrance. Among the eleven arrested were Terry Francois, Terrence Hallinan, and Tracy Sims. Willie and I arranged bond for them through Jerry Barrish, a young man just starting out with his own bail bond business.

After several more months of protests and a legal suit Peitchel brought against the picketers, the company and the demonstrators reached an agreement, ending both the discriminatory practices and the public picketing. This initial success in combating racial and employment discrimination ushered in a year of direct action and civil rights agitation in San Francisco.

In 1965, Willie Brown ran for Assembly again. He'd learned quite a bit from his lost run in the 1962 election. This time, he organized a better campaign committee drawn from many of the people he and I had met in our civil rights work. And, perhaps most importantly, US Representative Phillip Burton got behind him 100 percent, even lending him experienced campaign organizers from his own organization. Willie won the election, and he was sworn in in 1966.

John Burton, Willie Brown, and I have been good friends since my early arrival in San Francisco and my early participation in the Young Democrats with both of them. We have been friends for over sixty years.

That same year when Willie ran for Assembly, John Burton put me up for president of the Young Democrats. I was its first black president and served for one year. The Young Democrats made up the largest group of volunteers for Willie's campaign, and I organized a lot of them. But truthfully, Willie's growing reputation in the black community and the issues he championed drew the great majority of his campaign workers. They came from all walks of life and from all the area colleges. The liberal left embraced Willie's campaign wholeheartedly, and many Bay Area activists gravitated to him. The entire Hallinan family went all-in and was out ringing doorbells and handing out fliers for days.

After passing the bar, years before Willie was elected, I'd

gone to work for Richard Bancroft, who worked with Allan Brotsky. Bancroft was a brilliant black man who hired me and Ephraim Margolin, a white man, as associates with his firm on Polk Street. Later, as Bancroft's work expanded, he moved me and Richard Peritz, another associate, into a space further down Polk while he and Ephraim Margolin stayed in the original offices. As associates, we weren't paid a salary; instead, we earned a percentage of the income we generated. I did mostly personal injury and worker's compensation, gaining experience and expertise with each case. After a couple of years, I settled an injury case for $20,000, my largest settlement up to that point, and Bancroft got the majority of the fee, per our agreement. I realized it was time to go out on my own and stop generating more income for someone else than I was generating for myself. I talked it over with Ina, and in 1963, I hung my shingle outside an office on McAllister Street. My practice was off and running.

Much later, after I had become a judge, my friend Dante Cosentino and his wife, Antonia, asked us to go to Italy with them on vacation for several weeks. They had both lived there for years and spoke the language very well. It looked like a perfect vacation, which Ina and I sorely needed. Her mother saw me shaking my head as I pored over the brochures one evening, and she asked me about it.

"Why are you shaking your head, John? Aren't you and Ina looking forward to your vacation?" she asked.

"I'm not sure we're able to afford it, Bertha," I said.

Unbelievably, she gave us money to join Dante in Italy.

"Go on and take Ina," she said. "I added a little extra so you can cover side trips and emergencies," she said smiling. "I don't want you two to miss the trip of a lifetime just because of a few dollars."

Bertha's sister, Fanny, was that way, too. Once, when we were still living at Fanny's house, she was on a shoreside leave when she gave me enough for us to visit my mother in Saginaw —Ina had never met her. I was carping about how to pay for the trip and Fanny heard. Later, she slipped an envelope containing money under the door to our bedroom. I really did hit the jackpot with my wife and her family—another of my lucky stars!

Once we had children, our family also took trips every summer and drove across the country. Ina would map out the route and plan everything: where we were going to stop, where we were going to sleep, and things like that. I was responsible for driving all day, pitching the tents, all the grilling, and the multiple trips to the bathroom with our kids several times a night! Ina slept soundly.

We once were at a campground where they had recently had a tic outbreak. I set up two tents (one for the girls, one for the boys), Ina and I would sleep in the car. That night, after taking Jonathan to the bathroom we heard another camper say, "did it bite you?". When we got back to the campground, Jonathan said, "I'm not sleeping in the tent.".

I said, 'Ina, why don't you sleep in the tent with me?"

Ina said, "I'm not sleeping on the ground."

Needless to say, Jason and I slept in the tent that night. I might have gotten about 2 hours of sleep that night just to get up and start the whole process all over again.

In the next few years, I bought our house on Mount Olympus in addition to two rental properties. By 1977, I was a judge and my salary was $50,000 a year—less than I'd been making as an attorney. However, the job was more stable, had great benefits, and truly suited my personality. As much as anything else, though, I took the job as a tribute to my mother.

I have always been very respectful around women.

The Journey

Truthfully, women have been my world. There have only been a few important men in my life—two uncles, my first stepfather, and Robert's father were the most significant. I was mostly raised by women, and they're the ones I've learned the most from. They all taught me to always try to do my best, to be a good man, and to be a good person in everything I do. I haven't always succeeded, but I have always tried.

Chapter 15
My New Family

As a young boy, I reached the conclusion that I would never marry and that I would never have children. It had nothing to do with opposing the institution of marriage or disliking children. Instead, it had to do with what I experienced as a child myself and, more importantly, what I saw and experienced from others.

I used to see people with huge families, like my uncle and his wife and their thirteen children. Those children always seemed to be lacking something. They were not well-fed, well-clothed or well-housed. They were much worse off than I was. I made up my mind that I would never marry because I did not want to bring children into the world if I couldn't properly care for them.

Then, one year and three days after I married Ina and lost my single life, I was the father of a beautiful eight-pound-ten-ounce daughter. Tracy arrived on Christmas Day in 1961. Ever since, she has thought all the Christmas hoopla was for her.

That night on Christmas Eve, Ina and I were playing a card game while we waited for the proper time to go to the hospital. Shortly before midnight, we rushed to the hospital where Tracy was born just past midnight with minimum fanfare.

I had been admitted to practice law in California the previous June but was still struggling and fearful that I wouldn't be able to support a family. But shortly after Tracy joined us, the seeds that we had been planting began to sprout, and my career looked like it was taking hold. My fears had been short-lived. With Ina's help, and because she knew so many people, my lucky star proved to still be with me. Perhaps I should say Tracy was another of my lucky stars.

One time, I went to pick her up from daycare. She was in diapers, and they hadn't changed her. She wasn't walking yet, so she was scooting around on the floor on her butt while wearing a dirty diaper. When I picked her up, I lost it. It brought back memories of my cousins being dirty and not taken care of. I exploded.

On October 5, 1964, my fatherhood experience expanded when Kelly, our second daughter, was born. I should never have told her I was not at the hospital when she introduced herself to the world as she has never let me forget it. My plate was filling, but so was my constellation of lucky stars. I was happy with my life despite my initial fear of marriage and children. Actually, Ina had made me feel so comfortable with my new family life that my fear was subsiding. Before I knew it, we had another child. Jonathan was born on October 30, 1967. I wasn't at the hospital for his birth either, but when I arrived to discover a boy, I felt quite sure our family was complete.

After my new son arrived, I realized my view of family was as conventional as that of any man in that era. I had been perfectly happy with two beautiful daughters who were turning out to be curious, thoughtful, and bright. Surely, they were headed for great academic and other successes in life, enough to satisfy any father. But once this handsome and healthy baby boy joined us, I began having visions of a great athlete in addition to his many future academic accomplishments. Now I knew our family was complete!

But Ina had other ideas. She had been a medical social worker in child placement, where she saw the urgent and heart-breaking need for families to adopt young children who had no offense against them save that of being born. Unless they were taken in by a nourishing, supportive family by the time they were three years old, they were likely to suffer a life of hardship and privation with little chance for happiness and success. Ina had seen this every day, and she took her role seriously, often coming home with tears in her eyes for the prospects of another beautiful young child who did not deserve the rotten future they were facing.

Because of her background, Ina had deep and sincere concerns about the welfare of all children and felt she was now in a position to do her part in softening some of that. So one day, as I was merrily going about my regular business of thinking how our completed family was going to work together, she said to me, "John, Jonathan is going to be spoiled rotten being the only boy. Why don't we adopt another one to balance things out?" Being the frustrated athlete that I was, and seeing that resistance was futile—as it always was with Ina—I figured, *What the hell, another future scholar and athlete.* We adopted Jason, our second son, in August of 1970, when he was about one year old.

Our new little athlete was an immediate hit with the other

three, but I think Kelly was the first to really bond with Jason. He was a cheerful child and a bit mischievous, and they quickly became quite the pair around the house and the neighborhood, seemingly bound at the hip. Jason added much joy to our now complete household.

For years, the family was energetic and fun with this pack of new minds exploring at every opportunity. The children made new discoveries every day to investigate and learn from. I was constantly amazed at how much they could turn into laughter, fun, and play every single day. Family had become a source of joy and laughter for me—for us all—making every day profoundly richer and more interesting than the one before. My early fears had been unfounded. I was earning enough to support them all. Ina had known all along.

Ina was a fantastic mother to the children and oversaw their educational needs. Ina also planned all the entertainment for the children when they were growing up. I was always busy hustling, trying to make a living so everybody was well taken care of. Ina stopped working before Tracy was born, but she did everything else. In addition to raising four children, she was active in civic affairs. She called herself a professional volunteer, and she served on many boards and commissions in San Francisco, including the San Francisco Planning Commission and the YWCA—all while dealing with multiple sclerosis.

Then, when the children became teenagers, tragedy struck. We discovered that Jason was addicted to drugs. This was even more tragic because he had turned into such a superb athlete. His future seemed to be filled with all the promise and possibility of a career as a professional athlete. At sixteen, Jason was recruited to become a member of a new fast-paced semi-pro basketball league. It was for youngsters six foot two and under.

At six feet, Jason was small for pro ball, but he was fast and quick, a skilled ball handler and a deadly outside shooter. We were all ecstatic at this new opportunity, and I was proud that I might have had some part in guiding this fine young man into a successful life doing something he both loved and was very good at.

A professional scout who was associated with the league heard about Jason and flew out from New York to meet him, give him a tryout, and discuss the possibilities for his future. Jason missed two appointments, and the scout flew back to New York without meeting him. Later, Jason told me he had been high. He said, "The crack told me it was a waste of time." We were all devastated. So much talent and so much opportunity . . . so close together, yet ultimately so far apart. For the first time, I feared for the future of one of my children. We all did.

Jason dropped out of high school not long after that. The scourge of addiction had him by the throat and has rarely let up since. Like most addicts, his life has been a series of struggles to get clean, each followed by another failure to resist the demon, then some years living on the streets (or very close to them), getting high, and hustling dope, each day like the last, filled with the unquenchable drive for more—more dope. Jason is a wonderful person, but it's amazing what drugs can do to you.

He met a woman while he was in Delancey Street, a rehabilitation center, and they both graduated. They have a daughter together, and she lives in New York. When Jason's daughter was a child, I used to bring her to San Francisco to visit every year. But after she graduated from high school, things went badly for her. She now has two children of her own. I have never seen them.

I hear from Jason occasionally, and so do his former friends, who were so eager to accept and help him. He is still an addict, and that has led him to a series of jail and prison terms. He is out now and working on staying straight, looking for a way to fill a productive role in society. I am saddened by Jason's failures, but we are still hopeful . . . we are still trying. Both Ina and I still believe that joyful little boy is in there somewhere, fighting to get out. Maybe he will be successful this time. His family is still pulling for him. He is already considerably older than the average addict's lifespan.

As for my other three children, my mother would be proud. Ina and I now have three adult children who have graduated from college. Two have post-graduate degrees. All are leading happy, successful lives, and Ina and I are very thankful for that.

Dearman Family (l to r) Jason, Ina, John, Kelly,
Jonathan and Tracy and Sunshine (the cat)

My first daughter is Tracy, and she has a master's degree in business administration. She is divorced, and she put her children through school without her ex-husband's help. (Of course, I helped a little bit.) I have a vivid memory of picking Tracy up from the babysitter, holding her in my arms while driving (illegally!) through Golden Gate Park. I pulled over as I was suddenly overcome with this realization that I was now responsible for this little human. It reminded me of all of the fears that I had about marriage and children, and the responsibilities attached thereto based upon my own life in my younger years.

She has three children: two girls (Michelle Branch and Monica Branch) and a boy (Monte Branch). Michelle is a practicing nurse, Monica is working for a non profit agency as a coach/mentor and fundraising director. Monte is a property manager. Tracy took over Ina's mother's real estate business and has been very successful. She has about twelve employees.

I once made the mistake of telling my children that I would take care of them as long as they were full-time students. Kelly, my second daughter, took me up on that. She finished UC Berkeley with some off-the-wall major—I've forgotten what it was. Then she spent a year in St. Louis with the CORO Foundation. Then, when she came back, she went to law school on my dime. Once she finished law school, she still didn't get a job. She said, "Dad, I'm going to get my master's." After she graduated, I said, "Kelly, don't you think it's about time to start to work?" She finally did—after pursuing higher education for nine years straight. She practiced law as a deputy city attorney in San Francisco for many years, and, after realizing she did not want to practice law she started working in public service. She now proudly serves as the Executive Director for San Francisco's Department of Disability and Aging Services.

After she married, Kelly and her husband, Dwight, were looking for a home in San Francisco but couldn't find one. She came to me one day and said, "What if we buy your house? You can stay here and we'll take care of you." She and her husband have been living with Ina and me for the past twelve years. It has been a wonderful experience.

Kelly has two children, Nathan Moore and Nyla Moore. Nathan is interested in cooking and music. When he is not playing drums, he keeps a day job working at the federal building. Nyla is my youngest grandchild, and she is a budding actress. Actually, it seems like she has been acting for all of her life. I went to the hospital to see her when she was just two or three days old. She was already trying to talk then, and she hasn't stopped since.

Then there is my son Jonathan. He is a real estate broker, but he previously taught school for about eight years. Once he decided that he couldn't make a decent living in that profession, he began working in real estate. Jonathan has two daughters, Anika and Maya, who are both college graduates. Anika is a teacher. She's married now and has two children, little boys: J.J. Nealy and Grayson Nealy. Maya recently graduated from college and is now working for the San Francisco public school district as an analyst.

Although I never wanted children, I'm happy that I have them. It has been a wonderful experience being a father, a grandfather, and now a great-grandfather. I'll probably be a great-great-grandfather in another four or five years!

I'm also happy that I got married. Ina has been a good mate for over sixty years. When I think about it, it really is unbelievable that I got so lucky.

My mother's modest goal for me had seemed so far away when I was young and she brought me to Waco: for her twelve-year-old firstborn son to come out of the cotton fields, return to school, graduate, and maybe more. That goal has led to a career, a family, and a future bright beyond her wildest dreams. I used to tell my children what my mother told me years ago, and that was to depend on no one but yourself. My favorite expression to share with them was, "If you see me fighting with the bear, help the bear. I don't need it." I don't know how seriously my children took this advice, but they have done well for themselves.

Early in life, I didn't want a wife or children, but they have all made me a very happy man!

Chapter 16
Bar and Bench

When we were younger, Willie Brown and I used to talk about what we would like to do in the future—what our goals were. He wanted, more than anything, to be involved in politics, which he ultimately was. One day we were having lunch and he said, "You know, John, I think it would be great for you as a judge." We were two Texans, both from poor backgrounds, and the thought of being a judge was unbelievable to us at that time.

He said, "If I'm ever in a position, we're going to work on that and see about getting you that judgeship." That was early on, when we first started practicing together. Back then, African American attorneys started their practices in criminal law because that's the type of business we could get. However, I'd always been interested in personal injury work; in law school, my best grades were in that area, torts, which are acts that cause harm to someone's body or personal property, such as an assault or damaging someone's personal property. . I had always been fascinated with torts. Part of the reason I concentrated on practicing that phase of the law (but not the only reason) was that Melvin Belli had come to Wayne State during my final year of law school and talked about being the King of Torts.

From then on, I said, "One of these days, I'm going to be a personal injury lawyer." But first, I worked in criminal law. My first client was a man named Robert. I cannot recall his last name, but he was a pimp and a drug dealer, and that's how I started my practice.

Early on, Ina and I were out having dinner when we ran into a friend of hers, a black doctor she knew from childhood who had just opened a medical practice.

"John, do you do personal injury cases?" he asked. As new attorney this was my opportunity to fully get in to personal injury law. Up to this point I had done some cases but not as many as I wanted.

"My bread and butter," I said. "Think you could put me on your referral list?"

It was illegal then for attorneys to advertise or for doctors to refer cases to specific attorneys, and you had to be careful or you could get into hot water with the Bar Association. I knew that most doctors would vet a "short list" of ten or fifteen attorneys whose work they were familiar with, and getting on those lists meant the opportunity to earn a good reputation by winning settlements.

"Sure I can," he said. "But winning cases is up to you. And I'll keep track of how you do."

I was thrilled for the opportunity. I probably had one of the biggest smiles you've ever seen because that's exactly what I wanted. Dr. Johnson started referring people to me and I started taking a lot of personal injury cases, mostly from this doctor. Then another African American doctor came into town, Dr. Jackson. He heard about me and also started sending me cases.

When Willie ran for the Assembly the second time and won, he and I formed a legal partnership. (I made appearances on behalf of Willie when he was in Sacramento.) We also brought on a third attorney, Hiram Smith, and the firm became Brown, Dearman & Smith. I stopped doing criminal cases and focused primarily on personal injury work and workers' compensation, which was a form of personal injury. Willie and Hiram did primarily criminal cases.

Our practice continued for twelve years. We were not fabulously rich lawyers, but we got a lot of recognition because of Willie's involvement in politics. In fact, that's one of the reasons we didn't make a lot of money. A lot of people who came to the office said, "I voted for Willie. I'm one of his people, and I would like some legal information."

So, we gave a lot of free legal advice—at least, I did. When I was being honored for having been on the bench for thirty-one years, Willie spoke and said something to the effect of "John and I didn't make money because John didn't know how to charge. John was practicing social work instead of practicing law." It was somewhat true; I never could refuse someone help if I was able to give it. That law practice continued for more than a decade, and we had some decent cases. We also represented a few professional athletes, though I didn't have much to do with it—that was mostly Willie's area. Nate Thurmond, an NBA player for the Golden State Warriors, was one of our biggest clients. Another was Gary Lewis, a running back with the 49ers.

Those were fun years, and the firm somewhat helped me achieve my dream of being in a position to help people, especially people who could not help themselves. I guess that came from my social work background, but I enjoyed it.

One of the highlights of the practice was when Willie,

Hiram, and I opened the office at 1515 Vallejo two or three years before I became a judge. It was a fabulous office. We had a steam room and a jacuzzi. Just when I was getting used to it, I was contacted by Tony Kline, a lawyer who was a friend of Governor Jerry Brown and served as his affairs secretary. He was in charge of appointing judges.

Tony had been calling me and asking for names of minorities and women who were qualified and could be considered for judgeships. This was important because one of Governor Brown's promises had been to equalize the court with minorities and women. Tony was helping him to carry it out.

I recommended several people, two in particular. The first was Benjamin Travis, a friend of mine. He lived in Oakland and was appointed as a judge there. My second recommendation was Richard Bancroft, the first boss I worked for after passing the bar. He ended up being appointed as a judge in Alameda County.

I also recommended a female public defender. However, Tony called me up and said, "That last recommendation, we can't do it because she's a Republican."

Willie and I had talked about me being a judge years earlier, and now he was in a position to help me out. However, I thought the law office business was about to take off because I had just tried a case and received a decent judgment. I had also settled a case with a decent amount of money. As a result, I was feeling good. But I couldn't forget that I was being considered as a potential judge. While Willie and I had talked and joked about it in the past, the actual possibility was mind blowing to me. Unbelievable that I was being considered.

One night, I got a call from a friend of Tony Kline's. He said, "Why don't you submit your application?"

I said, "Nah, not now. Maybe later." The timing seemed off.

Governor Brown had announced that he was planning to run for president, and every assemblyman had endorsed him but Willie. I thought Governor Brown's office was trying to use me to gain Willie's support.

Then Tony Kline took me out to lunch and assured me that gaining political support had nothing to do with it. He said, "That's not the reason. Willie and I have had a chat, and Willie wants you to do it."

I was surprised. "Well, Willie hasn't said that to me," I said.

Willie called me up later and said, "What's this business I hear about you refusing to accept the judgeship?"

"I didn't refuse. I just said I didn't want it right now because of this political stuff going on. I don't want to be a part of that."

He said, "Don't worry about it. You go ahead and accept that appointment because this might be the last chance that you get."

So I did.

The author being sworn in as a judge in 1977

I was appointed to the Municipal Court, and I was sworn in

on my birthday, March 28, 1977. I served primarily in traffic court for a while, then the drunk driving court. I got into trials after a time, and suddenly, I was elevated to the Superior Court, where I remained for about twenty years. While there, I mostly did civil trials, but I also heard some criminal cases. Once, I spent about three months trying a murder case. It was not a death penalty-type case, but I still didn't like sending someone to prison.

Prior to joining the Superior Court, I spent a day at San Quentin because I wanted to see where I'd be sending people. When I visited the prison, a clerk showed me around the different sections, including the gas chamber—but what I remember most is the big yard where they let prisoners exercise and visit with one another. While I was there, a few prisoners were lifting weights. The guide told me that when they come into the yard after being in the cafeteria, prisoners are searched to make sure they don't bring any utensils that they could hide.

Right at that moment, we stopped by a big post. There was a hole in the roof with two boards covering it, making a little slot where prisoners could conceal things. The guide said something about not giving people a chance to bring out knives.

"You mean like this?" I said, reaching for a knife I saw stuck in the slot. I took it out and showed him.

"Oh my God," he said.

A few minutes later, I heard a prisoner say my name: "Judge Dearman."

Three prisoners were coming toward us, and the yard was empty except for them. I figured I was dead; the guide didn't have a weapon—he was just a clerk. I recognized the guy who'd said my name as someone I had sentenced to prison as part of a plea deal while I was sitting pro tem on the Superior Court. (In other words, I had been substituting for one of the regular judges.)

"Wow, Judge," he said. "How are you?"

"I'm fine," I said. "How are you?"

"I'm fine. I want you to meet some friends of mine." He introduced me to his friends and said, "This is the judge I was telling you about that saved my life."

He was praising me! Needless to say, I took a deep breath. That was the most memorable moment of my experience at San Quentin.

Aside from the murder case, the most unforgettable case from my time on the Superior Court involved a man who was being tried for rape and kidnapping. The victim was lesbian. When she testified, she said something to the effect of, "I told him that I liked women, too, just like he did, and I didn't enjoy men sexually. And he said, 'Shut up. You're not a man, and if you don't shut up, I'm going to cut your throat.'"

The trial lasted five or six days. When the defendant was brought in each day, his girlfriend was sitting in the audience. He would always say to me, "Your Honor, could I have a word with my girlfriend?" The bailiff would tell him to move on, but I would let him speak to his girlfriend.

When the case was over and he was found guilty, I sentenced him to about twenty years in prison. After the bailiff took the prisoner back to his cell after sentencing, he came back to me and said, "The defendant wanted to know why he was sentenced to the extent that he was. He said that because you're such a nice judge, it was hard for him to believe you could sentence him."

The bailiff's first name was Maurice. I said, "So, Mo, what did you tell him?"

"I told him that you had no other choice, that you were just following the law."

That was the truth. He had committed a horrible crime, and he deserved to spend time in jail. I probably would have cut the sentence if I could have, but not by much. Maybe I would have taken a year off to let him know I was thinking about him.

I spent most of my time with the Superior Court hearing civil jury trials, and I spent at least eight years presiding over back-to-back asbestos cases—it might have been as many as ten. Many of my peers recused themselves from those cases because they knew they would be lengthy, but I never did. They would say things like "I can't handle it because I have stock" or "I can't handle it because my wife is sick." Katy, my court reporter, likes to say that she was able to purchase income property because of all the asbestos cases.

I wasn't interested when Judge Grant, who was about to retire, said to me, "John, why don't you think about presiding in probate?" I'd already spent about twenty-two years in the Superior Court and didn't want to make a change with retirement just a few years off. On top of that, I'd dreaded my law school courses on wills, trusts, and taxes—the staples of probate. I enjoyed jury trials and didn't want to give that up for an area that I felt was boring.

A while later, Larry Kay, the supervising probate judge, was about to be elevated to the Appellate Court. He asked me to take the probate position. He said, "John, you'll love it."

I said, "I doubt it."

Even so, I ended up working in probate. Mary Quinn, director of the Probate Court, convinced me by assuring me it was easy work. Once I took the position, I found myself among the most professional group of people I had ever worked with.

They all knew what they were doing, they didn't mind doing it, and they taught me a lot.

I've never placed myself above anybody else, no matter what my job is. So, when I got to probate, I wanted everybody to know we were going to work together as equals no matter our job titles. I told everybody to call me John instead of Judge. I enjoyed being a judge, but it was my job—not my identity. Early in my judgeship, Ina and I were at some sort of function and someone introduced me as Judge Dearman. I said, "John Dearman is my name." And Ina said, "Yes, his mama didn't name him Judge. His mama named him John." That is how Ina is. She says what she thinks.

Mary Quinn, Christine Nahnsen (the assistant director), and Dorothy McMath (probate commissioner) took me under their wings and showed me the ropes. After about two months, I knew my way around a little bit and I began to really enjoy it, primarily because it reminded me of social work.

People would come before the court embroiled in a fight. There would be sisters and brothers—siblings fighting, sometimes over things that weren't even worth $200, but it would cause them to hate each other. I spent a lot of time trying to talk people into settling.

I remember three cases in particular. One time, two sisters were fighting over about $60,000 out of an estate worth more than $11 million. One sister had been advanced the $60,000 to pay for her child's education and didn't want it deducted from her share. I cajoled, tried being humorous, and finally told them that going to trial would cost each of them more than they were fighting over. They weren't deterred. Their positions had hardened so much by the time they went to court that their animosity had only increased. The predictable result was that their lawyers were quite enriched, and ultimately, the sisters vowed never to speak to each other again. Heartbreaking situations like that regularly arose in probate court, and it never ceased to amaze me how little some folks treasure their families when the going gets tough. My own priceless experiences with my family always informed me on the bench and helped me render fair and thoughtful decisions that were deeper than the letter of the law.

Another case involved two sisters fighting over something with no monetary value—perhaps a piece of furniture. I took them into my chambers and said, "Look, you guys are fighting over something that's worth little. I know it has sentimental value, but still, you're going to lose friendships."

"I don't care. I don't ever want to speak to her again," one of the sisters said.

"But if you go to court," I said, "you're going to spend all the money that you would have gotten, and it's not that much. The only people that are going to benefit from this will be the attorneys."

They hated each other. I don't know what happened, though, because the case didn't come before me again.

Then there was the case of the man whose wife had left money to their son when she died. The son's maternal grandmother was taking care of the boy, and the man wanted to take his son because of the money. I said I wanted to talk to him after the hearing. He was a muscular guy who had made threats, so Manuel, one of the court investigators, was concerned for my safety when I asked the bailiff to bring the man into a room off the courtroom. Manuel said, "Judge, do you want me to go in with you?"

"I can handle it," I said.

When I got into the room, I used expletives right away. "What the hell is going on, man? What's all this bullshit?" I had to talk street talk to get through to him. After about fifteen minutes, he and I were friends.

In the end, I liked probate because it gave me an opportunity to help people. I also enjoyed that my colleagues in probate were also interested in people and their welfare—it wasn't just me, and it wasn't just a legal thing. Probate was people-oriented, and that fit well with me and my personality.

Mary had also been right—probate *was* easy. That's because she, Christine, and the rest of the group prepared me well. Also, I could hear cases without doing all the necessary work that everyone else took care of. Before that, I never had a position where I got the praise and everybody else did the work. I was the judge, but I looked good because of the staff. Probate was one of my greatest experiences on the bench. I was there for nine years and got to know all the people I worked with. It was enjoyable to work with people who knew exactly what the probate department was all about, and they made my work easier.

I have to give credit to Mary Quinn, Christine Nahnsen, and those who worked under them. I would also like to recognize the clerk I worked with, Ella Yip, the bailiff I worked with, Rod Montgomery, and my court reporter, Katie Bersamin that I worked with for about forty years. It is wonderful being a judge when you get to work with such wonderful people. I'm a people person; I like working with people and doing things for them, and that's what the probate staff did. That made the job enjoyable.

I served a long time on the bench, and every year or two, the presiding judge changes. If the presiding judge had ever reassigned me outside of probate, I probably would have retired sooner. I stayed as long as I did because I was relaxed, happy, and having fun.

Chapter 17
From Cotton Fields to Mount Olympus

O ver the years, I've learned many lessons, and I want to share some of them. Some will apply only to young people. Others may be useful to everyone.

The first is to get an education. You can create your family life after you have developed yourself with an education and have something to share with others.

An education will also enable you to help others throughout your adult life. For instance, in my early years as a judge, I was able to be a presence to many young people. In one case, a young girl saw my likeness on a mural and asked her teacher if she could see me in court. I heard about her request and arranged to have her visit my courtroom. She asked a lot of questions. She'd also heard that I gave talks at schools and requested that I speak to her class, which I gladly did. While I don't know what path she took in life, I like to think that she was able to marshal her gifts and talents to get an education and share her knowledge with the world.

Once, I had a case in front of me where it was obvious that

the large young man who had been charged with acting violently acting violently was being used by a gang of young thugs to beat people up upon request. I asked him to come to my chambers. There, I told him I was concerned about him and said he was being taken advantage of. I told him I had chosen a particular place for him to serve his term because I knew they would help him learn how to handle himself and avoid being further exploited. I gave him my home phone number and told him he could call me anytime. As I left the courthouse that day, I overheard him in conversation with his mother. I heard him say with amazement, "That judge gave me his home phone number." I never heard from him and I don't know how his life unfolded, but I feel I may have been helpful to him.

Another case called for street talk. A young man who had been arrested was swearing, shouting, behaving disrespectfully, and creating chaos in court. I called him to the bench and quietly said, "Now listen, motherfucker, I'm trying to help you. So just stop with the swearing and sit down and behave. I can't help you if you keep acting like a fool." He did as he was told. A friend of mine was in court that day and we went to lunch later. He told me the young man was smiling when he went back to his seat after speaking to me at the bench.

Another lesson I learned was not to be afraid of working humble jobs. Don't be afraid to work hard and show initiative. Learn to work because that discipline will carry you far. Believe it or not, sweeping floors, acting as a short-order cook, shining shoes, busing tables, washing dishes, being an attendant at a golf course locker room, setting pins in a bowling alley, working in a car factory, cutting grass, sorting mail in post offices, acting as a security guard, or parking cars will give you learning experiences about people and the world that will carry you forward. I did all those things and learned a lot from each one.

Still another lesson I learned was to listen when people talked about what I should do with my life. I may not have acted on every suggestion, but I explored many of them—and when something really interested me, I took further steps. An example of this is taking a law class on a teacher's suggestion and later going to law school. The people who made the suggestions were acting in my best interests, I know, and they were my lucky stars.

I also learned to embrace change, or at least accept it. Life-changing events have turned out well for me. The first was moving in with my grandmother when I was five. She was a very lucky star. Moving to Waco to live with my mother when I was twelve years old also changed my life, and so did the two men she married. They acted as my daddies and were also lucky stars. One even adopted me and gave me his surname, Dearman. Other life-changing events included moving to Saginaw, Michigan, and eventually to my home of many decades, San Francisco.

In general, it's important to listen, watch for lucky stars, and appreciate change. Sometimes you only know an event's effect on you in hindsight. Listen to yourself and try to stay centered in yourself. Be open to new ideas and ways of conducting yourself. But always check in with yourself and ask whether you're taking the best course of action.

Now I have told my story to you, dear reader. It started in the cotton fields of Texas. It is a story marked by the lucky stars who guided me, enriched my thinking, and helped me move to the next phase of my life. It is also a story of hard work and humble jobs. I love my life and the families I've been fortunate enough to be a part of. I've known a lot of love and kindness in my lifetime.

The world has changed a lot since I started moving through

it, and that gives me another group to thank: those, both black and white, who helped move the United States from a terribly racist country where black men and women were denied basic rights and could be

accosted or even lynched on nothing more than an accusation, to a country where someone like me could build a story like mine. The United States has come a long way in civil rights and will go further still. I have tried to do my part in making the country better, and so have many of those I have been privileged to know.

Now, I live in a four-bedroom house on the side of Mount Olympus, a mountain in San Francisco's geographical center with a panoramic view of the city. On most Sundays, fifteen to twenty members of my extended family join me and my wife, Ina, for Sunday dinner—three generations of my family, the family I helped create and of whom I am most proud.

Now, I can vote. I can live where I want. I can eat where I want. I can go where I want. I feel satisfied that I have made my contribution to making this life and this country better. And, to my knowledge, I have not been called bastard or nigger in quite a while.

I am a very lucky man.

Acknowledgments

To my wife Ina, it's been a wild ride. To my mother-in-law Bertha Flemming for having so much faith in me. To my children and grandchildren for always keeping it interesting and making me such a proud father and grandfather. To my niece and nephews for being family first. To my brother, Robert, for sharing in some of these stories. Lastly to David McClure and Mary Joy Quinn for all of your writing. Without all of you this never would have happened.

Sources Used

https://www.archives.gov/research/african-americans/migrations/great-migration#:

https://www.tsl.texas.gov/ref/abouttx/secession/2feb1861.html

https://libraryguides.missouri.edu/pricesandwages/1930-1939

https://www.senate.gov/artandhistory/history/common/generic/FreedmensBureau.htm#:

https://marlintexas.com/falls-county-history/

https://www.tshaonline.org/handbook/entries/bell-county

www.ingramcontent.com/pod-product-compliance
Lightning Source LLC
Chambersburg PA
CBHW072338090426
42741CB00012B/2838